A SEARCH FOR A JUDICIAL PHILOSOPHY

KENNIKAT PRESS

NATIONAL UNIVERSITY PUBLICATIONS

SERIES IN AMERICAN STUDIES

General Editor

JAMES P. SHENTON

Professor of History, Columbia University

CHARLES A. LEONARD

A Search For A Judicial Philosophy

Mr. Justice Roberts and the Constitutional Revolution of 1937

National University Publications
KENNIKAT PRESS
Port Washington, N.Y. • London

Library of Congress Catalog Card Number: 77-139358

ISBN 0-8046-9009-X

Manufactured in the United States of America

Published by

Kennikat Press, Inc.

Port Washington, N.Y./London

To
Emily and Rose

Acknowledgments

I would like to express my gratitude for assistance in the preparation and completion of this work. First, and foremost, I should mention the Brothers of the Christian Schools of the Baltimore Province, through whose collective efforts the research for this study was made possible. The debt owed to Brothers F. Patrick Ellis, F.S.C., and E. Patrick Sheekey, F.S.C., for reading the entire work and to Mrs. Rita Kieffer for extraordinary pains in typing the manuscript is recognized.

The assistance of Miss Elizabeth Drewry and her staff at the Roosevelt Library, Hyde Park, N.Y. and Mr. Charles Hallam, Supreme Court Librarian, was invaluable.

A special word of appreciation is due to Dr. Paul C. Bartholomew of Notre Dame University for his inspiration, urgings, and vigilance.

Finally, the deepest debt of gratitude is owed to the late Brother Azades Gabriel, F.S.C., dean of De La Salle College, Washington, D.C., who strove to plant the desire for advanced studies in all of his students and who gently prodded those who continued toward higher degrees.

C. A. L.

Contents

List of Illustrations

A SEARCH FOR A JUDICIAL PHILOSOPHY

Introduction

Justice David J. Brewer once warned:

> It is a mistake to suppose that the Supreme Court is either honored or helped by being spoken of as beyond criticism. On the contrary, the life and character of its justices should be the objects of constant watchfulness by all, and its judgments subject to the first criticism. ... True, many criticisms may be, like their authors, devoid of good taste, but better all sorts of criticism than no criticism at all.[1]

Since the days of John Marshall, the finger of Supreme Court decisions has touched, at one time or other, every aspect of American life which could be brought under the Federal Constitution.[2] These probings by the Court have been painful at times, and have resulted in loud cries of opposition from those segments of our society which were adversely affected: The future Justice Felix Frankfurter noted this influence of the Court in his article in the *Encyclopedia of the Social Sciences* in 1934:

> Thus the most important manifestations of our political and economic life may ultimately come for judgment before the Supreme Court, and the influence of the Court permeate even beyond its technical jurisdiction. That a tribunal exercising such power and beyond the reach of popular control should from time to time arouse popular resentment is far less surprising than the infrequency of such hostility and the perdurance of the institution. .... Clashes of views, and very serious ones, there have been on the Court almost from the beginning, but these judicial differences have cut deeper than any differences as to old party allegiances; they involve differences of fundamental outlook regarding the Constitution and the judge's role in construing it. Whenever Supreme Court decisions have especially offended some deep popular sentiment, movements have become rife to curb the Court's power.[3]

1

During the first term of the New Deal, from March, 1933 to February, 1937, the volume of protest increased as, item by item, the legislative program of the administration was voided by the Court.[4] Remarks, on and off the record, by members of the administration indicated that the Court's continued obstruction would not be long endured. Walter Lippmann noted this feeling on the day prior to President Roosevelt's message to Congress on the reorganization of the Federal judiciary:

> Since Congress came back to Washington it has become evident that a storm is brewing over the judiciary; there is a large amount of accumulated resentment over the laws which have been outlawed, and a strong feeling that all kinds of necessary or desirable reforms are prohibited. Those who voice this sentiment say that the expressed will of the sovereign people is being frustrated.[5]

The overwhelming victory of the Democratic candidates in the 1936 campaign[6] led the administration to view the election as a popular mandate for its program. And though the Supreme Court, as an institution, had not been an issue in the Democratic campaign, its decisions were the subject of much debate. In addition, as Arthur Krock noted in an article in *The New York Times*, "The Republicans in the campaign repeatedly notified the voters that the President was dissatisfied with the workings of the Judiciary and, by new appointments to the Supreme Court and otherwise, would, if reelected, attempt sweeping reforms."[7] Therefore, in light of the election returns, it seemed that the Court must yield to the *vox populi*.

On February 5th, 1937, the President made his move against the "reactionary" bloc on the Court through the submission of the Judicial Reorganization Bill to Congress.[8] It was made to seem part of the overall New Deal reform of the Federal government, which also included reorganization of the executive branch. The reform of the lower courts was much needed, but the attempt to "pack" the Supreme Court through the addition of six justices was immediately seen as a poorly disguised effort to bring the Court's decisions into line with the economic and social philosophy of the New Deal.[9]

There followed 168 days of verbal and political warfare which ended in defeat of the President's proposal through recommittal, as was noted by Harold Ickes, Secretary of the Interior during the New Deal, on Sunday, July 25, 1937: "On Thursday the bill to reform the Supreme Court was recommitted to the Judiciary Committee with only twenty voting against it. That this was a terrific defeat for the President cannot be denied. ...The President has been beaten and beaten badly on his Court proposal."[10]

The reasons which led to the decisive defeat of this Rooseveltian policy are varied[11] – not the least being the apparent reversal by the Court of some of its previous views on social and economic legislation. This reversal has been titled a "constitutional revolution" by the late Professor Edward S. Corwin.[12] Specifically, the reversal consisted in a new view of the power of the states and of the Federal government in the area of labor legislation.[13] These original "switches" were followed by further amplifications of state police power and of federal power under the commerce clause.

The member of the Court whose vote began the trend of reversal of precedent was chiefly Owen Josephus Roberts.[14]

It is the purpose of this study to trace the views of Mr. Justice Roberts in context with those of the other members of the Court in the area of economic and social legislation on both the federal and state level. This study will consist of an analysis of the cases which were reveiwed by the Court during those pre-New Deal years when Roberts was a justice, and those of the first term of the Roosevelt Administration until the election of 1936. There will follow an analysis of the cases of the "switch" period, the second half of the October, 1936 term, and also a discussion of the influences which impinged upon the Court, in general, and upon Roberts, in particular, during this highly controversial span in the story of the United States Supreme Court. Finally, a survey will be made of the landmark cases in the area under study from 1937 to 1941, when Chief Justice Hughes retired, and Mr. Justice Harlan F. Stone was promoted to the Chief Justiceship, who with Roberts represented the, only pre-New Deal appointments remaining on the high bench. The author hopes thereby to make a statement on what constituted the "Constitutional Revolution of 1937" and Roberts' part therein.

Notes

[1] "Government by injunction," *National Corporation Reports*, XV 848 (1898), quoted in J. O'Meara, "Forward: The Supreme Court in the American Constitutional System," *Notre Dame Lawyer* XXXIII (1958) 521.

[2] James Kent, "A Lecture, Introductory to a Course of Law Lectures, 1824," quoted in Perry Miller, *The Legal Mind in America: From Independence to the Civil War* (Garden City, N.Y., 1962), p. 103.

[3] "Supreme Court, U.S.," XIV (1934), 480.

[4] John Gunther, *Roosevelt in Retrospect* (New York, 1962), p. 307.

[5] "Today and Tomorrow," *New York Herald-Tribune,* Feb. 4, 1937, p. 21.

[6] Richard B. Morris, *Encyclopedia of American History,* rev. ed. (New York, 1961), pp. 335 & 427. There were 331 Democrats in the House, 76 in the Senate, and 523 in the Electoral College.

[7] *New York Times,* Sunday, Feb. 7, 1937, Sec. IV, p. 3.

[8] Senate Bill 1932, *Congressional Record* LXXI [75th Congress, 1st Session], p. 7375. For an exhaustive study of the events leading to the presentation of the Court Bill see William E. Leuchtenburg's article, "The Origins of Franklin D. Roosevelt's 'Court-Packing' Plan" in *The Supreme Court Review, 1966* (Chicago, 1966), p. 347ff.

[9] *New York Times,* Sat. Feb. 6, 1937, p. 16.

[10] *The Secret Diary of Harold Ickes* (New York, 1954), Vol. II "The Inside Struggle, 1936-1939," pp. 170-171.

[11] William E. Leuchtenburg, *Franklin D. Roosevelt and the New Deal* (New York, 1963), p. 237.

[12] Edward S. Corwin, *Constitutional Revolution, Ltd.* (Claremont, California, 1941), pp. 64-65.

[13] *West Coast Hotel v. Parrish,* 300 U.S. 379 (1937); *National Labor Relations Board v. Jones & Laughlin Steel Corp.,* 301 U.S. 1 (1937).

[14] *New York Times,* March 30, 1937, p. 1.

Chapter I

The Court From 1930-1933

The Appointment of Owen Josephus Roberts

"When President Hoover was called upon in 1930 to choose a successor to Mr. Justice Edward T. Sanford," wrote Osmond Fraenkel five years later, "it was recognized that the future constitutional development of the country might depend upon his choice."[1] Subsequent events demonstrated the validity of that statement.

The sudden death of Justice Sanford at sixty-four made the choice of his successor all the more difficult. While on his way to the usual Saturday conference of the Court, the Justice stopped to see his dentist about a tooth which had been troubling him. During the examination he succumbed.[2]

Sanford's career on the court had been unspectacular.[3] Prior to his promotion to the associate justiceship from the federal bench in eastern Tennessee, a noted member of the New York bar, Charles C. Burlingham, had written to Chief Justice William H. Taft that Sanford was "vacillating and fussy. I know of one particular case in which he played the granny; I think that he would be overwhelmed on the Supreme Court. Of course, he can't vacillate there—he will be swept along—but he won't be the tower of strength you need."[4] Burlingham's view seems to have been borne out, for in 1939 Professor Thomas Reed Powell of the Harvard University Law School wrote in an evaluation of the Court during Sanford's term, "There came a period of uncertainty centered chiefly in Mr. Chief Justice Taft and Mr. Justice Sanford. Only one of them was needed to have a decision go as Justices Van Devanter, McReynolds, Sutherland, and Butler were certain to vote to have it go."[5]

The nomination of a North Carolina Republican, Judge John J. Parker of the 4th Circuit Court of Appeals, by President Hoover, to replace Sanford, at first seemed to some to be a "master political stroke."[6] However, the unrest of the times due to the economic panic of six months before,[7] Negro opposition voiced through the National Association for the

5

Advancement of Colored People, aroused because of a statement made by Parker in 1920 against the advancement of that race in politics,[8] and a 1927 decision[9] enjoining a labor union from interfering with the activities of non-unionized companies, which led to opposition by organized labor — all contributed to create an obstacle to confirmation. The liberals in the Senate were able to defeat the nomination by two votes—39 to 41.[10] The fight during 1969 and 1970 over the confirmation, first of Judge Clement F. Haynsworth of Virginia and, then, of Judge G. Harrold Carswell of Florida, in which the same interests groups as in 1930 successfully opposed Supreme Court nominees reminded many observers of the rejection of the nomination of Judge Parker.

One author theorizes that when the decisions of Judge Parker are compared with those of Justice Owen Josephus Roberts, Sanford's eventual successor, the liberals "would have been better off if they had supported" Parker.[11] Later, Judge Parker took part in liberalizing labor law through a notable opinion in *Virginia Railway Co. v. System Federation #40,*[12] which subsequently was upheld by the Supreme Court.[13] Judge Parker also wrote a memorable civil rights opinion in *Barnett v. West Virginia,*[14] where he ruled that in light of changes in opinion and personnel on the Supreme Court, the *Gobitis* rule[15] was probably no longer good law.[16] A view, which was later upheld by the High Court when West Virginia appealed.[17]

Senate rejection of the Parker nomination was an error: "The facts did not support the charges made against [him] and his record ever since has been that of an able, liberal judge."[18] Certainly, Mr. Roberts was not noted as being more liberal than the man whose name preceded his to the Senate, nor was he more qualified as a jurist; rather, as Walter Murphy points out, Parker "was probably more sympathetic to the social and economic aims of the liberals than Owen J. Roberts.[19]

Some authorities see in the rejection of Parker an attack on the Court rather than on the nominee himself,[20] while others hold that the incident was an example of political muscle-flexing on the part of the liberals and insurgent Republicans who, once having demonstrated their strength, did not wish to block Hoover's nominations any further.[21] *The Christian Century* expressed similar views of the Parker fight and the opposition to the appointment of Chief Justice Hughes some months earlier:

> The whole succession of incidents which began with the fight on the confirmation of Mr. Hughes, proceeded through the defeat of the nomination of Mr. Parker and reached its climax in the confirmation of Mr. Roberts has been immensely salutary. It has been salutary for the country at large, for it has given millions of citizens a new understanding of the powers of the Supreme Court and of the way in

which that Court when composed of conservatives can fasten a reactionary social and political policy on the nation. It has been even more salutary for Mr. Hoover and his advisors, for it has shown them the extent of public dissatisfaction with the Court as it has been and of the expectation that the President will use his appointing power to place on the supreme bench men who will construe the law liberally and with first regard for human rights.[22]

President Hoover sent the name of Owen Josephus Roberts to the Hill two days after the rejection of Judge Parker. There was much speculation about whose advice was followed in making the nomination—various names were mentioned as sponsors. The *Chicago Daily News* declared that Senator David A. Reed from Pennsylvania, a representative of the Mellon interests, had suggested Roberts.[23] On the other hand, Drew Pearson and Robert Allen stated categorically that it was at the suggestion of Mr. Justice Harlan F. Stone, whose advice against the Parker nomination had been ignored by the White House, that the Philadelphia lawyer was advanced to the high court. Roberts had been a special counsel for the government when Stone was Calvin Coolidge's Attorney General in 1924.[24] Senator George W. Pepper, also of Pennsylvania, was "accused" of using his influence to secure the nomination of Mr. Roberts. Pepper, subsequently, denied any participation,[25] and in 1940 former President Herbert C. Hoover wrote that "the name of Mr. Roberts, among others, was proposed by Attorney General [William D.] Mitchell. I selected Justice Roberts from among them after careful study of his record."[26]

The wisdom of appointing at that time another justice who had no judicial experience has been questioned. However, Professor Cortez Ewing, after careful study of the history of Supreme Court appointments, felt compelled to state:

> ... among those twenty-seven [justices without prior judicial experience] are many with whom each of us will violently disagree on constitutional interpretation. But I am still unconvinced that the selection of juristically experienced judges would have improved upon the contributions which these political appointees have made to the constitutional law of the United States.[27]

And John R. Schmidhauser noted:

> There is little in the history of the Supreme Court to suggest that justices with prior judicial experience were more objective or better qualified than those who lacked such experience. As a matter of fact, despite the examples of Holmes and Cardozo, some of the Supreme Court's most distinguished members, notably Marshall, Taney, Curtis, Campbell, Miller, Bradley, Hughes, Brandeis, and Stone, were totally lacking in this experience before their appointments to the Supreme Court.[28]

While lacking judicial experience, Roberts had the other qualifications to make a good judge. These were noted by the editors of the period. The Philadelphia *Evening Bulletin,* speaking editorially on May 9, 1930, declared, "it is somewhat humiliating to note that the eminent legal and judicial qualifications of Mr. Owen J. Roberts of this city are actually subordinated to, and conditioned upon, the appeal he has made to the progressive bloc in the Senate."[29] The *New York Herald-Tribune* referred to the nominee as "one of the outstanding practitioners before the Supreme Court" and as having "an unusual degree of experience, learning, and character of mind."[30] While *The Washington Post* noted, "Mr. Roberts does not possess judicial experience as Judge Parker does, but he does stand at the forefront of the American Bar, and his character and fairmindedness are above criticism."[31] The ultra-liberal *Philadelphia Record* found that "as a learned, high-minded and constructive lawyer of liberal convictions, Mr. Roberts commands public respect and will do much to strengthen public confidence in the Supreme Court."[32] It was an opinion which this same newspaper later had reason to question.

Four years after Mr. Roberts had joined the Court, Theodore C. Wallen had speculated that perhaps he was "only at the threshold of a great career."[33] Wallen also noted that Roberts, like Brandeis, had rendered important public service prior to his promotion to the Supreme Court; in both instances their activities were in non-political capacities.[34]

Owen J. Roberts' varied public and private career extended back to his graduation with highest honors from the University of Pennyslvania Law School in 1898. The new lawyer was immediately employed as a lecturer by his alma mater, where he gradually rose to the rank of full professor specializing in real property. In 1901 he was appointed first assistant district attorney for Philadelphia County, his first and only political position. Three years later, he returned to teaching at the Law School and to private practice, which included counseling the local public transportation facilities. Roberts resigned his position at the University in 1919 to give his full attention to the law firm of Roberts, Montgomery, and McKeehan, which he had help found seven years before.[35] In May, 1918 Roberts was named Special Deputy Attorney General for the prosecution of violations of the Espionage Act of 1917 by United States Attorney General Thomas Gregory. He successfully conducted a number of cases arising in the eastern Pennsylvania area.

In mid-February, 1924 the future justice came into national prominence as special counsel for the United States, which post he retained until his elevation to the Supreme Court in June, 1930. Senator Pepper, who had been one of Roberts' mentors in the Law School, is credited with placing his name before President Coolidge.[36] The post had been created for the purpose of investigating and prosecuting of the oil reserve scandals arising during the Harding Administration. Mr. Roberts, together with his co-counsel, former Senator Atlee Pomerene of Ohio, succeeded in having the oil lease to the Elk Hills reserve and contract for the Pearl Harbor Naval Fuel Oil Storage Project with companies controlled by Edward Doheny cancelled, and the termination of the Teapot Dome lease with Harry Sinclair. In addition, Secretary of the Interior Albert B. Fall was convicted on bribe-taking charges.[37]

Roberts pleaded many times before the high tribunal and, on occasion, was involved in a case of constitutional consequence. Among such cases were *Pennsylvania Hospital v. Philadelphia,* 245 U.S. 20 (1917); *Quaker City Cab Co. v. Pennsylvania,* 277 U.S. 389 (1928); *Liggett Co. v. Baldridge,* 278 U.S. 105 (1928); and his last case before becoming a member of the Court, *Baizley Iron Works v. Span,* 281 U.S. 222 (1930).[38] At the time Roberts was nominated to the high tribunal he was involved in a unique procedure on behalf of the Commonwealth of Pennsylvania in an original jurisdiction proceeding between New York and New Jersey over water rights.[39]

Though Roberts had represented large corporations during his years of legal practice, including on occasion the Pennsylvania Railroad, his colleagues held that he was not a "corporation lawyer" in the usual meaning of the term. He was, they maintained, temporarily employed by corporations, but it was not a "full time job."[40] The distinction was difficult for some to grasp, especially for later critics of Justice Roberts' voting and views on the Supreme Court.

Drew Pearson and Robert Allen believed that there were two great factors in the development of the future justice. The first was his wife, the former Elizabeth Caldwell Rogers, whom these authors view as a "Pere Joseph" figure throughout Roberts' career.[41] They maintain that Roberts, himself, was more moderate than his wife but argue that his opinions were influenced by his outspoken, reactionary, anti-New Deal spouse.[42]

> While she could not for a moment intrude her ideas on the legal details by which her husband arrives at his opinions, nevertheless her own opinions on such things as the New Deal, crop control, labor legislation, and class consciousness, expressed freely and with pithy vigor over the breakfast table during recent years, undoubtedly, have played a more decisive part in some of the recent decisions of the Supreme Court than some of the lawyers that argued them.[43]

The second factor, according to Pearson and Allen, was the city where Roberts was born on May 2, 1875, the city of "Brotherly Love and Big Incomes."[44] It seems that the authors are guilty of those preconceptions of which they accuse others, when they consider that the influence of the metropolis could be so one-sided as to stamp a "mid-Victorian" image on its sons, thus rendering them capable of such social and economic insensibilities which they impute to the Justice and his lady.

Just where Justice Roberts stood in political philosophy has been the subject of much controversey before, during, and since he served on the high bench. The confusion about his position is due both to a lack of political involvement[45] and to the fact that his public appearances were on behalf of government while his private activities were mainly as a representative of business interests. As the future justice, Robert H. Jackson, wrote in 1941, "the life of Justice Roberts has been much preoccupied with professional work of a highly creditable quality but which revealed little of his philosophy of government. His public service had been largely legal, rather than policy-making in character."[46]

In February, 1923 Roberts, a lifelong Republican, delivered a speech before the annual dinner of the Trust Company Division of the American Bankers Association. This speech was frequently quoted in later years to indicate his *anti-liberal* leanings. He deplored the multiplication of administrative agencies because, he said, "the businessman in America feels that he is doing business with a minion of government looking over his shoulder with an upraised arm and a threatening scowl."[47] Ernest Bates, for example, some twelve years later, noted that Roberts had thereby condemned the New Deal ten years before its birth.[48] However, if Roberts' remarks are read in context, they are no more illiberal than the position taken by Mr. Justice Brandeis whose opposition to bigness in government, including the early New Deal measures, as well as to business, is well known.[49]

Commentary on Mr. Justice Roberts' political posture is as confused and contradictory as is that on the early New Deal Court and Roberts' part in its change of mind in 1937. Views extend from one end of the spectrum to the other.

Merlo Pusey, biographer of Chief Justice Hughes, believes Roberts to have been basically a liberal.[50] *Outlook* declared in 1930 that "we expect to find Justice Roberts not infrequently, siding with Holmes, Stone, and Brandeis."[51] Five years later another author noted that the hope aroused at the Roberts' nomination that the dissenting three, Holmes, Brandeis, and Stone, would be more frequently victorious, had been fulfilled.[52] The

Scholastic declared in the same year that "on the whole Justice Roberts has been on the side of the liberals,"[53] while the *Chicago Daily News* editorialized at the time of Mr. Roberts' nomination that "his associates have been of the sort to justify the belief that, if he is confirmed, in dealing with problems of law his views will be both sound and progressive."[54] And one newspaper, which at a future date would single out Mr. Roberts as the sole cause of the New Deal's troubles with the Court, in an editorial titled, "Owen J. Roberts, Liberal, a Splendid Supreme Court Choice," stated:

> Mr. Roberts is not a crusading progressive on social and economic questions and, as a conspicuously successful lawyer, his abilities have been largely at the service of property interests. But four years ago, he was the first choice for Attorney General of so ardent and exacting a progressive as Clifford Pinchot. And his career indicates that on fundamental issues, public rights and human welfare, he would far more often be found in agreement with Justice Holmes, Brandeis, and Stone than with Chief Justice Hughes and the majority.[55]

Opposed to the foregoing views is Edward S. Corwin's remark that Roberts was considered conservative even in the conservative company of the Philadelphia bar,[56] and Frank R. Kent's observation that the nominee's record shows that he "is simply not a liberal."[57] The *New York Herald-Tribune* concluded that "if there is any meaning in labels, Mr. Roberts, the metropolitan corporation lawyer, is at least as conservative as Judge Parker. He is a member of the board of directors of several corporations."[58] At the same time *Outlook* pointed out that the Washington newsmen, who had hounded Hughes and Parker in their columns because of their conservatism, had avoided attacking Mr. Roberts in a similar vein because of their feelings of friendship toward him, but "few, if any, of [them] consider Mr. Roberts to be an economic liberal and none sympathize with the decisions that have flowed from the pleadings before the Court to which he has been named."[59] Finally, *Newsweek,* looking back to twenty-five years before, noted that "although considered a conservative when appointed to the Bench by Herbert Hoover, his vote decided many five-to-four rulings both for and against the New Deal."[60]

Standing between the extreme views detailed above are those who saw Mr. Roberts as a middle-of-the-roader. The authors of *The 168 Days* hold this view[61] and they are joined by the editors of *Fortune*[62] and *Newsweek*[63] magazines, and The Baltimore *Sun* who declared:

> Neither the liberals nor the conservatives can be absolutely certain in which direction his mind will move. The liberals have no such reason

to believe that he will, in general, throw his strength with the
Holmes-Brandeis-Stone group as they would if Chief Justice Cardozo
of New York had been appointed. The conservatives have no reason to
believe Mr. Roberts will join the Sutherland party on the Supreme
Court as they would have if Judge Parker had been confirmed.[64]

The Philadelphia *Evening Bulletin* added the following about the same
time:

> Mr. Roberts' whole life in his contact with public affairs in the
> city, as well as in the nation, has shown him to be a liberal in the true
> sense, progressive, forward-minded, always seeking to elevate the tone
> and level of political life and political morality. But also in a true
> sense conservative, seeking to square public policies with American
> traditions in the spirit of the United States Constitution.[65]

In 1942 William O. Trapp, who talked at great length with the Justice
while he was still on the Bench, concluded that Mr. Roberts was neither
liberal nor conservative; however, in the final analysis Mr. Trapp judged
that Mr. Justice Roberts would have to be classified as a moderate
liberal.[66]

Indeed, some authorities, for example, Thomas R. Powell, Walter F.
Murphy, and Fred Rodell, held that Roberts defied classification. And
Ernest Bates, writing in *The New Republic* in 1936, made the following
comparison:

> McReynolds, Hughes, and Roberts all had liberal backgrounds
> and were connected with government regulations of industry. Their
> subsequent conservatism apparently violating their original political
> approach is hence more interesting than the consistent, but quite
> traditional conservatism of Van Devanter, Sutherland, and Butler.[67]

Two men who knew Roberts as well as any of his non-court
associates take a view different from those set out above. Mr. John Lord
O'Brian, for fifty-two years a member of the Supreme Court bar, knew
Roberts socially, as well as professionally. He believes that the Justice was
a man who took a pragmatic rather than a theoretical approach to legal
questions.[68] And Albert J. Schneider, who was associated with the Justice
from his earlier Philadelphia days, and, except for the 1930 term was Mr.
Roberts' only law clerk, is in agreement.[69] Dean Erwin Griswold has
summarized this view of Roberts' thinking:

> In considering his approach to the problems which came to him,
> the essential fact to keep in mind, I think, is that he dealt with them
> as a lawyer. He was not a philosopher and did not attempt to be. He
> was not a sociologist, and did not think that lawyers should be

sociologists, at least while they occupied positions on the bench. He was no more interested, as the saying goes, in Mr. Herbert Spencer's *Social Statics* than he was in some other Justices' social ecstatics. He was not seeking goals. He was just trying to decide cases. ... As an active lawyer at heart, he thought that precedents and continuity were important, and he did not depart from them in any bursts of emotional enthusiasm.[70]

Despite this confusion about Mr. Justice Roberts' political philosophy, the only serious objection to his confirmation arose over his views on the 18th Amendment. In the 1923 address to which reference has been made above, Roberts denounced the Prohibition Amendment as the insertion of a "police regulation" into the Constitution, which was lowered thereby "to the status of a city ordinance."[71] Six years later, Mr. Roberts declined to serve on a commission established by President Hoover to investigate the enforcement of the Prohibition Law.[72] Frank R. Kent in his column of May 11, 1930, commented that "it seems that there ought to be some opposition to Mr. Roberts. It seems that while there is nothing in his record to indicate that he does not think the 14th & 15th Amendments to the Constitution perfectly splendid, he does not revere the 18th Amendment. In fact, he has expressed the view that it has no business in the Constitution at all."[73] The prohibition issue was raised publicly by Senator Morris Sheppard of Texas, but it failed to develop sufficient support to block confirmation.

On May 19, 1930, ten days after the President had nominated Mr. Roberts, Senator William E. Borah reported favorably on the nomination to the Senate on behalf of the Committee on the Judiciary, and the matter was placed on the Executive Calendar.[74] The following day Senator Charles McNary moved for a discussion of executive business in open session, and after Senator George Norris had validated the fact that the Judiciary Committee had given its unanimous approval, the Senate in action approaching record time—without roll call and in less than a minute—[75] confirmed the nomination of Owen Josephus Roberts to be Associate Justice of the Supreme Court of the United States. He took the oath and assumed his seat on June 2nd, the last day of the term.

The Twilight of Holmes

When Roberts assumed his seat, the Supreme Court was entering a period of transition. The character of the pre-1930 Court had been shaped to a great degree by the recently retired Chief Justice Taft. Fearing a sudden change in its membership, Taft had written to a friend in 1929, "I must stay on the Court in order to prevent the Bolsheviki from getting control."[76] If the members of the Court were diverse in many things, they had at least one common quality—a ripe age—the average was a little over sixty-eight. To Taft's chagrin, poor health forced his own retirement before the end of the year, and, by coincidence, Justice Sanford was to die on the same day as himself, March 8th of the following year. This gave President Hoover, whom Taft had suspected of liberal tendencies, two places to be filled on the Court.[77]

One historian of the period has noted that "like a legislature the Court had its right, left, and center."[78] Roberts was aware of the pull of these various forces within the high tribunal, and a short time before he took the oath, he told some of his friends that "he had made up his mind to vote with complete independence on the merits of each case."[79]

Since 1922 the dominant group on the Court had been composed of Justices Willis Van Devanter, James C. McReynolds, George Sutherland, and Pierce Butler—the "four horsemen" as they were frequently characterized by their critics. They were united by a belief in the doctrine of "constitutional fundamentalism" which excluded amendment of the Constitution, as they viewed it, by interpretation of the Court.[80] Professor T. R. Powell gave his views on the members of the group in the following terms:

> The four stalwarts differ among themselves in temperament. I think that Mr. Justice Butler knows just what he is up to and that he is playing God or Lucifer to keep the world from going the way he does not want it to. Sutherland seems to me a naive doctrinaire person who really does not know the world as it is. His incompetence in economic reasoning is amazing when one contrasts it with the excellence of his historical and legal . . . . Mr. Justice McReynolds is a tempestuous cad, and Mr. Justice Van Devanter is an old dodo.[81]

Van Devanter had been nominated to the Bench by President Taft in 1910. A native of Indiana, he had moved to Wyoming as a young man, where he had a spectacular legal career, which was climaxed by appointment as chief justice of the Supreme Court of the Wyoming Territory at 30. His career on the United States Supreme Court was a paradox; he was perhaps the most able legal thinker on the Court in the period, yet he wrote the least number of opinions. Some attribute his failure to write to arthritis, which made the mechanics of penmanship painful,[82] while others believe that the cause was more psychological than physical.[83] A memo from Justice Sutherland to the Chief Justice on the *Quaker City Cab* case[84] in 1928 is characteristic of the esteem in which Van Devanter was held by his brethren. "If Van Devanter writes the opinion, I shall unhesitatingly agree to it. If written by anyone else, I will agree to whatever you and he accept."[85] The Justice was well-beloved by his brethren, and his resignation—the first after the court fight of 1937— left a personal vacuum for all its members.

McReyonlds had been Woodrow Wilson's Attorney General, and his close association with the moving spirit of *The New Freedom* would have led one to believe that he would take a liberal view of the powers of government after his elevation to the Court. As frequently happens, however, this expectation remained unfulfilled, when he developed into the most outspoken conservative on the high court. McReynolds was considered a rude, sullen bigot[86] whom Taft had characterized as a "continual grouch."[87] Despite this uncomplimentary view, Alsop and Catledge tell us that his relationship with Roberts was most cordial.[88]

The chief spokesman for the *Conservative* group was George Sutherland, whose English birth seemed to endow him with the facility of pen characteristic of that people. A resident of Utah, he had represented that state in the United States Senate and, while there, had become a close friend of Warren G. Harding, who, as President, named him to the high bench in 1922.[89] Sutherland was an admirer of Herbert Spencer and his *Social Statics,* and in 1921 he gave expression to his views in an address to the New York Bar Association when he declared that the natural laws of supply and demand should be classified with the multiplication tables, the Sermon on the Mount, and the American Constitution.[90]

The junior member of the group, Pierce Butler, had been a corporation lawyer in Minnesota. Chief Justice Taft had maneuvered Butler onto the Bench in 1922 and looked upon him as a bulwark against the liberal wave which the Chief saw arising.[91] In 1929 Taft wrote to Butler "that the most that could be hoped for 'is the continued life of enough of the present membership ... to prevent disastrous reversals of our present attitude. With Van and Mac, and Sutherland and you and Sanford, there will be five to steady the boat .... We must not give up at once.' "[92] The nomination of a man of Butler's social background represented a change in the trend of the nomination of the period. And one wonders if his aggressiveness was not a reflex action against his humble origin. His last Chief, Hughes, considered him the most difficult man on the Court.[93]

It has been proposed by some that the geographical origins of the members of the Court influenced their views on governmental interference in the economic life of the country.[94] While it is difficult to determine the effect of geopolitical forces, it cannot be denied that the "westerners" did tend to look askance at legislative and administrative controls, while the "easterners" took a more liberal view.

The liberal group, which had been in the minority since the resignation of Justice John H. Clarke in 1922, included Justices Oliver Wendell Holmes, Jr., Louis D. Brandeis, and Harlan F. Stone. The relationship between Holmes and Brandeis was especially close, both on and off the Court. While their conclusions about the law were similar, the path each took to achieve them was different. Holmes found the basis for his reasoning in the *philosophy* of sociological jurisprudence, while Brandeis found his in its *practical application.* Though it was Holmes who had championed Roscoe Pound's thesis on the law, it was Brandeis who had first introduced it to the Court[95] in his brief in *Muller v. Oregon.*[96] After 1922 the familiar "Holmes and Brandeis, jj., dissenting" appeared with increasing frequency in the *United States Reports.*[97]

For years Holmes had fought for judicial restraint. "It is a misfortune," he had declared, "if a judge reads his conscious or unconscious sympathy with one side or the other prematurely into the law and forgets that what seems to him to be first principles are believed by half his fellowmen to be wrong."[98] And on another occasion he told Justice Stone [who was sixty-one at the time], "Young man, about seventy-five years ago I learned that I was not God. And so, when the people of the various states want to do something I can't find anything in the Constitution expressly forbidding them to do, I say, whether I like it or not, 'Goddammit, let them do it.' "[99]

Holmes was approaching the end of his thirty-year term when Roberts joined the High Court, and he was uncertain of the new man's position. He wrote to his friend, Harold J. Laski, "I foresee some clashes of opinion and am wondering what turn our new member will take. He makes a good impression, but as yet I have little notice of his characteristics."[100] The mental powers of the "Yankee from Olympus" were hampered by a body marked by Civil War scars and eroded by an active life of eighty-nine years. The familiar naps in the courtroom and conference chamber were becoming more and more frequent. On January 4, 1932 "Holmes & Brandeis dissenting" appeared for the last time in the *United States Reports* appended to the opinion of Mr. Roberts in *Arizona Grocery Co. v. Atcheson, Topeka, & Sante Fe Railway Co.;*[101] and one week later, Holmes read his last opinion. As one biographer has described the scene:

> When his time came, Holmes leaned forward, picked up the papers in *Dunn v. the United States.*[102] Spectators noticed how well he looked; the cheeks were pink against the white hair and mustache. But when he began to read, Holmes' voice faltered, thickened. He shook his head impatiently and went on. But what he said was barely audible beyond the first row of benches.

At the noon recess, Holmes left the Courtroom with the other justices, ate his box lunch, and returned to the Bench. When the Court rose at four-thirty, he got his hat and coat, walked over to the clerk's desk. "I won't be down tomorrow," he said.

That night Holmes wrote his resignation to the President.[103]

Benjamin N. Cardozo, Chief Justice of New York, was nominated as Holmes' successor. His name had been brought forward on a number of previous occasions, but his Jewish ancestry and the fact that New York was already represented on the Court had caused him to be passed over. In 1932 because there were already two New Yorkers on the Bench, Mr. Justice Stone offered to resign his seat "so that the nation might have the benefit of Cardozo's great learning."[104] Holmes himself, though not participating in the choice of his successor, had indicated that his preference was for Cardozo whose philosophy he considered close to his own.

On March 2nd Cardozo took the seat which traditionally had been occupied by New Englanders and associated with such names as Joseph Story, Benjamin Curtis, Horace Gray, and, most recently, Holmes. A quiet, intellectual bachelor, Cardozo had already earned a reputation as a legal philosopher and a practical jurist prior to his elevation to the Court.[105] In a prophetic moment in 1921 he had written, "My duty as a judge may be to objectify in law not my own aspirations and convictions and philosophies, but of the men and women of my time. Hardly shall I do this well if my own sympathies and beliefs and passionate devotions are with a time that is past."[106] He strove to activate these words during his all too short term on the Court.

With Holmes' departure Brandeis took over the leadership of the dissenters. His name had been etched in American legal history in 1908 as a result of his brief in the *Muller*[107] case. Eight years later, Brandeis brought his crusade for economic democracy with him to the Supreme Court, and these views nearly blocked his confirmation. William Howard Taft and six other past presidents of the American Bar Association opposed the nomination and noted their position in a statement to the Senate Judiciary Committee. "Taking into consideration the reputation, character, and professional career of Mr. Louis D. Brandeis, he is not a fit person to be a member of the Supreme Court of the United States."[108] The real basis for opposition, according to John Schmidhauser, was Brandeis' lack of sympathy for the values which these leaders of the bar cherished.[109]

Mr. Justice Brandeis' views on the New Deal were not clear as yet; he opposed bigness in any form in which property rights might overwhelm human rights, yet he favored government intervention to protect those

human rights. He exercised much influence in policy making during the
first years of Franklin D. Roosevelt's administration through his contact
with the young lawyers recently arrived in the Capital. The weekly teas at
the Brandeis' apartment brought together many of the "names" in
government for counsel and direction.[110]

In contrast to the usual picture of the gentle justice was the one
which his friends sometimes saw of a proud, imperious, and at times
overbearing man.

The third member of the group, Stone, had come to the Court after a
noted academic career, which was capped by a nine-month period as Calvin
Coolidge's reforming Attorney General. At first, he was "a sensible,
practical conservative, drawn to Butler and Van Devanter, mistrustful of
Holmes . . . and positively repelled by Brandeis."[111] Dean Griswold tells us
that Stone was in no way a disciple of Holmes and Brandeis though he
gradually came to hold the same views but for different reasons.[112] At
times, however, he came to question his own thinking in light of the
majority's consistent rejection of change and the fact that men of ability as
Hughes and Roberts, were unconvinced by his views.

The cleavage between the two groups was not so sharp as the
publicity of the day attempted to make it seem, nor did it apply to any
specific piece of legislation, but rather to the long-range consequences of a
movement.[113] Indeed, Professor Swisher informs us that "Stone was no
more of a radical reformer than were Holmes and Brandeis, but the three
of them [and we might add Cardozo] and an increasing number of people
throughout the country took the position that the Court should not use
the device of judicial review to curb social legislation they disliked unless it
was clearly prohibited by constitutional language.[114] And as Stone wrote
to Felix Frankfurter in April, 1930, "It is not a contest between
conservatism and radicalism, nearly so much as a difference arising from an
inadequate understanding of the relation of law to the social and economic
forces which control society."[115] A study of the voting in the years
immediately following Roberts' accession to the Court reveals how few
cases were presented to the Justices which would cause open conflict.[116]
In the 204 decisions in the area of federal and state economic power,
which were handed down during the 1930 to 1932 terms, 173 were
unanimous, i.e., in 85 percent there was complete agreement. As Samuel
Hendel wrote in his analysis of the Court under the leadership of Charles
Evans Hughes, "The early Hughes Court represented an uneasy compromise
between the *laissez-faire* and the social welfare conceptions of the
state."[117]

Standing between the two camps on the Court were its newest members, Chief Justice Charles Evans Hughes and Associate Justice Roberts, who had been named to the Court within four months of each other. Hughes' career had been, by far, the more illustrious of the two. After a period of successful law practice and some teaching experience at Cornell University Law School, he served as governor of New York from 1907 to 1910, when he was named to succeed Justice David J. Brewer on the United States Supreme Court. In 1916 he gave up his seat on the Court to run as Republican presidential candidate against Woodrow Wilson. It is interesting to note that, according to former Justice Felix Frankfurter, this was the one act that Hughes regretted during his life.[118] Wilson's victory forced Hughes' return to private practice, but five years later he was called upon by President Harding to become Secretary of State. In 1927 he became the American representative on the Permanent Court of Arbitration (The Hague Tribunal) and he was elected to the Permanent Court of International Justice (The World Court) the following year. Two years later, he was nominated by President Hoover to succeed William Howard Taft as Chief Justice of the United States.[119]

During his earlier term on the Court he had been known for his liberal view of state and federal economic controls as a result of his opinions in the *Minnesota* and *Shreveport Rate* cases.[120] However, opinion varied on what the new Chief Justice's views on the same constitutional questions were in 1930, and a bitter fight developed over his confirmation. The main issue, besides his representation of "big business" with its accompanying lucrative fees, was his resignation in 1916 to run for office.[121] Following a violent three-day debate, however, he was confirmed by a vote of 52 to 26.[122]

Hughes' eleven-year administration of the Court is almost unanimously recognized as one of the great periods in its history. Writing in 1941, the then Attorney General, Robert H. Jackson, declared:

> . . . At no time in my governmental service, even at times of which I am most critical, have the Justices rated as a "lot of mummies." It has been a sharply divided Court, but it has not been an inferior or contemptible Court. Charles Evans Hughes has been a Chief Justice in the great tradition. Each side of questions on which the Court has disagreed has been represented by Justices of ability and earnestness and deep conviction.[123]

Mr. Justice Roberts, who served under Hughes' leadership for eleven years, referred to him as an "administrative master" who was able to hold his Court together on most occasions, many more than he is credited with, as will be demonstrated below. In addition, "men whose views were as sharply opposed," Roberts noted, "as those of Van Devanter and Brandeis, or those of Sutherland and Cardozo, were at one in their admiration and affectionate regard for their presiding officer."[124] Former Justice Frankfurter has numbered Hughes among the three greatest Chief Justices of the United States, along with Marshall and Taney.[125] And another commentator notes:

> No Chief Justice controlled his flock so firmly as did Hughes, whom most students and observers of the Court, as well as those who served with him, have generally regarded as the most effective—even if on occasion somewhat arbitrary—organizer, leader, and disciplinarian along these lines since Mr. Chief Justice Marshall's regime .... Be that as it may, Mr. Chief Justice Hughes was immensely popular as a leader of his bench, and he was the only member of the Court to whom Mr. Justice McReynolds would defer.[126]

As demanding a critic of the Court as Max Lerner was forced to concede that Hughes was the very model of a Supreme Court judge in bearing and demeanor.[127]

The accusation has been made that the Chief Justice used his powers of persuasion in an unseemly manner in order to change votes. His biographer has answered that charge thus:

> The idea is absurd to anyone who knew the court from the inside. No man of any intelligence would have attempted to dominate Brandeis, Butler, or Roberts. Hughes recognized that the court was composed of judges of wide experience, deep learning, independent views, and profound convictions. Everyone's brains, as he used to say, were on the table. It was ridiculous to suppose that the brethren could be swayed from any settled habits of thinking by high-powered arguments or emotional appeals. Consequently, Hughes made no such appeals. We have Stone's word that the Chief's influence upon "the efficiency and morale of the Court ... cannot be exaggerated." But Stone attributes that influence solely to Hughes' "passion for prompt and faithful performance of the work of the court," and to his "painstaking care and unflagging energy."
> Nor did the Chief Justice solicit support for his views outside the conference. He had only contempt for the kind of chief who would take a judge aside and say, "Can't you see the tight spot we're in; you've got to help us out." He knew, of course, that the four conservatives conferred together on specific cases. But he would neither join their circle nor sponsor a rival one. While his door was always kept open to any member of the Court who wished to discuss any kind of problem, he reserved his views of cases before the court (with one or two exceptions) for expression at the conference where all the Justices would be present.[128]

And Mr. Justice Roberts, who, himself, was supposed to have been the object of Hughes' pressure on occasion, declared in 1948:

> Chief Justice Hughes was a stickler for proprieties ... I am sure that it was part of a well thought out program that the Chief Justice, after the argument of the case and prior to the conference, did not discuss the merits of that case or the probable disposition of it with any of his brethren. He absorbed the arguments and the briefs of counsel .... [But] what his conclusion was, none of us knew until he announced it at conference. He neither leaned on anyone else for advice nor did he proffer advice or assistance to any of us, but left each of us to form his own conclusions to be laid on the table at conference in free and open discussion.[129]

Professor T. R. Powell noted a shift toward the liberal position when Hughes and Roberts came to the high bench. "A perceptible swing of the pendulum," he called it.[130] There are those who credit Hughes alone for this movement, maintaining that Roberts simply followed his lead. That this was not certain can be seen from a series of articles written by Irving Brant in 1937 which attempted to demonstrate that Hughes was not a liberal at all.[131] Brant's findings were not widely accepted, however, and most felt that, in general, the Chief had not repudiated his earlier liberal views. Arthur Krock noted in *The New York Times*, "... Mr. Chief Justice Hughes was supposed to have abandoned the liberalism of his youth. More and more, it is becoming clear that this was a popular delusion, fostered by newspaper cartoons and editorial epithets."[132]

Professor Carl Brent Swisher sees both Hughes and Roberts occupying the "middle ground, shifting back and forth between liberal and conservative positions."[133] This view is supported by most of the commentators of the period, including many of the journalists. At least one author, however, believes that Hughes was the "swing man," not Roberts.[134] On the other hand, Fred Rodell makes a strong argument for the opposite view:

> ... Charles Evans Hughes is regularly catalogued by legal historians as having shared the balance of power between the liberal and conservative wings of the Court .... What the Court records prove is that Hughes held no such power at all. True, his votes did veer, as did Roberts's from one side to the other; but never once in a major case did he cast the deciding vote; for never once in a major case was Hughes to the right of Roberts. Thus, with five brethren to the right of him and three clearly to the left, Hughes could only choose whether a conservative decision should be scored 5-4 or 6-3; he could never determine that a decision be liberal unless Roberts, the Court's swinging keystone, came along. Proof of this lies in the simple fact

that Hughes dissented several times—and always on the liberal side—
in the big cases that came up during that drastic age, whereas Roberts
never dissented once. It was Roberts who, for practical purposes,
steered the Court that Hughes headed, whenever the Justices called
them close.[135]

The discussion of cases that follows proposes to determine which
view is correct.

Cases & Comment

Professor Swisher interprets the economic rulings of the Court from
1919 to 1933 in the following way:

> Supreme Court decisions between the first World War and the New
> Deal reflected the steady expansion of state and federal regulatory
> power over economic enterprise and the desires of the judiciary to
> establish barriers against the overextension of such power all along the
> line. Cases involving state regulations were so numerous and varied as
> to discredit gloomy predictions of the decimation of the states in the
> face of growing federal authority. The principal limitations upon state
> authority resulted not so much from the expansion of federal
> regulatory power as from judicial holdings that state regulation
> violated some provision of the constitution. The decisions reflected
> concern of the courts about the increasing obvious departure of the
> United States from laissez-faire principles. They had their counterpart
> in the other decisions similarly limiting the powers of the federal
> government.[136]

In the three terms prior to the arrival of the New Deal legislation
before the Court, that tribunal was presented with fifty-six cases involving
questions of federal power in the economic sphere, exclusive of tax suits.
Of this number the largest single group was centered on the control of
interstate commerce and the laws implementing that control. Justice
Roberts, some nineteen years later, declared that "once the doctrine was
established that, in order to protect the power of regulation [of interstate
commerce] in the national field, federal agencies might interfere with state
regulation, a wide door was open for economic and welfare legislation on
the national scale, and much legislation followed."[137] In this period before
the change of view in 1937, the Court made some final attempts to limit
the definition of "interstate commerce."

While the I.C.C. was supported in seventeen of the twenty-eight times
it appeared before the Court, most of these decisions were merely
restatements of well-established principles. In 1931, however, the Justices

veered from the line of precedents traceable to the *Shreveport Rate Case*[138] and ruled through the Chief Justice, who in 1914 had fathered that precedent, that the Commission had made an "inexpedient exercise" of its recognized power to bring intrastate rates in balance with those charged in interstate transportation.[139] It might be noted that this case was decided by a unanimous Court and therefore had the support of those members who in future days would attack Mr. Justice Roberts publicly, as well as privately, for substituting his judgment for that of a duly constituted policy-making body. On the final day of the term, however, the Court did uphold the commission's decision in similar circumstances in two cases.[140]

The Court was asked to rule on the effect which the economic conditions brought on by the Depression, should have on railroad rates. The case was *Atcheson, Topeka, and Sante Fe R. v. U.S.*[141] The Chief Justice again speaking for the high court declared:

> There can be no question as to the change in conditions upon which the new hearing was asked. Of that change we may take judicial notice. It is the outstanding contemporary fact dominating thought and action throughout the country. As the interstate Commerce Commission said in its recent report to Congress,[142] "a depression such as the country is now passing through is a new experience to the present generation."[143]

However, in a similar case in the following term Mr. Justice Roberts declared for a unanimous Court:

> The Commission is not bound to allow existing unreasonable rates to stand solely because revision will in some degree adversely affect carriers suffering from economic depression. The decision in the *Sante Fe* case is not to be extended to require a rehearing in every rate case for changed economic conditions, however insignificant the effect of the order on carrier revenue. The rule announced, while intended to safeguard substantial rights of the railroads, may not be invoked where its application would disenable the Commission to protect the interest of the public.[144]

The powers of the I.C.C. were challenged in non-rate matters in fifteen cases during the 1930 to 1932 terms, and in eleven decisions the vote was in favor of the commission, in all but two cases, unanimous. In one of the more significant decisions, *United States v. Chicago, Milwaukee, St. Paul & Pacific Railroad*,[145] the Court in a 5-3 division ruled that the Commission had no supervisory jurisdiction over the reorganization of a bankrupt railroad. In a preview of things to come the Court declared that

The power to regulate commerce is not absolute, but is subject to the
limitations and guarantees of the Constitution, among which are those
providing that private property shall not be taken for public use
without just compensation and that no person shall be deprived of
life, liberty, or property without due process of law. . . . . Both liberty
of contract and the right to property here are involved. The contrast
was valid and had been so adjudged by the court having jurisdiction of
the foreclosure and sale. The parties to it were willing and were
entitled to have the contract executed according to its terms. There is
no power in any department of the government to order otherwise.
. . . *Any legislative or administrative edict which purports to
empower the carrier to take the property without compensation and
dispose of it,* not as the contract provides, but as the governmental
body may direct, *must fail as a futile attempt to accomplish what the
Constitution does not permit.* [146] [Italics supplied]

Mr. Justice Stone once indicated that it was here, when Roberts voted with
the majority, that he felt that the latter began to drift away from the
liberal side.[147] It is true that this is the first time that the Justice
disagreed about governmental powers with the more liberal members of the
Court, but his later votes would show him to be still frequently in the
company of Holmes, Brandeis, and Stone. Later in the year, the Court
ruled again that arbitrary and unreasonable regulation of railroads was a
violation of due process of the 5th Amendment and that in the case at bar
the I.C.C. had acted in such a manner.[148]

In *McBoyle v. United States*[149] nine Justices decided that the
National Motor Vehicle Theft Act, as then on the statute books, did not
apply to the theft of aircraft.

After Benjamin N. Cardozo had replaced Justice Holmes, the Court
speaking through Justice Sutherland unanimously decided that the Pure
Food and Drug Act was sufficiently explicit to provide the executive with
guides in the execution of congressional policy. The Court then went on to
repunctuate the law, and in this grammatical exercise Justices Brandeis,
Stone, and Cardozo refused to join. The majority noted that "the
legislative power of Congress cannot be delegated . . . . But Congress may
declare its will, and after fixing a primary standard, devolve upon
administration officers the 'power to fill up the details' by prescribing
administrative rules and regulations."[150]

During this period the Court was called upon to make four decisions
involving anti-trust legislation. In *Swift v. United States*[151] a 4-2 Court
ruling through Mr. Justice Cardozo declared that though size is not the
only constituent of a monopoly, it does provide the atmosphere in which it
thrives and, in this case, did violate the Sherman Anti-Trust Act. While in

Atlantic Cleaners & Dyers v. United States[152] the Court broadened the definition of "trade" in the Act to include the definition of Mr. Justice Story. "Wherever any occupation, employment, or business is carried on for the purpose of profit, or gain, or a livelihood, not in the liberal arts or in the learned professions, it is constantly called a 'trade.'"[153] The *Appalachian Coals, Incorporated v. United States*[154] case, announced just nine days after the inauguration of President Franklin Delano Roosevelt, offered, so some thought, an augury of the Court's attitude toward the National Industrial Recovery Act which was in the legislative mill and would be for three more months. Speaking through Chief Justice Hughes and with Mr. J. McReynolds as the lone dissenter, the Court dismissed an anti-trust suit against a bituminous coal producers' association, which had been established to provide fair competition through price and production controls. *The New York Times* commented that the "Chief Justice's words would give new courage to cooperative associations of businessmen."[155]

A case which received little attention at the time but which presaged the mind of the Justices on federal control of labor-management relations was decided in April, 1933. On the surface it was a victory for labor, but at best it was pyrrhic. In *Levering & Garrigue v. Morrin*[156] the Court reaffirmed that a labor strike in an industry within the state was beyond the federal legislative power, even if, as the employers contended in this instance, the strike by preventing the consumption of building materials interrupted their flow in interstate commerce. There would be similar contention in the *Carter* case,[152] where it was ruled that mining labor conditions which resulted in strikes did not affect interstate commerce.

Three Federal Employers' Liability Act cases were presented to the high tribunal for adjudication during these years. In each the Justices unanimously refused to extend the coverage of the act to (1) a stationary engineer in an interstate commerce depot; (2) railroad shop maintenance workers; (3) a mechanic working on an out-of-service steam engine.[158]

Governmental power fared somewhat better in cases involving other regulatory and administrative agencies. Three of the five decisions upheld the power challenged. In *Federal Trade Commission v. Royal Milling Co.*[159] a divided Court upheld the commission's prohibition of certain advertising practices in the flour industry, and in *Federal Radio Commission v. Nelson Brothers Bond & Mortgage Co.*[160] it was unanimously decided that the commission had unlimited freedom in the allocation of commercial radio licenses. However, in *Federal Trade Commission v. Raladam*[161] the commission's order was voided because the Court felt it was based on a health issue rather than one of fair

competition and, therefore, was beyond the Federal Trade Commission's competence.

Another aspect of jurisdiction was discussed and decided in *Crowell v. Benson:*[162] "By an involved process of reasoning and in the face of a devastating dissent," wrote Carl Swisher, "[Hughes] recaptured for the courts power to redetermine facts designated as 'jurisdictional facts' previously determined by administrative agencies."[163] Specifically, the majority of five ruled that a court might set aside the findings of an agency and substitute jurisdictional facts of its own or order a new trial. The divided tribunal found this to be required in order to maintain the independence of the judicial branch. "Harmony among the judges was shattered," wrote Hughes' biographer,[164] and in a thirty page dissent in which he was joined by Stone and Roberts, Brandeis chided the majority for deciding questions not brought up in the arguments of counsel and for preempting the powers of the agency without letting the administrative procedure run its course. However, the "jurisdictional fact" doctrine was written into the law and it remained in force until 1946; since then its application has been on the wane,[165] though Congress has promoted it in the Administrative Procedures Act of 1946 and the Taft-Hartley Act of 1947. Its application between 1932 and 1946 was erratic; indeed, in the year following its adoption, the Court took a step backward in *Voehl v. Indemnity Insurance Co.*[166] The Chief Justice, who had written the *Crowell* opinion, declared for a unanimous court that the findings of a deputy commissioner, when authorized by law, are conclusive if based on the evidence presented.

In the area of governmental tax immunity there were a number of notable decisions in this three-year period. The positions taken by the Court were varied and contradictory, but as Mr. Justice Roberts wrote sometime later, "in no field of federal jurisprudence has there been greater variation and uncertainty."[167] Despite this criticism the Justice challenged the view of Mr. Justice Frankfurter that Congress should determine what was, and what was not, immune when he declared:

> The power is in the Court and nowhere else. It would be to make a mockery of state sovereignty if Congress could override it at will beyond redress in the Court in which is reposed the decision of cases arising under the Constitution. So to hold could, in effect, be to make Congress the final arbiter, to the destruction of the national harmony, the preservation of which the Constitution commits to the judiciary.[168]

When the Court ruled in favor of immunity from the federal tax, it was by a split vote, while the Justices were unanimous in those instances where the tax was upheld. Chiefly, the controversies centered around the question of what was, and what was not, a state instrumentality. In *Willcuts v. Bunn*[169] a capital gains tax on the sale of municipal bonds was upheld, while in *Group #1 Oil Corporation v. Bass*[170] an income tax on the profits of a corporation after the states' royalties were removed was given the judicial nod. However, in *Burnet v. Coronado Oil & Gas Co.*[171] the high Court, splitting five-to-four, voided a tax on income from minerals leased from the state. The majority through McReynolds declared that "We accept as settled doctrine that the United States can lay no tax on [state] governmental instrumentalities."[172] The precedent cited was *Gillespie v. Oklahoma*,[173] and the majority tried to distinguish it from their own decision in *Group #1 Oil Co.*, above, but, as Justice Roberts noted after he had left the Court, it was "a case really indistinguishable."[174] The dissenting four, Brandeis, Stone, Roberts, and Cardozo, had their day nine months later in *Burnet v. Jergens Trust*[175] when a unanimous court speaking through Mr. Roberts declared that the *Gillespie* and *Coronado* precedents were to be strictly read and therefore were not binding in the case at bar, since the state in this instance was not acting as a "trustee of an express trust with regard to the lands leased."[176]

In *Indian Motocycle Co. v. United States*[177] the Court took twenty-five months and a reargument to decide in favor of the exemption of a municipality from a federal tax on its purchase of motorcycles for its police force. The majority found that "where the principle [of immunity] applies, it is not affected by the amount of a particular tax or the extent of the resulting interference, but is absolute."[178]

In one other case the power of the federal government was held to be unlimited even against the claim of immunity by state instrumentalities.[179] Robert E. Cushman indicates that in this case the court dropped its position that a tariff is a tax, since if it were merely a tax the immunity principle would have to be employed.[180]

There are two federal tax cases in which Roberts spoke for the Court during this period which demonstrate his approach to legislation. The first, *Poe v. Seaborn*,[181] was also his first opinion for the Court. Dean Griswold considers Roberts' approach characteristic of his work during the next fifteen years.[182] The case involved a tax on community property, and added to its complexity was the fact that there were two lines of precedent to support opposing solutions. This was to be true of many of the questions presented to the Court during Roberts' tenure. The Justice's attack was that of a lawyer rather than that of an accountant, and as a lawyer he turned to the statute. The result turned on the legislative meaning of the word "of."[183] Griswold noted that the Chief and [Justice] Stone, according to rumor, wished to dissent, but according to the tradition of no dissents to the inaugural opinion of a Justice, they simply "took no part."[184] The second case[185] presented a question of double taxation and Roberts' approach was similar to that in *Poe*—what was the meaning of the legislature? This case is noteworthy for an additional reason. Roberts inserted a dictum on the relation of administrative interpretation and legislative confirmation of it. "The repeated reenactment of a statute without substantial change may amount to an implied legislative approval of a construction placed upon it by executive officers."[186] The Justice then cited his own opinion in the *Poe* case.

In the area of the 18th Amendment Roberts wrote an opinion for the Court. That he would be assigned is an interesting insight into the Chief Justice's method of assigning cases, since, it will be recalled, Roberts' position on the Prohibition issue had been brought up at the time of his nomination. The opinion is notable for another reason as well, for the Justice included a comment in it which would clash with his position in *United States v. Butler*[187] some five years later. "The 10th Amendment was intended to confirm," he declared, "the understanding of the people at the time the Constitution was adopted that the powers not granted to the United States were reserved to the States or to the people. *It added nothing to the instrument originally ratified* [italics supplied] and has no limited and special operation, as is contended, upon the people's delegation by Article V of certain functions to the Congress."[188] In the *Butler* decision, the Justice wrote:

> From the accepted doctrine that the United States is a government of delegated powers, it follows that those not expressly granted, or reasonably to be implied from such as are conferred, are reserved to the states or the people. To forestall any suggestion to the contrary, the Tenth Amendment was adopted. The same proposition, otherwise stated, is that powers not granted are prohibited.[189]

Roberts' record in the area of federal powers is closely allied with the record of the Court as a whole. In the seventy-eight cases decided, he dissented three times from anti-government positions taken by the Court and only once from an opinion supporting it. He wrote twenty-one opinions for the Court, twelve of which favored governmental activity. The Court voted forty-eight times to uphold the government and thirty times against the government. While the Court split in thirteen anti-government decisions, it divided in only eight pro-government cases.

When state economic powers were challenged during the 1930 to 1932 terms, the Court upheld the activity in all but twenty of the ninety cases, and in two more, state action was partially upheld and partially voided. That in eighty-two percent of the cases the Court was unanimous, further supports the claim that the Chief was able to establish a unified Court.

In only one case and partially in another did the Justices uphold the immunity principle against state taxation. Both decisions dealt with the freedom of national banks from state taxation. A tax on all banks not levied on other domestic corporations was held void in *Iowa-Des Moines National Bank v. Bennett*,[190] while in *Union Bank and Trust Co. v. Phelps*[191] the tax on state banks was upheld, but that on national banks was struck down. A non-discriminatory tax on all corporations including national banks was upheld in *First National Bank v. Louisiana Tax Commission.*[192]

During this period the Court reversed itself on the immunity of material which was protected by a copyright. In *Education Films Corporation v. Ward*[193] a divided Court, while retaining the precedent that copyrights are federal instrumentalities, ruled that they were not immune from state taxation on the royalties. The failure to openly overrule precedent, while it was actually being done, resulted in much criticism. Sixteen months later, as if in reply, the high tribunal erased the precedent that copyrights were federal instrumentalities in *Fox Film Corporation v. Doyal*[194] and therefore were not immune from federal taxation. In doing so the Court specifically overruled *Long v. Rockwood*[195] which had originally extended the cloak of immunity to patents and copyrights.

Similarly, these three years saw the rejection of the view that federally-licensed power plants were immune from state taxes.[196] Likewise, carriers under contract to the government were held liable to non-discriminatory vehicle taxation,[197] and in *Storaasli v. Minnesota*[198] Justice Roberts speaking for a unanimous Court declared that a soldier living on a military reservation was required to pay the state license fee on his auto. And finally, the Court held that the income of a corporation, a part of whose income was from federal, state, and municipal bonds, had to pay a corporation profits tax.[199]

This relaxed attitude toward tax immunity was characteristic of the position of the Court toward legislation in general and was exemplified in the view of state taxation to interstate commerce which was sustained in twelve of fifteen challenges.

A tax on railroad property for the construction of highways was unanimously sustained,[200] and a tax on fuel used on interstate trains but stored within the state was upheld, as well.[201] In this last case, *Nashville, Chattanooga, and St. Louis Railway v. Wallace,* the Court was called upon to rule on the side issued of whether it had jurisdiction over state "declaratory judgments" in view of the constitutional limitation of the federal judiciary power to "cases and controversies."[202] Mr..Justice Stone speaking for the brethren declared:

> The Constitution does not require that the case or controversy should be presented by traditional forms of procedure, invoking only traditional remedies. The judiciary clause of the Constitution defined and limited judicial power, not the particular method by which that power might be invoked. .... Whenever the judicial power is invoked to review a judgment of a state court, the ultimate constitutional purpose is the protection, by the exercise of the judicial function, of rights arising under the Constitution and laws of the United States. The states are left free to regulate their own judicial procedure.[203]

Similarly, fuel used on interstate airplanes was held liable to state taxation.[204]

A companion case to *University of Illinois v. United States*[205] was decided a month and a half prior to that reassertion of the absoluteness of the federal power over foreign commerce. In *Anglo-Chilean Co. v. Alabama*[206] the high bench ruled that nitrates imported and kept in the "original package" were not subject to state tax; on the other hand, the Justices upheld a license tax on a corporation which built and maintained an international toll bridge.[207] Justice Butler noted that the appellant has the burden of establishing the fact upon which the challenge of unconstitutionality rests, and that the corporation did not do so.

One other case of note in the field of taxation of interstate commerce was *Utah Power & Light Co. v. Pfost,*[208] in which the nine members of the Court decided that a power company which sold some of its electricity out-of-state was liable to state taxes. Justice Sutherland speaking for the Court commented thus on the *separability clause:*

> While [the] declaration is but an aid to interpretation and not an inexorable command, it has the effect of reversing the common law presumption, that the legislature intends an act to be effective as an entirety, by putting in its place the opposite presumption of divisibility; and this presumption must be overcome by considerations that make evident the inseparability of the provisions or the clear probability that the legislature would not have been satisfied with the statute unless it had included the invalid part.[209]

Finally, two far-reaching tax disputes were brought to the Court in *State Board of Tax Commissioners v. Jackson*[210] and *Liggett v. Lee,*[211] in both of which Roberts spoke for the majority. In each case the Justices were called upon to rule on discriminatory taxation of chain stores. In the former, an Indiana graduated license tax based on the number of stores owned by an individual or corporation; in the latter case the high bench voided a special tax on the property of chain stores, while upholding a higher rate of taxation on storage space of chain stores than on that of wholesalers who supply independent retailers. The long range effect of these decisions was the return to a small degree to the states' control over monopolies within their borders.

In two of the three rate cases presented to the Court for determination, the decision of the administrative body was upheld.[212] In *Railroad Commission v. Maxcy*,[213] however, the Justices ruled once more that the specific rate set by the commission was confiscatory and therefore void. On the other hand, in the four cases argued during the 1930 to 1932 terms on the *method* of rate determination, the Court ruled favorably in the areas of telephone,[214] natural gas,[215] and electricity.[216] In this last case, *Los Angeles Gas & Electric Corporation v. Railroad Commission,* the Court made its position on the matter of the method of rate determination explicit:

> The legislative discretion implied in the rate making power necessarily extends to the entire legislative process, embracing the method used in reaching the legislative determination as well as that determination itself. We are not concerned with either, so long as constitutional limitations are not transgressed. When the legislative method is disclosed, it may have a definite bearing upon the validity of the result reached, but *the judicial function does not go beyond the decision of the constitutional question. That question is whether the rates as fixed are confiscatory.* [italics supplied] And upon that question the complainant has the burden of proof, and the Court may not interfere with the exercise of the State's authority unless confiscation is clearly established.[217]

Further, in *O'Gorman & Young v. Hartford Fire Insurance Co.*[218] the Court ruled favorably on the power of the state to set insurance rates.

In 1951 Mr. Justice Roberts commenting on the power of the state to control interstate commerce, noted:

> By the end of the last century there had come to be three recognized types of regulation. First, the interdiction by criminal statute of interstate transportation of specified commodities and persons. Secondly, the interdiction of concerted action, whereever localized, directed at the destruction of free competition in interstate trade, and, thirdly, regulation of activities of those engaged in interstate

transportation by the aid of legislative delegate, which should implement and enforce the declared purpose of Congress.

From the first, it has been understood that state action, though authorized or required by state law, if in conflict with a valid exercise of the commerce power by Congress, must give way; and this is so although, except for the exercise of the power of Congress, the state regulation would be valid. Thus in order to effectuate the commerce power of the federal government, it may become necessary to modify or abrogate state power.[219]

The Court was called upon to rule on state activity in all of these listed areas during the pre-1937 period.

The Justices looked kindly upon the state regulation of railroads, even those engaged in interstate commerce, in six of the eight cases reviewed. In the two exceptions, the state's attempt to force a railroad to build a cattle underpass was struck down,[220] and its discretion in the application of the Federal Employer's Liability Act was limited by the rules established by the federal Supreme Court.[221]

The Justices were just as liberal in their views of state power over highways. A number of cases challenging the right of the state to control interstate carriers were heard, and the Court upheld the determination of the route of the carrier,[222] the size and weight of the trucks,[223] and a tax for the patrolling and maintenance of the roads.[224] In *Stephenson v. Binford*[225] the tribunal ruled that the highways are public property and their use for gain by private, as well as public, carriers was subject to state control.

When we move to a consideration of the area of business control, we find that the Court did not abandon its favorable attitude toward state action. In twenty-five cases decided with opinions, nineteen upheld that state, eighteen unanimously; and four of the six negative votes were nine-to-nothing. It is difficult to reconcile these statistics with the traditional view of the judicial veto.

In the control of domestic corporations the state was upheld in eleven of thirteen trials. The most notable decision in this field was that in *New State Ice Co. v. Liebmann*,[226] which gained notoriety as a dismal forecast of evil days to come. By a six-to-two vote the Court struck down an Oklahoma statute which regulated through the requirement of a license the number of competitors in the ice business. The state had declared this particular trade to be "affected with the public interest" and therefore viewed its regulation as a valid exercise of its power. The Justices ruled otherwise, but Mr. Justice Brandeis, who was joined in dissent by Mr. Justice Stone, warned the Court of the effect of their decision:

To stay experimentation in things social and economic is a grave responsibility. Denial of the right to experiment may be fraught with serious consequences to the Nation. It is one of the happy incidents of the federal system that a single courageous state may, if its citizens choose, serve as a laboratory, and try novel social and economic experiments without risk to the rest of the country. This Court has the power to prevent an experiment. We may strike down the statute which embodies it on the ground that, in our opinion, the measure is arbitrary, capricious, or unreasonable. We have the power to do this, because the due process clause has been held by the Court applicable to matters of substantive law as well as to matters of procedure. But in the exercise of this high power, we must be ever on our guard, lest we erect our prejudices into legal principles. If we would guide by the light of reason, we must let our minds be bold.[227]

But the *Chicago Daily News* challenged the dissenters:

What is the proper test of reasonableness in social and economic experimentation? Clearly—experiments repugnant to the federal Constitution or to the constitution of the state concerned, cannot be sanctioned by the courts. ... Manifestly, the federal Supreme Court adheres to the old logical test of a public utility, the expediency of a monopoly from the standpoint of public interests. Those who favor a different test should assume the burden of proving the necessity and propriety of the departure.[228]

The *Wall Street Journal* took a different view and acutely stated what the ensuing constitutional battle was to deal with: "this case involves no conflict between property rights and individual or 'human' rights. The Court divided only over the question how far a state government can go by itself in altering the American scheme of existence."[229]

It is, therefore, enlightening for the student of the Court who pages through volumes 282 to 289 of the United States Reports to find that the right of the state to regulate business was upheld in an overwhelming number of cases, albeit in traditional areas. The Justices upheld the regulation of natural gas,[230] insurance,[231] advertising,[232] investments,[233] machinery sales,[234] grain contracts,[235] oil production,[236] and banking.[237] Though, as Justice Roberts some time later admitted, a few of these cases were two-headed coins. Both the *Champion Oil* and *Utah Power & Light* decisions had rejected the extension of interstate commerce control to mining, manufacturing, and allied areas of production, since they were considered "purely local activities."[238]

In addition to the *Liebmann* case, the only other voiding of state business regulation was *Sterling v. Constantin,*[239] where the use of martial law to control oil reserve depletion was struck down. Merlo Pusey summarized the details in these words:

> In the dark days of the depression, Texas had sought to reduce the flow of oil from the wells capable of producing five thousand barrels a day to a mere two hundred barrels. The legality of the order had been challenged, a federal court had issued a temporary injunction against its enforcement. By way of retaliation Governor Sterling had shut down all the wells in several counties and tried to justify this resort to martial law by declaring that "insurrection and riot" in the oil counties were beyond civil control.[240]

All of the cases in this area, except *New State Ice* and Utah "Blue Sky" law (*Porter*), were unanimous opinions. The Court also upheld the control of out-of-state corporations even to the extent of complete exclusion from doing business within the state.[241]

State bankruptcy proceedings were upheld in all but two cases. The Justices voided only a limitation on bankruptcy proceedings[242] and restated the supremacy of the federal law in cases when there was a conflict.[243]

Nine members of the Court upheld the right of the state to regulate the importation of non-potable alcohol under the Webb-Kenyon Act,[244] and by a similar vote sustained the right of the state to require certification of freedom from disease for cattle brought into the state.[245]

In the area of workingman's compensation, the Court supported the application of a Vermont law in *Bradford Electric Light Co. v. Clapper,*[246] while in *Ohio v. Chattanooga Boiler Co.*[247] the state was held to be empowered to recover from an out-of-state employer for payment made from its compensation fund. This support of compensation laws in light of the subsequent voiding of social legislation was not as unusual as might be supposed, since it was based on well-established though not unanimous precedents. However, some states still viewed such laws as "Robin Hood" statutes based only on financial discrepancy and not based on any meaning of justice.[248]

In summary, during the 1930 to 1932 terms the Court ruled on some aspect of the economic powers of government one hundred and sixty-nine times. Its decisions were unanimous in one hundred and thirty-three instances, and in one hundred-eighteen occasions it ruled in favor of federal or state action. It is recognized here that numbers do not of themselves show a liberal court. Each case must be weighed as to its implications, as the *New State Ice* case must be, and the subsequent acceptance or rejection as a precedent. What the statistics do demonstrate is the inaccuracy of the usual picture of the Court during this period as the "nine old men" swinging with reckless abandon right and left with their judicial scimitars decapitating all attempts of government, state and federal, to serve the people.

Justice Roberts' position during this period coincided almost exactly with that of the Court as a whole. Frankfurter and Hart give the following score of the Justice's votes during this period: 1930 term — 24 opinions for the Court, one dissenting opinion and one other dissenting vote; 1931 term — 22 opinions and three dissenting voltes; 1932 term — 22 opinions, one dissenting opinion and two other dissents.[249] Roberts' dissents in the field of governmental economic controls were in:

> *International Paper Co. v. United States* 282 U.S. 399 (1931). The Secretary of War was held liable for seizure and use of property when not acting under the war powers and payment was ordered.

> *Coolidge v. Long* 282 U.S. 582 (1931). An attempt by Massachusetts to tax a trust fund after the gift was consummated was voided. In a thirty-two page documented opinion Roberts speaking for Holmes, Brandeis, and Stone declared, "no exercise of a governmental power, whether it be that of taxation, police, or eminent domain, though it make less valuable the fruits of a private contract, can be said to impair the obligation thereof." (p. 638)

> *Crowell v. Benson* 285 U.S. 22 (1932). The Court reinterposed the judiciary between the administrator and the law in the determination of jurisdictional facts.

> *Burnet v. Coronado Oil & Gas Co.* 285 U.S. 393 (1932). The Court reinstated the view that a lease from a state for minerals is its instrumentality and therefore immune from federal taxation.

> *Federal Trade Commission v. Royal Milling Co.* 288 U.S. 212 (1933). The Commission's order forbidding certain practices of a flour firm was upheld. This was the only dissent of the period in which Roberts voted against a majority which had upheld governmental action.

The Justice's record during his first three terms, as that of the Court itself, is one favoring governmental activity in the area of economic controls. Professor T. R. Powell noted this fact when he commented in 1939, "with the advent of Mr. Chief Justice Hughes and Mr. Justice Roberts there again came a perceptible swing of the judicial pendulum."[250]

Notes

[1] O. Fraenkel, "Five-to-Four Decisions of the Supreme Court," *United States Law Week*, May 12, 1935, p. 21. (1010).

[2] C.H. Butler, *A Century at the Bar of the Supreme Court of the United States* (New York, 1942), p. 207. Former Chief Justice Taft died the same day. 281 U.S. V.

[3] Perhaps, Mr. J. Sanford's most notable decision was *Gitlow v. New York* 268 U.S. 652 (1925), which, as Paul C. Bartholomew noted in his *Leading Cases on the Constitution* (4th Ed. Paterson, New Jersey, 1962) p. 101-2, "has long been regarded as a 'landmark' decision because here for the first time the Court held portions of the 'Bill of Rights' applicable to the states by means of the 14th Amendment."

[4] January 15, 1923, quoted in W.F. Murphy, "In His Own Image: Mr. Chief Justice Taft & Supreme Court Appointments," *Supreme Court Review, 1961* (Chicago, 1961), p. 182.

[5] "Changing Constitutional Phases," *Boston Law Review* XIX (1939), 514.

[6] A.T. Mason, *The Supreme Court from Taft to Warren* (Baton Rouge, 1953), p. 74.

[7] Fraenkel, *loc. cit.*

[8] A.H. Schlesinger, Jr., *The Age of Roosevelt*, Vol. III: *The Politics of Upheaval* (Boston, 1960), p. 428.

[9] *U.M.W.A. v. Red Jacket Consolidated C & C Co.*, 18 Fed. 2nd 839.

[10] J.P. Harris, *The Advice and Consent of the Senate* (Berkeley, 1953), 127.

[11] J.P. Frank, *Marble Palace: The Supreme Court in American Life* (New York, 1958), p. 48.

[12] 84 Fed. 2nd 641 (1936).

[13] R.L. Stern, "The Commerce Clause and the National Economy, 1933-1946," *Harvard Law Review* LIX (1946), 676.

[14] 47 F. Sup. 251 (1942).

[15] 310 U.S. 586 (1940).

[16] W.F. Murphy, "Lower Courts' Checks on Supreme Court Power," *American Political Science Review* LIII (1959), 1026.

[17] 319 U.S. 624 (1943).

[18] Harris, p. 485.

[19] Murphy, *Congress and the Court* (Chicago, 1962), p. 53.

[20] Schlesinger, p. 485.

[21] C.B. Swisher, *American Constitutional Development* (2nd rev.; Cambridge, Massachusetts, 1954), p. 779.

[22] "Confirming Mr. Roberts," XLVII (1930), 677-678.

[23] May 9, 1930, p. 1.

[24] Pearson & Allen, *The Nine Old Men* (Garden City, New York, 1936), p. 112.

[25] G.W.P. to William O. Trapp, September 23, 1942 in W.O. Trapp, "The Constitutional Doctrines of Owen J. Roberts" (unpublished Ph.D. dissertation, Cornell University, 1943), p. 65; G.W. Pepper, *Philadelphia Lawyer* (Philadelphia, 1944), p. 231.

[26] Trapp, p. 63.

[27] C. Ewing, *Judges of the Supreme Court, 1789 to 1937* (Minneapolis, 1938), p. 119.

[28] J. Schmidhauser, *The Supreme Court: Its Politics, Personalities and Procedures* (New York, 1961), p. 54.

[29] p. 8.

[30] May 10, 1930, editorial page.

[31] May 10, 1930, p. 6.

[32] May 10, 1939, p. 6.

[33] "The Supreme Court—Nine Mortal Men," *The Literary Digest* CXVII (1934), p. 45.

[34] *Ibid.*, p. 9.

[35] E.R. Keedy, "Owen J. Roberts and the Law School," *University of Pennsylvania Law Review* CIV (1955), pp. 318-320.

[36] Pepper, p. 197.

[37] R.T. McCracken, "Owen J. Roberts—Master Advocate," *University of Pennsylvania Law Review* CIV (1955), p. 326.

[38] Trapp, pp. 35-43, *passim.*

[39] McCracken, p. 330.

[40] Trapp, p. 31.

[41] Pearson & Allen, p. 141.

[42] *Ibid.*, pp. 152-53.

[43] *Ibid.*

[44] *Ibid.*, p. 141.

[45] B.F. Wright, *The Growth of American Constitutional Law* (New York, 1942), p. 110.

[46] R.H. Jackson, *The Struggle for Judicial Supremacy* (New York, 1942), p. 84.

[47] *New York Times,* February 16, 1923, p. 7.

[48] E. Bates, *The Story of the Supreme Court* (Indianapolis, 1938), p. 287, footnote.

[49] Schlesinger, pp. 220-221.

[50] Interview with Merlo Pusey, March 14, 1963.

[51] "Trend of Events," CLV (1930), pp. 175-176.

[52] Fraenkel, *loc. cit.*

[53] "Who's Who in the News," XXVI (1935), p. 21.

[54] May 9, 1930, p. 1.

[55] *Philadelphia Record,* May 10, 1930, p. 6.

[56] E.S. Corwin, *Constitutional Revolution, Ltd.* (Claremont, California, 1946), p. 75

[57] *The Sun* (Baltimore), May 11, 1930, p. 1.

[58] May 23, 1930, editorial page.

[59] "Backstage in Washington," CLV (1930), 100.

[60] "Obituary," May 30, 1955, p. 57.

[61] J. Alsop & T. Catledge (Garden City, New York, 1938), pp. 5-6.

[62] "The Supreme Court," May 1936, VIII, 192.

[63] "The Supreme Court's Hardworking Balance Wheel," May 18, 1935, p. 15.

[64] May 22, 1930, p. 12.

[65] May 10, 1930, p. 8.

[66] Trapp, p. 349.

[67] "McReynolds, Roberts, & Hughes," LXXXVII (1936), 232.

[68] Interview with John Lord O'Brian, March 26, 1963.

[69] Interview with Albert J. Schneider, August 1, 1962.

[70] E.N. Griswold, "Owen J. Roberts as a Judge," *University of Pennsylvania Law Review* CIV (1955), 336.

[71] *The New York Times,* February 16, 1923, p. 7.

[72] M.J. Pusey, *Charles Evans Hughes* II (New York, 1952), 620.

[73] *The Sun* (Baltimore), p. 1.

[74] U.S., *Congressional Record,* 71st Congress, 2nd Session, LXXII, 9115.

[75] Philadelphia *Evening Bulletin,* May 21, 1930, p. 1.

[76] Schlesinger, p. 455.

[77] A.T. Mason, *The Supreme Court from Taft to Warren* (Baton Rouge, 1958), pp. 68-69.

[78] J.M. Burns, *Roosevelt: The Lion & The Fox* (New York, 1956), p. 230.

[79] Trapp, p. 342.

[80] Schlesinger, p. 458.

[81] *Ibid.,* p. 457.

[82] Murphy, *The Supreme Court Review* 1961, p. 166.

[83] Schlesinger, *loc. cit.*

[84] *Quaker City Cab Co. v. Pennsylvania,* 277 U.S. 399.

[85] J.F. Pascal, *Mr. Justice Sutherland, a Man against the State* (Princeton, 1951), p. 259.

[86] H.J. Abraham, *The Judicial Process* (New York, 1962), p. 178. He refused to speak to Justice Brandeis during his first four years on the Court.

[87] Murphy, *The Supreme Court Review* 1961, p. 166.

[88] Alsop & Catledge, p. 6.

[89] Schlesinger, pp. 456-457; 461.

[90] V. Wood, *Due Process of Law* (Baton Rouge, 1951), p. 103.

[91] Murphy, *The Supreme Court Review,* pp. 168-176. See also D. Danielski, *A Supreme Court Justice is Appointed,* for a detailed account of Butler's nomination.

[92] Schlesinger, p. 455.

[93] Pusey, p. 670.

[94] W. Mendelson, *Capitalism, Democracy and the Supreme Court* (New York, 1960), pp. 96-97; C. Curtis, *Lions under the Throne* (Boston, 1947), p. 98.

[95] H.S. Commager, *The American Mind* (New Haven, 1959), pp. 380-381.

[96] 208 U.S. 412 (1908).

[97] Griswold, p. 334-335.

[98] Oliver Wendell Holmes, *Speeches* (Boston, 1934), p. 101 in P.E. Jackson, *Wisdom of the Supreme Court* (Norman, Oklahoma, 1962), p. 224.

[99] Drew Pearson's Column, April 27, 1941 quoted in C. Curtis, *Lions under the Throne* (Boston, 1947), p. 281.

[100] *Holmes-Laski Letters,* ed. M.D. Howe (Cambridge, Massachusetts, 1953), p. 1291, October 24, 1930.

[101] 284 U.S. 370 to 390.

[102] 284 U.S. 390.

[103] Bowen, pp. 378-379.

[104] A.T. Mason, *Harlan Fiske Stone: Pillar of the Law* (New York, 1952), pp. 336-337.

[105] Schlesinger, p. 461.

[106] Cardozo *The Nature of the Judicial Process* (New Haven, 1921), p. 173.

[107] *Muller v. Oregon* 208 U.S. 412 (1908).

[108] Schmidhauser, p. 17.

[109] *Ibid.*

[110] Schlesinger, pp. 220, 223.

[111] Schlesinger, p. 462.

[112] Griswold, p. 335.

[113] Jackson, p. 82.

[114] C.B. Swisher "The Supreme Court, a Need for Re-evaluation," *Virginia Law Review* XL (1954), 842.

[115] Mason, *Stone,* p. 302.

[116] Vols. 282 to 289 of the United States Reports.

[117] S. Hendel, *Charles Evans Hughes and the Supreme Court* (New York, 1951), p. 136.

[118] "Chief Justices I Have Known," *Virginia Law Review* XXXIX (1953) 882 ff. in A.F. Westin, *An Autobiography of the Supreme Court* (New York, 1963), p. 228.

[119] Pusey, Vols. I & II, *passim.*

[120] 230 U.S. 352 (1913); 234 U.S. 342 (1914).

[121] Pusey, II, 655.

[122] *Ibid.,* p. 659.

[123] Jackson, p. xix.

[124] O. Roberts, "Charles Evans Hughes: The Administrative Master," *Memorial Address before the Association of the Bar of the City of New York*, December 12, 1948 in Westin, p. 210.

[125] Frankfurter, p. 883.

[126] Abraham, pp. 178-179.

[127] M. Lerner, "The Great Constitutional War," *Virginia Quarterly Review* XV (1942), 533.

[128] Pusey, pp. 675-676.

[129] Roberts, pp. 209-210.

[130] T. Powell, *loc. cit.*

[131] I. Brant, "How Liberal Is Justice Hughes?" *The New Republic* XCI, 295-332.

[132] A. Krock, "Supreme Court Decisions Upset Some Fixed Beliefs," March 6, 1934, p. 24.

[133] C.B. Swisher, p. 920.

[134] Abraham, p. 306.

[135] F. Rodell, p. 223.

[136] C.B. Swisher, p. 813.

[137] "American Constitutional Government: The Blueprint and the Structure," *Boston University Law Review* XXIX (1949), 25.

[138] 234 U.S. 342 (1914).

[139] *Florida v. United States*, 282 U.S. 194 (1931).

[140] *Georgia Public Service Commission v. United States*, 283 U.S. 765 (1931); *Alabama v. United States*, 283 U.S. 776 (1931).

[141] 284 U.S. 248 (1932).

[142] 45th Annual Report, December 1, 1931; House Document #30, 72nd Congress, 1st Session, p. 114.

[143] 284 U.S. 248, 260 (1932).
[144] *United States v. Northern Pacific Railroad,* 288 U.S. 490, 494 (1933).
[145] 282 U.S. 311 (1931).
[146] *Ibid.,* pp. 327-28.
[147] Mason, *Stone,* p. 311.
[148] *Chicago, Rock Island & Pacific Railroad v. United States,* 284 U.S. 80 (1931).
[149] 283 U.S. 25 (1931).
[150] *United States v. Shreveport Grain & Elevator Co.,* 287 U.S. 77, 85 (1932).
[151] 286 U.S. 106 (1932).
[152] 286 U.S. 427 (1932).
[153] *Ibid.,* p. 436 – *The Schooner Nymph* 18 Fed. Cas. 506, $10,388.
[154] 288 U.S. 344 (1933).
[155] March 15, 1933, p. 16.
[156] 289 U.S. 103 (1933).
[157] *Carter v. Carter Coal Co.,* 298 U.S. 238 (1936), which voided the first Guffey Coal Conservation Act.
[158] *Chicago & Northwestern R. v. Bolle* 284 U.S. 74 (1931); *Chicago & Eastern Illinois R. v. Industrial Commission of Illinois* 284 U.S. 296 (1932); *New York, New Haven & Hartford R. v. Bezue* 284 U.S. 415 (1932).
[159] 288 U.S. 212 (1933).
[160] 289 U.S. 266 (1933).
[161] 283 U.S. 643 (1932).
[162] 285 U.S. 22 (1932).
[163] C.B. Swisher, *American Constitutional Development,* p. 912.
[164] Pusey, p. 706.
[165] C.H. Pritchett, *The American Constitution* (New York, 1959), pp. 499-500.
[166] 288 U.S. 162 (1933).
[167] O.J. Roberts, *The Court & the Constitution* (Cambridge, Massachusetts, 1951), p. 9.
[168] *Ibid.,* p. 34.
[169] 282 U.S. 216 (1931).
[170] 283 U.S. 279 (1931).
[171] 285 U.S. 393 (1932).
[172] *Ibid.,* 400.
[173] 257 U.S. 501 (1922).
[174] O. Roberts, p. 26.
[175] 288 U.S. 508 (1933).
[176] *Ibid.,* 516.
[177] 283 U.S. 570 (1931).
[178] *Ibid.,* p. 575.
[179] *University of Illinois v. United States* 289 U.S. 48 (1933).
[180] R.E. Cushman, "Social and Economic Control Through Federal Taxation," *Minnesota Law Review* XVIII (1934), 767.
[181] 282 U.S. 101 (1930).
[182] Griswold, p. 337.
[183] *Ibid.,* pp. 337-338.
[184] *Loc. cit.*

[185] *Old Colony Railroad v. Commissioner,* 284 U.S. 552 (1932).

[186] *Ibid.,* p. 557.

[187] 297 U.S. 1 (1936).

[188] *United States v. Sprague* 282 U.S. 716 (1931), 733-34.

[189] *United States v. Butler,* p. 68.

[190] 284 U.S. 239 (1931).

[191] 288 U.S. 181 (1933).

[192] 289 U.S. 60 (1933).

[193] 282 U.S. 379 (1931).

[194] 286 U.S. 123 (1932).

[195] 277 U.S. 142 (1928).

[196] *Susquehanna Power Co. v. Maryland Tax Commission* 283 U.S. 291 (1931); *Broad River Power Co. v. Query* 288 U.S. 178 (1933).

[197] *Alwood v. Johnson* 282 U.S. 509 (1931).

[198] 283 U.S. 57 (1931).

[199] *Pacific Coast, Ltd. v. Johnson* 285 U.S. 480 (1932).

[200] *Memphis & Charlestown Railway v. Pace* 282 U.S. 241 (1931).

[201] 288 U.S. 249 (1933).

[202] United States Constitution, Article III, section 2, paragraph 1.

[203] 288 U.S. 264 (1933).

[204] *Eastern Air Transport Co. v. South Carolina Tax Commission* 285 U.S. 147 (1932); *Edelman v. Boeing Air Transport Co.* 289 U.S. 249 (1933).

[205] 289 U.S. 48 (1933).

[206] 288 U.S. 218 (1933).

[207] *Detroit International Bridge v. Tax Appeal Board* 287 U.S. 295 (1932).

[208] 286 U.S. 165 (1932).

[209] *Ibid.,* p. 184.

[210] 283 U.S. 527 (1931).

[211] 288 U.S. 517 (1933).

[212] *Wabash Valley Electric Co. v. Young* 287 U.S. 488 (1933); *Public Service Commission v. Great Northern Utility Co.* 289 U.S. 130 (1933).

[213] 282 U.S. 249 (1931).

[214] *Smith v. Illinois Bell Telephone Co.* 282 U.S. 133 (1930).

[215] *Western Dst. Co. v. Public Service Commission* 289 U.S. 130 (1933).

[216] 289 U.S. 287 (1933).

[217] 289 U.S. 304-305 (1933).

[218] 282 U.S. 257 (1931).

[219] *The Court & The Constitution,* p. 41.

[220] *Chicago, St. Paul, Minnesota & Omaha Railroad v. Holmberg* 282 U.S. 162 (1930).

[221] *Chesapeake & Ohio Railroad v. Kahn* 284 U.S. 44 (1931).

[222] *Bradley v. Public Utility Commission* 289 U.S. 92 (1933).

[223] *Sproles v. Binford* 286 U.S. 374 (1932).

[224] *Contintental Baking Co. v. Woodring* 286 U.S. 352 (1932).

[225] 287 U.S. 251 (1932).

[226] 285 U.S. 262 (1932).

[227] *Ibid.,* p. 311.

[228] March 23, 1932, Editorial, p. 16.

[229] March 23, 1932, Editorial, p. 8.

[230] *Twin City Pipe Line v. Harding Glass Co.* 283 U.S. 353 (1931).

[231] *Hardware Dealers' Insurance Co. v. Glidden Co.* 284 U.S. 151 (1931).

[232] *Packer Corporation v. Utah* 285 U.S. 105 (1932).

[233] *Porter v. Investors' Syndicate* 286 U.S. 461 (1932).

[234] *Advance-Rumely Thresher Co. v. Jackson* 287 U.S. 283 (1932).

[235] *Dickerson v. Uhlmann Grain Co.* 288 U.S. 188 (1933).

[236] *Bandini Petroleum Co. v. Superior Court* 284 U.S. 8 (1931); *Champion Refining Co. v. Corporation Commission* 289 U.S. 88 (1933); *Gant v. Oklahoma* 289 U.S. 88 (1933).

[237] *Albie Street Bank v. Bryan* 282 U.S. 767 (1931); *Shriver v. Woodbine Savings Bank* 285 U.S. 467 (1932).

[238] O.J. Roberts, *The Court & The Constitution,* p. 43.

[239] 287 U.S. 378 (1932).

[240] Pusey, p. 723.

[241] *Railway Express Agency v. Virginia* 282 U.S. 440 (1931).

[242] *Royal Indemnity Co. v. American Bond & Mortgage Co.* 289 U.S. 165 (1933).

[243] *New York v. Irving Trust Co.* 288 U.S. 329 (1932).

[244] *McCormick v. Brown* 286 U.S. 329 (1932).

[245] *Minz v. Baldwin* 289 U.S. 346 (1933).

[246] 286 U.S. 145 (1932).

[247] 289 U.S. 439 (1933).

[248] R.E. Rhodes, Jr., "Due Process and Social Legislation in the Supreme Court—A Post-Mortem," *Notre Dame Lawyer,* XXXIII (1957) 13.

[249] F. Frankfurter & H. Hart, "Business of the Supreme Court in the October Term, 1933," *Harvard Law Review,* XLVIII (1935), 254-55.

[250] Powell, p. 514.

Chapter II

The New Deal in Court
1933–1936

The rulings of the Court in the area of governmental activity which have been considered thus far have offered little which could be called revolutionary. Decisions like *Packer Corporation* and *Appalachian Coals* seemed to presage a liberal view toward increased governmental activity, but they were offset by *New State Ice* and the continued restrictive interpretation of interstate commerce. The test of a new view came with the invasion of Washington by the victors in the election of 1932.

The First Hundred Days

How the Court would react to the results of the election with its apparent overwhelming mandate for the Democratic Party was not clear. It was obvious that if the Democratic Platform of 1932[1] were to be implemented, the new administration would have to grasp the helm of the ship of state firmly and bring it around into new and uncharted waters.[2] So there came to the country a radically new relationship between government and the economy, for, as Dexter Perkins notes, "The Roosevelt era represented substantial alterations in the economic order. The balance between the most important groups was substantially changed."[3]

Just what did occur on that November day was perhaps veiled to most of the citizens of the period. "Did the Court realize what happened?" asks Charles Curtis, and answering his own question, he continues:

> Of course, some of them did. Brandeis and Stone, and Cardozo did. Roberts must have known, but the others, Van Devanter, McReynolds, Sutherland, and Butler seem to have been taken by surprise. At least they thought it would blow over. Anyhow, all of them, particularly the Chief Justice, had a difficult job of statesmanship before them, a more difficult job than any of their predecessors.[4]

Perhaps the most curious thing about the election was the fact that even those who had elected Roosevelt were not sure of what he would do.[5] Indeed, two Supreme Court Justices, Holmes and Stone, had not favored the President in the election, despite their reputation as liberals. The recently retired Holmes wrote to Harold J. Laski a few weeks after the November balloting; "As to the election, if I had a vote, it would be for Hoover—without enthusiasm—Roosevelt when I knew him struck me as a good fellow with rather a soft edge, years ago."[6] And it was a known fact that Stone was a political ally, as well as a personal friend of Hoover.[7]

With perhaps more prophecy than he anticipated, T.R. Powell had written fifteen years before the coming of the New Deal:

> State and federal legislation, regulation of what we have hitherto considered "private business" — legislation with which we are going to become more and more familiar as the months pass—is almost certain to lead to a permanent enlargement of the class of public service businesses. Such enlargement may in time bring us again much nearer than we are at the present to the role of early common law that every business is a common calling, owing to the public the duty of reasonable service.[8]

That the new administration should act as swiftly as it did in 1933 was due to the catastrophic conditions created by the Depression.[9] However, not all serious thinkers, not even all liberals, Justice Stone for example, felt that the feverish activity was required or even justified.[10] In the Inaugural Address President Roosevelt had intimated the intent of the new ground to act. "I shall presently urge upon Congress," he declared, "in a special session detailed measures for the fulfillment [of my program], and I shall seek the immediate assistance of the several states."[11] The newly inaugurated President went on:

> I am prepared under my constitutional duty to recommend the measures that a stricken nation in the midst of a stricken world may require. These measures, or such other measures as the Congress may build out of its experience and wisdom, I shall seek, within my constitutional authority, to bring to speedy adoption.[12]

Under the New Deal the nation entered upon a period of planned economy, the extent of which even Roosevelt, with his aristocratic background probably did not intend. In his search for a route out of depths to which the depression had plunged the nation's economic life, the President yielded to his more radical advisors and "drifted into" government control.[13] However, the earlier New Deal measures were welcomed by businessmen, as well as workers, as the salvation of the American System. "The preservation of our democratic form of government," declared Abraham Epstein in 1937, "can be accomplished only through the establishment of security for our people; for no society can endure if it exposes the majority of its members to grave and continuous hazards and injustices."[14] And the late Edward S. Corwin echoed similar views when he offered the judgment that "the only way to restore dual federalism as a viable method of political control in the field of industry would be to break up the industrial structure."[15] This view left the alternative of federal control in order to achieve some degree of order in the industrial chaos of 1933. To the challenge that this would destroy the federal form of government, the *Cornell Law Quarterly* answered, "when the Supreme Court fears to reduce the states to dependencies of the nation, it fails to realize that so far as industry is concerned, economic forces have already accomplished the reduction. It is conceptualism to invalidate national social legislation upon the ground that it invalidates 'rights' which the states are powerless to exercise."[16]

Yet the executive and legislative branches were but two legs of the governmental tripod, and lacking the support of the third, the judiciary, the program would topple. As one commentator noted, "Franklin D. Roosevelt came to power in 1933 with his party in the majority in both Houses of Congress. But they would have to reckon with [the] concept of judicial supremacy which had an uncertain number of devotees among the Justices of the Supreme Court."[17] The New Dealers looked to past decisions of the Court as an indication that it, too, might *follow the leader*. The commerce clause seemed the strongest peg upon which to hang much of the legislation considered to be essential to the program. As Professor Charles Hyneman pointed out, "the reasoning in *Stafford v. Wallace*[18] gave President Franklin Roosevelt and his supporters ground for hope. . . that they could use the language of the commerce clause to justify a vast program of legislation. . . ."[19] That case seemed to repudiate the traditional view of commerce as the transportation of goods and persons. On the other hand, as noted in the preceding chapter, the Court continued to employ the restrictive definition of interstate commerce into the early thirties.

Undaunted by dismal prognostications, Roosevelt on the day following the inauguration issued a call for the promised special session of Congress and he bombarded it with messages, directives, and bills for passage.[20]

Robert H. Jackson called it "the most active period in American legislative history."[21] On March 16th the agricultural measures were sent to the Hill; on the 21st the Civilian Conservation Corps, Reconstruction Finance Corporation, and Federal Emergency Relief Bills, and on March 29th suggestions for control of the stock exchanges. In April the Tennessee Valley Authority and Home Owners' Load Corporation were proposed, followed in May by a request for railroad control and the National Industrial Recovery Act. The congressional scorecard on New Deal measures was good; there was rapid action in terms of the administration's desires, but the speed with which the laws passed took its toll in terms of the quality of the formulation of the laws. Frankfurter and Hart commenting on the legislative activity of the 1st session of the 73rd Congress wrote:

> Some of these enactments will lapse with time; others, repeal will terminate. But most of the new legislation, it is safe to assume, will constitute additions to the permanent structure of federal laws. ... neither careful draftmanship nor conscientious administration can avert the steady and difficult process of judicial distillation of the meaning of the complicated new legislation.[22]

Interspersed among the above measures was the abandonment of prohibition on March 22nd and of the gold standard on April 19th.

Professor Mason summarized the national temper as the One Hundred Day Congress adjourned:

> A hundred days of the New Deal had encouraged people in all walks of life to lift up their heads in hope and look to the future. But the long hill upward was tortuous; swift congressional achievements had not yet brought relief from the ravages of depression years. The state legislatures also had to tackle problems of jobless workers, debt-ridden farmers, and bankrupt business. Over this unprecedented outpouring from the legislative mill, both national and state, loomed the lethal threat of unconstitutionality.[23]

and Professor Swisher added,

> Not much was heard about the Supreme Court as the vast program of the New Deal got under way. Some doubts as the constitutionality of parts of the program were hesitantly expressed. It was widely believed that the crisis would be over before the Supreme Court could have an opportunity to act....[24]

The fact of the matter was that the New Dealers tried to ignore the question of constitutionality publicly, even though "the administration advisors were well aware of [the Supreme Court's] 'brooding omnipresence.' "[25] It would be a year before the New Deal would appear before the high tribunal for its first test and, therefore, as Robert McCloskey noted, "for a time the issue hung in doubt, and there was reason to believe that the Court would call upon its affirmative precedents, uphold national and state New Dealish innovations, and thus maintain a position on the margin of the political arena."[26] "To watchers of the future, only one thing seemed sure" recalled Charles and Mary Beard six years later, "since the judges were divided in opinion, Chief Justice Hughes and Justice Roberts held the fate of the Court, if not the New Deal, in their hands and they were not devoid of political acumen and experience."[27]

Federal Cases and Comment

On February 5, 1934, Justice Roberts, speaking for a unanimous bench, announced the decision in *Booth v. United States*[28] in which the reduction of the salary of retired federal judges under the Independent Offices Appropriations Act of June 1933 was voided. The reduction was part of the economy drive of the new administration, and its voiding was followed by a second blow in *Lynch v. United States*,[29] which struck down the congressional repudiation of veterans' insurance privileges in the Economy Act of March 1933. It might be noted that, as part of the Hughesian diplomacy, this latter opinion was assigned to Justice Brandeis, whose ties with the New Deal young men have been established above.

With these cases there was noticeable a perceptible shift of the Court from a liberal to conservative construction of state and federal power which occurred during the next three years. The man mostly responsible for this drift to pre-1930 positions was Owen J. Roberts, and he was joined from time to time by Chief Justice Hughes. But as one commentator wrote:

> Charles Evans Hughes is regularly catalogued by legal historians as having shared the balance of power between the liberal and conservative wings of the Court that sat intact through the first four years of the New Deal. What the Court records prove is that Hughes held no such power at all. True his votes did veer, as did Roberts' from one side to the other; but never once in a major case did he cast the deciding vote; for never once in a major case was Hughes to the right of Roberts. Thus, with five brethren to the right of him and three clearly to the left, Hughes could only choose whether a conservative decision should be scored 5–4 or 6–3; he could never determine that a decision be liberal unless Roberts, the Court's swinging keystone, came along. Proof of this lies in the simple fact that Hughes dissented several times—and always on the liberal side—in the big cases that came up during that drastic age, whereas Roberts never dissented

once. It was Roberts, for practical purposes, who steered the Court that Hughes headed, whenever the Justice called them close.[30]

In the area of federal taxation there was a record of unfavorable votes in the period from 1933 to 1936; in only five cases of the twenty reviewed did the high tribunal uphold the government when an interpretation of the federal taxing power was required. Two exceptions are found in *Ohio v. Helvering*[31] and *Helvering v. Powers*,[32] both of which dealt with a tax on the state when it enters a business in competition with private corporations. The first case involved the sale of liquor and the second, the administration of a railroad. In addition, in *Wainer v. United States*[33] a federal tax on engaging in the liquor business was found not to be a form of licensing.

During this period the justices showed a perceptible move toward a stricter view of non-revenue uses of the taxing power, amounting almost to a repudiation of *McCray−Doremus−Hampton−University of Illinois*[34] line of precedents and a return to the principles of *Bailey v. Drexel Furniture Co.*[35] In three opinions, all written by Roberts, the Court took a dim view of non-revenue purposes of the taxing power. In *United States v. Constantine*,[36] nominated by a commentator as one of Roberts' most controversial opinions,[37] and in a companion case, *United States v. Kesterson*,[38] the Court held that it was a usurpation of the police power of the states for the federal government to impose a tax on the importation of spiritous beverages into those states where their sale was prohibited. In a preview of his thinking in the Agricultural Adjustment Act case[39] Roberts declared:

> If in reality [a tax is] a penalty it cannot be converted into a tax by so naming it, and we must ascribe to it the character disclosed by its purpose and operation, regardless of name. Disregarding the designation of the exaction, and viewing its substance and application, we hold that it is a penalty for the violation of state law, and as such beyond the limits of federal power.[40]

In response Justice Cardozo, joined by Justices Brandeis and Stone, similarly in a foretaste of the latter's dissent in *Butler,* revealed:

> The judgment of the Court rests upon the ruling that another purpose, not professed, may be read beneath the surface, and by the purpose so imputed the statute is destroyed. Thus the process of psychoanalysis has spread to unaccustomed fields. *There is a wise and ancient doctrine that a court will not inquire into the motives of a legislative body or assume them to be wrongful.* ... The warning sounded by this court in the *Sinking-Fund Cases,* 99 U.S. 700, 718, has lost none of its significance. "Every possible presumption is in favor of the

validity of a statute, and this continues until the contrary is shown beyond a rational doubt. *One branch of the government cannot encroach on the domain of another without danger.* The safety of our institutions depends in no small degree on a strict observance of this rule." I cannot rid myself of the conviction that in the imputation to the lawmakers of a purpose not professed, this salutary rule of caution is now forgotten or neglected after all the many protestations of its cogency and virtue.[41] (Italics supplied.)

By the time the *Hoosac Mills Case (United States v. Butler)* arrived before the Court, 1935, a year disastrous to the New Deal, was drawing to a close. The National Recovery Administration had trembled in January[42] and fallen in May;[43] and in the same month the Railroad Retirement Act had been voided,[44] and "the intra-mural judicial war, developing since 1930, now reached its climax."[45] Roosevelt himself noted some years later that the NRA decision had "cast a long shadow of doubt" over the entire New Deal program.[46] But as *The Washington Post* pointed out, the NRA was only given a *coup de grace,* but the AAA was in the middle of its vitality when it was struck down,[47] and Ernest Bates declared "regardless of the ultimate economic wisdom or unwisdom of the [Agricultural Adjustment] Act, it admittedly worked much more successfully than the NRA."[48]

There is some debate over the efficacy of the act and as to just what section of the farm population it aided. Some viewed the statute itself as "inept" since the taxing power is the weakest foundation in the Constitution for a broad regulation.[49] But as will be indicated later, the taxing sections were not the key portions of the act as far as recovery was concerned, as the subsequent passage of the Soil Conservation Act of 1936 and the Agricultural Adjustment Act of 1938 demonstrated. Another aspect of the weakness of the bill was the fact that the tax could be passed on to the consumer by the processor through a rise in prices. The administration attempted to reduce the likelihood of this by amending the act in 1935 to require proof that the processor had not passed the tax on in order to initiate a taxpayers suit.[50]

As early as June 17, 1935 the White House had expressed anxiety over the constitutionality of the act.[51] So that when the Boston Federal District Court entertained a suit by the government to recover for unpaid taxes from a bankrupt company, the administration's attention was directed northward. The court of original jurisdiction upheld the act against the protest of the receivers for the Hoosac Mills Co., but the Court of Appeals reversed this ruling. Representative Martin Dies wrote to Roosevelt advising him that in light of this decision and the probability that the Supreme Court would uphold the Court of Appeals, the Act should be amended immediately to conform with the appeals court's ruling.[52] The interest of the President in the case itself is demonstrated by a request to the Attorney General for a copy of the government's brief which had been praised by the Attorney General.[53] On November 25th the Solicitor General notified the President that the case had been set for argument on December 9th.[54] The oral argument extended over two days, the 9th and the 10th, and *Newsweek* described the scene for its readers: "Rudy Vallee got a seat in the Supreme Court chamber, so did the Archbishop of York. But...on Monday of last week [2000 people waited outside] when the largest crowd ever tried to attend a Supreme Court hearing. Up before the Court was a suit of less significance to crooners and prelates than to farmers and politicians."[55] On the 10th the Court turned its attention to the Bankhead Cotton Allotment Act:

> The Solicitor General tried to show that the railroad and farmer were not really in dispute [but] just trying the constitutionality. Justices Hughes, McReynolds, Van Devanter, and Roberts let loose with a hail of stinging questions. . . . The Solicitor General blanched and swayed, "I'm afraid I'm going to have to ask the Court's indulgence." He sank down, half fainting. The amazed Justices adjourned fifteen minutes before their usual four-thirty closing. Deputy Marshal Thomas E. Waggemann dashed up to the Solicitor with aromatic spirits of ammonia. "Oh, look," a little girl spectator exclaimed, "the marshal is going to arrest Mr. Reed for annoying the Court.[56]

Just how much anger was carried into the conference room cannot be known, but one commentator speculated that opinion and the dissent give a glimpse, for "in reading that discussion one senses that drama of the debate that must have taken place in conference. Dignified judicial utterance could not cloak the fact that feeling must have run high before the final vote. And it can be surmised that the minority's charge of abuse of power against the majority rankled most of all."[57]

The voting in the case is a matter of much discussion. It is known that Mr. Justice Brandeis did not reveal his vote until the day following the conference,[58] and the bitterness of Stone's dissent at first almost cost him the support of the elder liberal justice.[59] The vote of the Chief was also a matter for speculation. Harold Ickes relayed the information that Cummings told the cabinet at a meeting on February 14, 1936 that Hughes was willing to go either way and, had Roberts voted to sustain the act, the Chief Justice would have joined him.[60] The authors of *The Nine Old Men* related the following incident:

> A few days after [the AAA decision] Justice Stone bumped into Professor Henry Schulman of Yale, one of his former students, who said he had a very indiscreet question to ask regarding the AAA decision.
> "It's not contempt of Court to ask a question," Stone replied.
> "Well, to be blunt, Mr. Justice," Schulman said, "did Hughes change his decision in the Triple A case?"
> "While I can't answer that," Stone replied with a twinkle in his eye, "if that were stated as a fact, I should be unable to prove the contrary."[61]

Hughes' biographer answered the detractors:

> The rumor of Hughes changing his vote is equally devoid of substance. While he was zealous in safeguarding the prestige of the Court, his profound sense of integrity never permitted him to alter his judgment in a case before the Court for the sake of creating a better impression.[62]

In view of the strength of character of the Chief Justice, one tends to agree with Professor Mason that "the story seems incredible."[63] Subsequent to the vote, Roberts was assigned to write the opinion, which fact Pearson and Allen found surprising in light of the position taken by the Justice in the *Nebbia*[64] case eighteen months before. They speculated that the reason Hughes did not write it himself, as he was wont to do when in the majority in an important case, was that the Chief was less than enthusiastic about the majority position. On the other hand, Edwin McElwain gave a most plausible explanation for the assignment of *Butler* to Roberts:

> In situations where the Court was divided, [Hughes] would assign the case to the Justice nearest the center for the purpose of preventing any extreme opinions. This he did in the first AAA case, where the opinion was assigned to Mr. Justice Roberts, and the result was a very narrow decision which adopted the Hamiltonian-Story view of the general welfare clause though it struck down the particular tax as in substance a regulation of local affairs.[65]

The fact that the counsel for the respondents, former Senator George Wharton Pepper, was a close friend and patron of the justice caused some raised eyebrows. The canons of legal propriety seemed to have been violated, as Fred Rodell noted, "to the slight offense of those who were fastidious about the emulation of Caesar's wife by Supreme Court Justices, Pepper's protege wrote the Court's opinion that answered Pepper's ...prayer.[66] Charles and Mary Beard found that the suggestion that Roberts should have refrained from writing the opinion "was hypercritical and implied that a judge must necessarily be influenced by what he knows as a man and feels as a friend."[67]

The *Butler* opinion, which Dean Griswold believed to be Roberts' most spectacular one,[68] represented a high point in the Justice's authorship of Court opinions; and it is to be regretted that in writing it he abandoned his *Nebbia* position. As Griswold noted:

> It seems fairly clear at this date that Roberts took too much of an "old view" approach in this case, that he was too firmly tied to the past. . . . Though I have no knowledge of the fact, I am inclined to think that he later came to have some doubts about the correctness of the *Butler* decision.[69]

In October, 1935 the Court had moved into its new multimillion dollar home from its old quarters in the Old Senate Chamber across the plaza in the Capitol Building.[70] So the A.A.A. decision was the first New Deal case to be decided in the new palace.

The official reporter's treatment of the case in *297 U.S. Reports* is unusual, not only in its length (88 pages) but also because of the inclusion of some of the oral argument of Solicitor General Reed and attorney G.W. Pepper, including the latter's famous peroration: "Indeed may it please your honors, I believe I am standing here today to plead the cause of the America I have loved; and I pray Almighty God that not in my time may 'the land of the regimented' be accepted as a worthy substitute for 'the land of the free.' "[71]

With what Griswold called "Roberts' lawyer-like approach" the Justice begins the opinion with a clear statement of the question to be settled, "in this case we must determine whether certain provisions of the Agricultural Adjustment Act, 1933, conflict with the Federal Constitution."[72] Justice Roberts divided his answer into three parts prefaced with a clear statement of the law and a precis of the adjudication up to the moment. The first section took up the matter of the taxpayers' standing and the separability of the two stages dealt with in the law; the second part dealt with the nature of the spending power of the federal government; and the third studied the coercive nature of the agricultural control program. The opinion concluded with an attack on the philosophy of government which could foster such a plan.

In the matter of standing, the Justice distinguished the present case from *Massachusetts v. Mellon*[73] because in the present instance the monies used under AAA are for an unauthorized purpose. Konefsky reminds us that the same charge was brought up in the precedent cited and that, like *Butler,* the *Mellon* law[74] was condemned because the states were being tempted "to surrender part of their sovereignty (in the present case, individuals were losing their freedom) by the offer to them of financial assistance."[75] However, it must be noted that in dissenting, Justice Stone evidently stipulated the question of standing, since he ignored this point. It was neglected, perhaps, because of the haste with which he composed his opinion,[76] or it might be that it was dropped in the modified version which resulted when both Roberts and he agreed to make changes in their respective works.[77]

Mr. Justice Roberts rapidly passed over the declared emergency nature of the program,[78] and he also rejected the possible separation of the taxing and spending parts of the measure by declaring, "passing the novel suggestion that two statutes enacted as a single scheme should be tested as if they were distinct and unrelated, we think the legislation now before us is not susceptible of such separation and treatment."[79]

He then proceeded to tie the taxing to the spending aspects of the bill as part of the scheme of regulation, concluding with the words "we conclude that the act is one regulating agricultural production; that the tax is a mere incident of such regulation and that the respondents have standing to challenge the legality of the exaction."[80]

The Justice moved to the spending power which he considered "the great and controlling question in the case," because if the appropriation is valid, then the tax stands.[81] It is difficult to follow the Justice's reasoning at this point. He seemed to say that a tax is not a tax because it is part of the regulation of agriculture, but if the regulation of agriculture would be valid, then the tax is valid also.[82] But before detailing the nature of the spending power, the Justice inserted what Roscoe Pound calls the "slot machine" theory of judicial review:[83]

> When an act of Congress is appropriately challenged in the courts as not conforming to the constitutional mandate, the judicial branch of Government has only one duty,—to lay the article of the Constitution which is invoked beside the statute which is challenged and to decide whether the latter squares with the former. All the court does, or can do, is to announce its considered judgment upon the question. The only power it has, if such it may be called, is the power of judgment. *This court neither approves nor condemns any legislative policy.*[84] [Italics supplied.]

For the first time in constitutional law[85] the nature and extent of the national spending power received a detailed discussion by the Court. After detailing two views, Roberts accepted the Hamiltonian notion over that of Madison as being the "true construction" as one which is proved by the study of the works of "public men and commentators."[86] Mr. Justice Roberts found "that the power of Congress to authorize expenditures of public monies for public purposes is not limited by the direct grants of legislative power found in the Constitution,"[87] and he conceded that "every presumption is to be indulged in favor of faithful compliance by Congress with the mandates of fundamental law."[88]

The Justice then swept aside all that he had built in favor of the use of the power by a declaration that the purpose of spending in this statute "invades the reserved rights of the states."[89] The majority had added to the 10th Amendment the word *expressly, a limitation,* which as Professor Mason demonstrates, Congress had specifically rejected when the Bill of Rights was being debated.[90] It will also be recalled Roberts himself had declared in *United States v. Sprague* that the 10th Amendment "added nothing to the instrument as originally ratified."[91]

Roberts cited precedents for the rejection of the law and ignored the line of precedents which could have been employed to uphold it. One is reminded of the incident related by Professor Corwin:

> Years ago a student of mine, after leaving Princeton, went to Washington where he took a course of lectures in Constitutional Law at George Washington University. One of the lecturers was Justice Harlan, [who] remarked..."if we — meaning the Court — don't like an act of Congress, we don't have much trouble to find grounds for declaring it unconstitutional."[92]

The heart of Justice Roberts' opposition seems to be expressed in the following quoted from the opinion:

> The regulation is not in fact voluntary. ... The power to confer or withhold unlimited benefits is the power to coerce or destroy. ...Contracts for the reduction of acreage and the control of production are outside the range of [federal] power. ... The congress cannot invade state jurisdiction to compel individual action; no more can it purchase such action. ... The United States can make the contract only if the federal power to tax and to appropriate reaches the subject matter of the contract. ... If the act before us is a proper exercise of the federal taxing power, evidently the regulation of all industry throughout the United States may be accomplished by similar exercises of the same power.[93]

The whole case, then, turns on the coercive nature of the regulation, and we are informed by one of the participants that this matter was not even discussed in the conference.[94]

The Justice then cited some of the possible "evils" which would flow from such federal compulsory control of industry if NRA had been validated and therefore would result as well if the instant law were upheld. He then tempered the fierceness of his attack by declaring that "these illustrations are given, not to suggest that any of the purposes mentioned are unworthy, but to demonstrate the scope of the principle for which the government contends...."[95]

A reading of the opinion reveals that the Justice had fallen into a logical, as well as legal, error by equating the taxing and spending power and therefore freely substituting one for the other. He accomplished this by a rhetorical question: "If the taxing power may not be used as the instrument to enforce a regulation of matters of state concern with respect to which the Congress has no authority to interfere, may it, as in the present case, be employed to raise the money necessary to purchase a compliance which Congress is powerless to command?"[96] The most serious condemnation of the taxing portions of the bill was that one group is taxed for the benefit of another, but the validity of the tax itself would be upheld if this were the only challenge; so said the Justice:

> The word *tax* has never been thought to connote the expropriation of money from one group for the benefit of another. We may concede that the latter sort of imposition is constitutional when imposed to effectuate regulation of a matter in which both groups are interested and in respect of which there is power of legislative regulation.[97]

Since there was no such power, the tax was void.

"The decision produced one of the most passionate dissents in the history of the Court," Dexter Perkins declared. "The language of Justice Stone went far beyond what was necessary to a decision of the *Butler* case. It was, in effect, a severe commentary on the Court itself. When a Supreme Court Justice of high reputation used such language, it was easy to understand the attitude of the administration."[98] James MacGregor Burns described that reaction:

> In the White House, Roosevelt was talking to Secretary of War Dern when a secretary came in with the bad news on a slip of paper and laid it before him. Eager reporters crowded around Dern afterward: How had the President reacted to the news? "He just held the sheet of paper in front of him," said Dern, "and smiled."
> The smile was significant. To this decision Roosevelt would enter no dissenting opinion, no "horse-and-buggy" remark. The situation had gone far beyond such talk. More than any other previous decision, Attorney General Robert H. Jackson later remembered, the *Butler* case had turned the thoughts of men in the administration toward the impending necessity of a challenge to the Court. Roosevelt's smile was that of a fighter ready for the struggle ahead, perhaps too of a tactician watching his opponent overextend himself.[99]

Two days later at the Jackson Day Dinner the President advised his hearers, "It is enough to say that the attainment of justice and the continuation of prosperity for American agriculture remain an immediate and constant objective of my Administration."[100]

The reaction outside of political circles was varied and vociferous. At Ames, Iowa the six members of the majority were hanged in effigy.[101] The press as usual was split in its views on the decision. The *New York Daily News* warned that "it remains to be seen whether the people will consent to be governed by a body of nine old men, all of whom were appointed by presidents who are now dead or repudiated."[102] While *The New York Herald-Tribune* thought the opinion was "a model of clarity and trenchant reasoning, ranking with the great decisions of the Court,"[103] *The Cleveland Plain Dealer* declared that "so broad is the decision and so unequivocal in its language of negation that one can scarcely escape the conviction that at least most of the remaining New Deal laws are scheduled for the block as fast as the Court has time to pass final judgment on them."[104] And the *Philadelphia Record* vigorously protested that "the Supreme Court may call agriculture a purely local matter all it wants, but the city council of Dubuque will find it impossible to change the price of a 'purely local' commodity, wheat, even by half a penny a bushel. The prices are fixed in Chicago."[105] *The New York Times* found it difficult to accept the gloomy prophecies made after the fall of AAA, since the "AAA has served effectively as a temporary bridge across a gully to more solid ground."[106]

Most interesting of the reactions to the decision by members of the administration was that of the Solicitor General, as expressed when he addressed the New York State Bar Association two weeks after the opinion had been announced:

> Though I am one who most deeply regrets the result of the *Butler* case, I find very real cause for hope in the future in the language of Justice Roberts upon the welfare clause. ... It would not be surprising, if from this holding ... there will flow an important line of decisions validating Federal legislation in the fields of agriculture, social welfare, and labor relations. ... History may well repeat itself with *United States v. Butler* as a starting point.[107]

On the Monday following the announcement of the *Hoosac Mills* decision the Court ruled unanimously, again through Justice Roberts, that the 1935 amendments to the Agricultural Adjustment Act were also invalid and that the impounded monies, collected as taxes, had to be returned to the taxpayers.[108]

Another aspect of the federal spending power came before the Court in a number of land bank cases. In *Federal Land Bank v. Gaines*[109] and

Federal Land Bank v. Warner[110] the Federal Farm Loan Act was upheld in its application. But on Black Monday, May 27, 1935 the Court voided another act which proposed to aid the farmer. In *Louisville Joint Land Bank v. Radford*[111] the Frazier-Lemke Amendments to the Federal Bankruptcy Act were held to violate the boundary which the 5th Amendment sets around the bankruptcy power of Congress.[112] Justice Brandeis speaking for a unanimous Court suggested an alternate method to Congress, "If the public interest requires, and permits, the taking of property of individual mortgagees in order to relieve the necessities of individual mortgagors, resort must be had to proceedings by eminent domain; so that, through taxation, the burden of relief afforded in the public interest may be borne by the public."[113] Though such judicial admonitions are unusual, in light of the poor draftsmanship of the bill, they seemed to be in order. Indeed, the bill had been opposed by the administration leaders themselves.

As an aside, it might be noted that there was some doubt in the mind of the Chief Justice as to the advisability of announcing three blows at the New Deal on the same day, as *Schechter*[114] and *Humphrey*[115] were ready to be delivered on the same day as *Radford*. Brandeis, who was considered the unofficial representative of the New Deal on the Court, saw no reason to postpone it.

Seven months later, a unanimous Court upheld the ruling of the Wisconsin Supreme Court which voided that portion of the Federal Home Owners' Loan Act of 1933 permitting the conversion of state savings and loan associations into federal associations without the consent of the chartering state and on the vote of only a bare majority of the stockholders.[116]

In February of 1935 the Court had given approval, by a majority of one vote including that of Justice Roberts, to the repudiation of the gold clause in private contracts,[117] and in effect, in government contracts as well, for though the action was held unconstitutional, bondholders could not sue for damages.[118] The dissenters declared, through Mr. Justice McReynolds, that the repudiation in public contracts was immoral as well as unconstitutional: "loss of reputation for honorable dealing will bring us unending humiliation; the impending legal and moral chaos is appalling."[119] Not a few commentators felt that the majority agreed with the minority, but ruled as they did to prevent financial confusion.[120] McReynolds has been quoted as declaring, "as for the Constitution, it does not seem too much to say that it is gone."[121] However, in a subsequent "accurate" copy prepared by the Justice, the sentence does not appear.[122]

In 1936 there were heard a number of cases involving the power of the Secretary of Agriculture to set rates for the stockyards and the marketing agencies associated with them. The Court followed the precedent set in *Stafford v. Wallace*[123] to sustain the Secretary's power.[124] However, in *Morgan v. United States*[125] the justices voided a set of rates which were based on evidence not heard by the Secretary but by one of his assistants.

The Court continued its favorable view of the activity of the Interstate Commerce Commission with some exceptions. In eleven of the sixteen cases presented to it, the Court supported the commission's power or procedures. In only one of the five unfavorable cases did the Court split, and in that one, only because the Justices of the majority felt that the rates were not based on the evidence presented.[126] The Court continued to accept the *Shreveport*[127] doctrine in regard to discrepancies in state rates over interstate rates.[128] Writing some time later, Roberts noted:

> There can be no question of the correctness of the decision in the *Shreveport* case. The power to regulate interstate rates was incontestable. But if action required by the state law, in carriage within the state were to be allowed to disrupt and destroy the efficacy of the order regarding interstate rates, the power of the national legislature under the commerce clause would be nullified.[129]

The Federal Trade Commission and Federal Communications Commission fared as well before the high tribunal. In *Humphrey's Executor, Rathbun, v. United States*[130] the issue was not so much the independence of the Federal Trade Commission, which the Court upheld, but the removal power of the president,which was held to be limited to the reasons and procedures established by Congress. The decision was, however, as a defeat for the New Deal reform program.[131] "Indeed," wrote Schlesinger, "before making the removal, Roosevelt had consulted with James M. Landis, who had been Brandeis' law clerk at the time of the Myers[132] decisions". . . . (Landis supported the President's action in light of that precedent.) "But the new decision conveyed the clear impression, not that the Court had changed its mind, but that Roosevelt's action had been high-handed and lawless.[133]

In only two cases did the Court void the commission's action, and in both, the vote was split and Roberts was with the majority. The first ruling was in *Arrow-Hart & Hegeman Electric Co. v. Federal Trade Commission*,[134] where a five-to-four court speaking through Roberts voted against the application of the Clayton Anti-Trust Act to a holding company which controlled competing companies. Walter Gellhorn wrote to Justice Stone that the opinion showed that "Justice Roberts was suffering from one of his astigmatic spells."[135] The second decision, *Jones v. Securities Exchange*

Commission, [136] also involved an attempt to thwart the authority of a commission. The Securities and Exchange Commission had been established in June 1934 and had assumed administration of the Federal Securities Act of 1933 from the Federal Trade Commission.[137] The details of the case are given by the official reporter:

> The day before a registration statement filed with the Securities and Exchange Commission would have become effective... the Commission began a proceeding... challenging the truth and sufficiency of the statement and notified the registrant to appear at a hearing some weeks later and show cause why a stop order should not issue suspending its effectiveness. Thereafter, the Commission's subpoena was served on the registrant commanding him to appear and testify and bring designated books and papers. The registrant then gave formal notice that his statement was withdrawn and submitted motions to quash the subpoena, which he declined to obey, and to dismiss the proceedings. The Commission, however, persisted in the investigation and obtained from the District Court... an order requring the registrant to appear before the Commission and answer questions.[138]

The majority ruled that the forced investigation of the applicant's books was comparable to "star chamber" proceedings,[139] and declared that "an investigation not based on specified grounds is quite as objectionable as a search warrant not based upon specific statements of fact. Such an investigation, or such a search, is unlawful in its inception and cannot be made lawful by what it may bring, or by what it actually succeeds in bringing to light."[140] Mr. Justice Cardozo, in dissent, pointed out to the majority that there had been for months "a standing Regulation giving warning to [the registrant] and to the world that without the consent of the Commission there could be no withdrawal of a statement once placed on files."[141] The Justice continued:

> Recklessness and deceit do not automatically excuse themselves by notice of repentance. ... A statement wilfully false or wilfully defective is a penal offense to be visited, upon conviction, with fine or imprisonment. ... There will be only partial attainment of the ends of public justice unless retribution for past is added to prevention for the future.[142]

Five years later Roosevelt commenting on the decision noted that "its effect was bound to hamper the work of the Commission and to seek to discredit the motives and manner of operation of this agency set up to protect investors from fraud and dishonesty."[143]

Anti-trust legislation was invoked on four occasions during this period, and in all instances the prosecution was upheld. Three are worthy of note. In *Local 167, International Brotherhood of Teamsters v. United States*[144] the labor union was held liable to prosecution when it controlled the prices and sales of poultry either at the origin or destination of commerce. The present case was within the *stream of commerce* doctrine which traced its origin to *Swift & Co. v. United States*.[145] In light of the present decision the Court could have upheld NRA, had the Justices wished to consider this case as a precedent. A second case in this category involved the publication and circulation of a farmer's journal.[146] The nine members of the high tribunal ruled that such activity was interstate commerce and, therefore, subject to the Sherman Anti-trust Act. In a third case, *Sugar Institute v. United States*,[147] the Sherman Act was applied to an industry-wide association and its fifteen members for some forty-five practices including price regulation through hidden agreements. One is forced to agree with Robert L. Stern that "there would appear to be no difference in the constitutional power to protect interstate commerce against unduly high prices, as in the Sherman Act, and excessively low prices, as in the New Deal legislation."[148]

During these years also the Court was called upon to rule on the use of the commerce clause to support a federal criminal statute, the Federal Kidnap Act of 1932 and its 1934 amendments. In *Gooch v. United States*[149] the Justices unanimously upheld this extension of the meaning of the commerce clause.

"By the Spring of 1935," wrote Ernest Bates,

> the effects of the New Deal began to be manifest. . . . .In a word the New Deal had fulfilled its purpose—or at least [the purpose of Big Business] - and it was now time to do away with it.
> Coincidentally, with this changed attitude of Big Business there came a change in the decisions of the Supreme Court. The first real blow at the New Deal was struck on May 6, 1935, when the Court voided the Railroad Retirement Act by its decision in *Railroad Retirement Board v. Alton R. Co. 295 U.S. 330.*[150]

It has been debated whether the *Panama Oil* case or the *Railroad Board* decision was the first anti-New Deal blow. Walter Murphy suggests that special circumstances surrounding *Panama* rule that decision out.[151] During the years immediately preceding the coming of the New Deal, the Court had refused, as has been demonstrated above, to extend the coverage of the Federal Employer's Liability Act to non-operating employees of the railroads. And, while the President had signed the Crosser-Dill Bill, he did express serious doubts about its constitutionality. Though the Act was not an integral part of the New Deal Program, its voiding was considered an ill-omen for similar measures of the administration. And, therefore, it is interesting to note that even the Justices who voted to uphold the bill were not unanimous in their approval of the policy. Stone had declared privately, "if I had been a member of Congress, I am certain I would have voted against it."[152] The question of validity did not rest, however, on its merit as policy but as a constitutional use of the commerce power.

Roberts, speaking for the five man majority, summarized the opinion, rather than read it, because "it was too long."[153] He said:

> ...The Act is invalid because several of its inseparable provisions contravene the due process of law clause of the Fifth Amendment. We are of the opinion that it is also bad for another reason which goes to the heart of the law, even if it could survive the loss of the unconstitutional features....The Act is not in purpose or effect a regulation of interstate commerce within the meaning of the Constitution.[154]

But the rationale of the decision, at least in view of the emphasis placed by the Justice, seemed to be in the faulty philosophy behind the pension program as a means of providing good interstate service:

> Assurance of security it truly gives, but quite as truly, if "morale" is intended to connote efficiency, loyalty, and continuity of service, the surest way to destroy it in any privately owned business is to substitute legislative largess for private bounty and thus transfer the drive for pensions to the halls of Congress and transmute loyalty to employer into gratitude to the legislature.[155]

But the constitutional defect was found to lie in the fact that "the Act denied due process of law by taking the property of one and bestowing it on another."[156]

The Chief Justice, who spoke for many beside his three colleagues,[157] declared in dissent:

> The gravest aspect of the decision is that it does not rest simply upon a condemnation of particular features of the ... Act, but denies to Congress the power to pass any compulsory pension act for railroad employees. If the opinion were limited to the particular provisions of the Act, which the majority might find objectionable and not severable, the Congress would be free to overcome the objectives by a new statute.... It is not our province to enter [the] field [of pension plans], and I am not persuaded that Congress, in entering it for the purpose of regulating interstate carriers, has transcended the limits of authority which the Constitution confers.[158]

One commentator believed he saw other reasons for the split beyond constitutional principles. Fred Rodell wished to rest the decision on the fact that the majority five all had been railroad lawyers prior to their accession to the high bench.[159]

The decision was a shock to the New Dealers for numerous reasons. First, the Court's view that the federal government had no jurisdiction in the area of labor-management relations was an ill-omen for subsequent legislation in that field. The fear was strengthened by the apparent repudiation of the decision made by eight of the nine members in 1930 in the *Railway Clerks Case*,[160] which could have been used to uphold the Retirement Act. Secondly, in light of the liberal view expressed by Roberts fourteen months before in the *Nebbia* case, the *Retirement* opinion seemed to be a change of mind, and indeed it was taken by some to signify that the Justice was lost to the New Deal.[161]

The devastation caused by the decision was recognized by the White House. In a letter to Sam Rayburn, representative from Texas, Roosevelt wrote that "the Attorney General suggests that in view of the sweeping character of the Supreme Court in the Railroad Retirement case, it would be unwise to attempt to secure new legislation at this session of Congress."[162] The President's judgment was probably based on a letter which he had received from Cummings on June 4th[163] and a memo in which the Attorney General noted:

> The case was always a difficult one, but the form the opinions took would seem to indicate such a marked cleavage in the Supreme Court that it may be, and probably is, a forecast of what we may expect with reference to almost any form of social legislation that Congress may enact.[164]

The New York Herald-Tribune and *The Washington Post* echoed much of the editorial comment of the day when they pointed to the weakness of the composition of the bill.[65] But the liberal *Philadelphia Record* termed the decision "a threat to democracy" but declared that "Monday's decision. . .may prove a blessing in disguise, since Congress will set up a social security system on general welfare and not on regulation of commerce."[166] On the same day The *Record* printed a political cartoon illustrating the view which the liberals took of Roberts' part in the decision.[167] (See p. 63)

Between January 7, 1935 and May 25th of the following year the Supreme Court voided twelve congressional statutes,[168] and during the same period approximately 1600 injunctions against the execution of federal laws had been issued by federal judges.[169] As Al Smith quipped, the courts had begun to throw "the alphabet out the window three letters at a time."[170] The first attack on a New Deal statute had come in December, 1934 when section 9(c) of the National Industrial Recovery Act

"MIGHTY CASEY HAD STRUCK OUT."   —By Jerry Doyle

was challenged before the Court. The administration had been hunting for a test case and one from the petroleum industry seemed to be the best choice. This was especially true because of Roberts' familiarity with the problems of the industry dating from his work with the Teapot Dome scandals, especially with the cutthroat competition prevalent at the time.[171] The opportunity for the Court to rule came in *Panama Refining Co. v. Ryan*[172] and a companion case, *Amazon Petroleum Corporation v. Ryan.* The Justices were asked to review a reversal of decrees enjoining federal officers from implementing the petroleum code of NRA and the executive orders which enforced the act.[173] When the case got to oral argument, an amazing fact was uncovered. Assistant Attorney General Harold M. Stephens on his own initiative told the Court that through an administrative error the penalty section of the executive order had been omitted from the official copy when the order was revised.[174] The oversight had been discovered when a conscientious government attorney, while preparing the case, had checked the document.[175] The government, therefore, had been arresting, indicting and jailing persons for violations of "a law that did not exist."[176] In addition, during an exchange between Justice Brandeis and lawyer Stephens it was revealed that the codes were not generally available to the public.[177] Therefore, one benefit of the case was the initiation of the publication of the *Federal Register,* which contains in official form all orders and regulations affecting the public.

Because of the insertion of this side issue into the case, the Court never ruled on the issue of the validity of the codes because the penalty paragraph had been omitted from the executive order. Instead, the main issue became the question of the delegation of power which would permit such a situation to arise. For the first time the Court voided congressional legislation for this reason.[178] The Chief Justice declared:

> It establishes no criterion to govern the President's course. It does not require any finding by the President as a condition of his action. The Congress in sec. 9 (c) thus declares no policy. . . . So far as this section is concerned, it gives to the President an unlimited authority to determine the policy and to lay down the prohibition, or not to lay it down, as he may see fit. And disobedience to his order is made a crime punishable by fine and imprisonment.[179]

The majority of eight justices found that this part of NIRA was void. Justice Cardozo, on the other hand, found criteria in two statements of Congress in the bill: first, that the act was to "eliminate unfair competitive practices," and, second, "that it was to conserve natural resources,"[180] and, therefore, he felt the section should be upheld. Harold Laski writing to Justice Holmes felt that "Cardozo had much the best of the argument."[181]

The *Herald-Tribune* commented editorially that "...the blank check theory of government is finished...."[182] While *The Washington Post* considered the decision a reprimand to Congress not to attempt to avoid its duties,[183] the *Philadelphia Record* felt that it represented "no menace to the New Deal."[184]

Congressional reaction to the *Panama* decision was the passage of the Connally Oil Control Act,[185] which was extended to 1942 and was never successfully challenged. It was upheld by implication in *United States v. Powers.*[186]

In April, 1935 a case involving the NIRA, which is usually glossed over in discussions of the act, was decided. In *United States v. Arizona*[187] the Court unanimously refused to permit NRA to assume surveillance of the construction of Boulder Dam. Justice Butler noted that "the Recovery Act discloses no intention to require the Chief of Engineers' recommendations in respect of proposed improvements shall be made to the Administrator instead of to the Congress."[188]

However, there was still the matter of the real test of the NRA; and in March, 1935, when Stanley Reed replaced J. Biggs Crawford as Solicitor General, it was believed that the test would soon come.[189] Since late 1933 there had been a case involving the lumber code in the federal courts. It was appealed to the Supreme Court, but while the case was being prepared by the Justice Department, it was discovered that there had been some deception on the part of the government attorneys in the lower courts. Rather than risk a test on such a record, the Solicitor General requested, and the Court granted, a dismissal of the case on April 1.[190] The general public, aroused by the press, viewed the dismissal as a manifestation of bad faith and an admission by the administration that it was afraid to test the National Industrial Recovery Act.[191] "...There can be but one inference," charged the *New York Herald-Tribune*, "from this extraordinary conduct, that the Justice Department felt sure that the NRA was in its fundamentals unconstitutional, and that the Supreme Court was about to hold so."[192]

On April 3rd Donald Richberg, Chairman of the National Industrial Recovery Board, telegraphed the President that the government was expediting an appeal from the Circuit Court in New York, which would help quiet the criticism. On the following day Thomas Corcoran, a White House advisor, on the urging of Felix Frankfurter, frantically tried to stop the rush to get a test case before the Court despite the bad press.[193] Because of his closeness to Justice Brandeis, Frankfurter knew of the

general opposition to NRA as "having gone too far."[194] On April 10th
Reed requested instructions from the President as to a course of action,
and the next day the Solicitor General followed up with a notification that
the defendants had petitioned for a writ of certiorari. Mr. Reed warned of
the weakness of the case, but he advised the President that the government
would have to act immediately if they wished to have the case heard at the
1934 term of the Court.[195] He was advised to support the petition, and
on April 15th certiorari was granted.[196]

There were valid reasons for pushing the case despite the fears of
Frankfurter, who, incidentally, was one of the most influential persons
with the President at this time. Not the least powerful was the fact that
the law had been upheld by the Court of Appeals for the 2nd Circuit, one
of the most respected, and had been supported by the eminent jurist
Learned Hand.

The case[197] was argued on May 2nd and 3rd; Donald Richberg had
been invited to assist the Solicitor General with the oral presentation of the
case because of his familiarity with the intricacies of the code program.
The government was at a disadvantage because it was widely known that
the program was on the verge of collapse, though Jackson tells us that the
administration was about to ask for a complete overhaul of the bill before
it expired in June, had the Court sustained the principles of the
program.[198]

Briefly stated, the NRA was the broadest attempt at governmental
control of the national economy through the commerce power that had
ever been made. A bit prematurely Edward S. Corwin foresaw the
reduction of the importance of judicial review in the determination of
national policies with the coming of "Nira."[199] The genesis of the program
can be traced to the United States Chamber of Commerce, which saw in
the favorable view of the Court on the voluntary codes in the *Appalachian
Coals* case an opportunity to extend the principle through the addition of
the penalty power to the President's supervision of the codes. However,
when Congress added the protection of collective bargaining and provisions
for minimum wage and maximum hour determination, the business community balked.[200]

Mr. Justice Roberts, looking back some fifteen years later, summarized
the facts of the case:

> An attempt was made to enforce the act against a small butchering
> concern in Brooklyn. The attempt was justified on the ground that

the materials received by the defendant had passed to him through the channels of interstate commerce. ...[the Court held] the commerce had ceased when the butcher's activities began and that his practices in marketing his commodity could not be said to affect interstate commerce so as to be regulable by federal authority.[201]

An obvious weakness in the government's case was the nature and size of the industry challenged. While the company imported chickens from New Jersey and Pennsylvania, all of its sales were within New York. This rendered the charge that the government was attempting to control local business all the more forceful. The government invoked the *Shreveport* doctrine to justify its control of intrastate business which affected interstate commerce. It was hoped by this tactic to draw the vote of the Chief Justice, who had authored the precedent cited, and hopefully also, the vote of Justice Van Devanter who had supported Hughes' position and had penned complimentary remarks on the draft of the opinion.[202] Indeed, in writing the present opinion, the Chief took cognizance of the precedent but he declined to apply it in the instance of a small business. "The undisputed facts," he declared, "thus afford no warrant for the argument that the poultry handled by the defendants at their slaughterhouse markets was in a *'current'* or *'flow'* of interstate commerce...."[203] He then attempted to distinguish the precedent of one year's standing in the *Local 167 IBT* case by stating that the manipulation of wages by the union *affected* interstate commerce, while the practices in the instant case did not.[204] And so the Chief Justice summarized the ruling of the Court:

> It is not the province of the Court to consider the economic advantages or disadvantages of such a centralized system. It is sufficient to say that the Federal Constitution does not provide for it. ....We are of the opinion that the attempt through the provisions of the code to fix the hours and wages of employees of the defendants in their intrastate business was not a valid exercise of federal power.[205]

The Court had brushed aside the "emergency" nature of the legislature when it ruled that "extraordinary conditions do not create or enlarge constitutional power,"[206] and on one of the last occasions it restated the concept of *dual federalism*. Hughes noted that "such assertions of extraconstitutional authority were anticipated and precluded by the Tenth Amendment ...."[207] In addition, the Justices could have avoided the interstate commerce issue and ruled simply on the basis of the delegation of power, which they had already had in the *Panama* case; one close observer of the judicial process believed it was dangerous for the Court to enter this area[208] and, in light of the rulings in 1937, embarrassing as well.

This time Justice Cardozo joined his brethren, and in a concurring opinion, required by his dissent in *Panama*, he explained his change:

> The extension becomes wide as the field of industrial regulation. If that conception shall prevail, anything that Congress may do within the limits of the commerce clause for the betterment of business may be done by the President upon the recommendation of a trade association by calling it a code. *This is delegation run riot.* No such plenitude of power is susceptible of transfer. . . . Nothing less is aimed at by the code now submitted to our scrutiny.[209] (Italics supplied.)

Mr. Justice Brandeis had noted in approving the opinion that "this is clear and strong—and marches to the inevitable doom. It seems to me to be ready for delivery on Monday—and I hope that will be possible."[210] The following incident amplifies his view of the law: Brandeis called Corcoran into the robing room after the session had ended and warned:

> This is the end of this business of centralization, and I want you to go back and tell the President that we're not going to let this government centralize everything. It's come to an end. As for your young men, you call them together and tell them to get out of Washington — tell them to go home, back to the states. That is where they must do their work."[211]

It was, as Eriksson has noted, "undoubtedly the hardest blow by the Supreme Court to the New Deal" because it was unanimous.[212] Roosevelt's reaction mirrors the surprise of the administration:

> When the news reached the White House, the first question the President asked was "Where was Brandeis?" "With the majority," replied one of his legal advisors. "Where was Cardozo? Where was Stone?" he queried. "They too were with the majority."[213]

And some four days later at his press conference F.D.R. declared:

> . . .In spite of what one gentleman said in the paper this morning, that I resented the decision. Nobody resents a Supreme Court decision. You can deplore a Supreme Court decision, and you can point out the effect of it. You can call the attention of the country to what the results of that decision are if future decisions follow this decision.[214]

And further in the conference he told the nation what he thought the result was: "We have been relegated to the horse-and-buggy definition of interstate commerce."[215]

Not a few commentators believed, however, that the President was relieved to have the program out of the way. Max Lerner reflected on the question some years later:

> ...Who was it that killed the NRA? Was it the Supreme Court by the Schechter decision? Or was it Hugh Johnson and Donald Richberg through the administrative chaos within the NRA and the poor selection of a test case? Or was it the President who might have asked Congress to put through a revised act, as he did afterward with the AAA but who welcomed a chance to get the albatross off his neck. My own guess would be a combination of all three.[216]

We might add a fourth cause: "...It had already lost public support and the backing of important interests."[217]

Not all the letters arriving at the White House condemned the decision. Henry L. Stimson, who was to become Secretary of War in the War Cabinet in 1940, reprimanded the President thus:

> ...I think that for you to speak as if a single decision could overthrow this long honorable growth, adjusting itself intelligently to the growing needs of our country and as you are reported to have put it, throw us back to a "horse and buggy age," was a wrong statement, and an unfair statement and, if it had not been so extreme as to be recognizable as hyperbole, a rather dangerous and inflammatory statement.

To which F.D.R. replied:

> Once more, of course, the press reporting is not exactly adequate. They left out the beginnings of several sentences which ran thus: "If certain sentences in this decision are carried to their logical conclusuion, the following would be the result, etc. [sic][218]

Newspaper comment was favorable, in general, toward the decision. The *New York Herald-Tribune* saw the Court as the continuing protector of the Constitution,[219] while the *Chicago Daily News* declared that "constitutional government has returned to America."[220] The *Philadelphia Record*, which supported the striking down of the NRA, felt that the Court's declaration on interstate commerce created a power dilemma: "first, we have too much regulation of business, now we have none at all."[221] Arthur Krock, in his column "In Washington" two years after the *Schechter* decision, was amazed that "as good a lawyer as Donald Richberg could ever have been willing to stake his legal reputation that the government would win so narrow a test . . ."[222] And prophetically, but prematurely, *The New York Times* declared that "great significance attaches to the ruling out by the court of business [control] which 'merely affects interstate commerce.' That same clause . . .occurs in the Wagner Labor Bill. If it remains there and another judicial test is made, the consequences will be expected to be the same as in the rejection of the NIRA as unconstitutional."[223]

Because the statutory base had been destroyed in the *Schechter* decision, all of the codes collapsed. Congress began to legislate the little NRA during the second hundred days in an attempt to salvage something of the program. The notable statutes of this period were the Guffey-Snyder Coal Act of 1935 and the National Labor Relations Act of the same year.[224]

The Bituminous Coal Conservation Act had been formulated by the operators and miners and was then submitted to Congress by Senator Joseph Guffey and Representative John Snyder, both of Pennsylvania. It was an attempt to re-establish the successful bituminous codes which had been voided as a result of the *Schechter* decision. It provided the machinery for the fixing of minimum prices and a separate provision for the establishment of minimum wages and maximum hours. A heavy penalty tax was to be levied on those producers who did not accept the code. The bill specified that it was to be applied only to "transactions directly affecting interstate commerce."[225]

A controversy arose even before the bill's passage as the result of a letter from F.D.R. to Sam Hill, chairman of the House sub-committee conducting the hearings. "I hope your committee will not permit doubts as to the constitutionality, however reasonable," the President wrote, "to block the suggested legislation."[226] The anti-New Deal press took up the sentence and used it to impugn F.D.R.'s honesty.[227] Schlesinger justifies the statement by noting that "Roosevelt's point was orthodox enough, but the expression was unquestionably maladroit. He might better have written 'doubts as to unconstitutionality,' which is what he meant . . . ."[228] Charles Curtis would explain it another way:

> Congress acts first and so acts unhampered by doubts raised by or respect owed to others' opinions. Its duties to the Constitution do not include fear of a veto. No more should they include apprehension of the Court's disapproval. Roosevelt was quite right in what he wrote to

a member of the House Ways and Means Committee on the Coal Control Act.[229]

Despite the clamor the bill passed and became effective on August 30, 1935.

On the same day James Carter, President and one of the three members of the board of directors[230] of the Carter Coal Co., protested at a meeting of the board that the law was unconstitutional and moved that the Company refuse to participate. The other members of the board voted him down, and Carter sued in the Federal District Court in the District of Columbia to prevent the company from joining the coal code. His action had all the earmarks of collusion, but the procedure was valid—James Carter's lawyer had seen to that.

The District Court ruled that the labor provisions were invalid in light of the *Schechter* decision, but that the price-fixing machinery was valid. Since Congress had declared the separability of the two parts and it was the price-fixing which was being challenged, Judge Adkins refused to issue the injunction. In another case, *Tway Coal Co. v. Glenn* the federal court in Kentucky had already ruled that both sections were valid. Both cases were brought on appeal to the high bench at the same time.[231] The states of Illinois, Indiana, Kentucky, New Mexico, Ohio, Pennsylvania, and Washington filed *amici curiae* briefs in favor of the law.[232] Arguments were heard on March 11th and 12th, and it took sixty-eight days for the Justices to decide the fate of the act, the longest period of study of a New Deal statute which the Court made.[233]

The Court split in an unusual fashion in deciding *Carter v. Carter Coal Co.*:[234] "The Supreme Bench Splits 5-1-3," read the *New York Herald-Tribune* headline.[235] The opinion is long, as is the dissent, and together with part of the oral argument and briefs, covers over one hundred pages of the *United States Reports*.

Sutherland recognized, as had the courts of original jurisdiction, that the coal industry was in dire straits. But he ignored the emergency nature of the enactment and directly attacked the tax as a penalty, and, citing the *Butler* decision among others, he declared that "...if the act in respect of the labor and price-fixing provisions be not upheld, the 'tax' must fall with them."[236] The Justice then held that the general welfare clause was limited to the enumerated powers by declaring:

...nothing is more certain than that beneficent aims, however great or

well directed, can never serve in lieu of constitutional power. . . . We
shall find no grant of power which authorizes Congress to legislate in
respect of these general purposes unless it be found in the commerce
clause.[237]

Sutherland then goes on to restate the traditional view that mining is not
commerce.[238] And for the last time the Court held:

> . . .The extent of the effect [on interstate commerce] bears no logical
> relation to its character. . . . Much stress is put upon the evils which
> come from the struggle between employers and employees over the
> matter of wages, working conditions, the right of collective bargaining,
> etc., and the resulting strikes, curtailment and irregularity of produc-
> tion and effect on prices; and it is insisted that interstate commerce is
> *greatly* affected thereby. . . . The relation of employer and employee
> is a local relation. . . . An increase in the greatness of the effect adds
> to its importance. It does not alter its character.[239]

Justice Roberts correctly characterized this opinion in later years as "the
high water mark of the doctrine that Congress cannot regulate local
activities."[240]

The majority then went on to find that the price-fixing sections,
which were being challenged, but not ruled on, and the labor sections,
which were not challenged but were ruled on, were inseparable, despite the
clear declaration of Congress in section 15 to the contrary.[241] Justice
Sutherland further stated:

> In the absence of such a provision [of separability], the presumption
> is that the legislature intends the act to be effective in its entirety —
> that is to say, the rule is against the mutilation of a statute; and if
> any provision be unconstitutional, the presumption is that the remain-
> ing provisions fall with it. The effect of the statute is to reverse this
> presumption in favor of the inseparability and create the opposite one
> of separability. Under the non-statutory rule, the burden is upon the
> supporter of the legislation to show the separability of the provisions
> involved. Under the statutory rule, the burden is shifted to the
> assailant to show their inseparability. But under either rule, the
> determination, in the end, is reached by applying the same test—
> namely, What was the intent of the lawmakers?[242]

And on the following page, he concluded that ". . . the statute should be so
construed as to justify the conclusion that Congress, notwithstanding,
probably would have not passed the price-fixing provisions of the code" if
a motion to strike out the labor provisions had been approved during the

legislative debate.[243]

Wishing to keep Mr. Justice Roberts in the majority, Sutherland had to avoid anything which would clash with the position taken by the former in his *Nebbia* opinion, so he avoided the price-fixing question by declaring:

> The conclusion is unavoidable that the price-fixing provisions are so related to and dependent upon the labor provisions...as to make it clearly probable that the latter being held bad, the former would not have passed. . . . The price-fixing provisions of the code are thus disposed of without coming to the question of their constitutionality. . . ."[244]

The Court splintered badly in the *Guffey* decision—even the Chief Justice, who seemed to have abandoned his *Shreveport* doctrine in *Schechter,* could not abide Justice Sutherland's tenuous logic. "I agree," he wrote, "that. . . the so-called tax is not a real tax, but a penalty; . . . that production—in this case mining—which precedes commerce, is not itself commerce . . . . But that is not the whole case," he continued. "The Act also provides for the regulation of the prices of bituminous coal sold in interstate commerce and prohibits unfair methods of competion in interstate commerce."[245] The Chief threw a barb at Mr. Justice Roberts when he declared that "we are not at liberty to deny to the Congress, with respect to interstate commerce, a power commensurate with that enjoyed by the states in the regulation of their internal commerce." He then directed the reader to "see *Nebbia v. New York*, 291 U.S. 502."[246] Hughes would have taken Congress at its word on the matter of separability, and he chided the Court for *imagining* what Congress would do when it had already signified its intent.

Mr. Justice Cardozo attacked the majority for closing its eyes to the fact that the labor troubles at the mines have kept coal out of interstate commerce, and the resulting shortage of fuel has become a matter "vital to the national economy."[247] Speaking for Justices Brandeis and Stone, he concluded his dissent with an exposure of the real error in the majority's position:

> ...The attack upon the statute in its labor regulations assumes the existence of a controversy that may never become actual. . . . What the code will provide as to wages and hours of labor, or whether it will provide anything, is still in the domain of prophecy. The opinion of the Court begins at the wrong end. To adopt a homely form of

words, the complainants have been crying before they are really hurt.[248]

The Court, it seems, had repeated a technical error similar to the one made in the *Butler* decision—that of ruling on a section of the law in which the petitioner had no standing.[249]

As in all New Deal decisions, the reaction of the press was diverse, though mainly favorable toward the Court. *Time* wrote that "further federal attempts to regulate industry are seemingly doomed. A shadow of doubt is cast on the validity of the National Labor Disputes Act."[250] The *Washington Post* took a different view: "The Supreme Court does not close the door upon alternate methods of combating demoralization and providing for collective bargaining within the industry."[251] And the *Cleveland Plain Dealer,* usually pro-New Deal, declared that "this newspaper believes that now that the Guffey Coal Act is out, it will profit the industry."[252] The Philadelphia *Evening Bulletin* suggested that "the decision leaves unaffected the legislative power of the states," and this power should be used to solve the problems of the coal fields.[253] The Baltimore *Sun* editorialized that "the lay mind may be somewhat baffled as to the precise legal differences between [the *Schechter* and *Carter* cases]. Such distinctions, however, are the breath of legal learning."[254] The *Chicago Daily News* warned that "Guffey Decision makes Constitution an Issue,"[255] and the *Philadelphia Record* launched an attack on judicial review in general, though it conceded that "the Supreme Court's decision serves one service: even if our economic progress is impeded, it shows that the Constitution is what the Justices say it is,"[256] which brought a rejoinder from a local radio commentator, surprising in light of his usual pro-New Deal views: "we play by the rules of the game. The Supreme Court called Guffey out at the bag, therefore we go along. The editorial in the *Record* is unfair."[257]

It seemed to many that Roberts had repudiated his liberal *Nebbia* views, but a participant in the National Labor Relations Act cases which were soon to come to the Court still held hope at the time that Roberts had not been lost entirely. And the Secretary of the Interior revealed an interesting reaction of the President at this time to the failure of the New Deal to get past the Court:

> ...From what the President said today and has said on other occasions, ...he is not at all adverse to the Supreme Court declaring one New Deal statute after another unconstitutional. I think he believes that the Court will find itself pretty far out on a limb before it is

through with it, and that the real issue will be joined on which we can go to the country.[258]

In reference to the *Carter* decision and the *Ashwander*[259] case, Frankfurter and Fisher wrote that "in the whole history of the Court there have been few more striking examples of the interplay between explosive political issues and intricate technicalities of procedure than several cases at the last two terms."[260]

The Justices ruled on the Tennessee Valley Authority six weeks after the *Butler* case had been decided, and it was the next "New Deal" item to come to the Court after that voiding of the agricultural program. It must be recalled that just as the Railroad Retirement Act had not originated as a part of the New Deal program, neither did T.V.A. The Muscle Shoals project had been developed as a war measure in 1916, and after several attempts to sell the power plant to private investors after the war had failed, George Norris, the progressive senator from Nebraska, sponsored legislation in 1922 to create a government corporation to produce power and fertilizer to stimulate the development of the Tennessee River Valley. President Coolidge "pocket-vetoed" the measure in 1928, and a similar law was vetoed by President Hoover in 1931. T.V.A. became an issue in the campaign in 1932; and the new Congress passed the law for the third time, and F.D.R signed it in May, 1933.[261]

"With anti-judicial feeling at a new high," wrote Professor Mason, "Chief Justice Hughes suddenly interrupted the New Deal's headlong rush down the steep decline leading to the lethal chamber of the judiciary."[262] And in a letter to Senator Norris in August, 1936, Irving Brant, a newspaper man with contacts both on the Court and at the White House, wrote:

> After a preliminary line-up on the TVA case must have revealed itself in the court, Stone talked about the Court's attitude toward New Deal legislation with an alarm concerning the future which would have been illogical, or at least unlikely to manifest itself, if the Court had then swung even in part from the trend revealed by the AAA decision. . . . But public reaction against the Hoosac Mills decision persuaded the Court to follow precedents and uphold the T.V.A."[263]

Arthur Krock tells us that the government attorneys had gained wisdom from their experience with the Court, and so they de-emphasized the social experiment aspect of the Authority, and also "hired themselves a very smart lawyer, John Lord O'Brian of Buffalo, once an Assistant

Attorney General in a Republican Administration."[264]

The issue at bar was the technicality of the right of minority non-voting stockholders of the Alabama Power Company to sue to prevent the fulfillment of a contract of their company with T.V.A. Did they have such a right? Brandeis, Stone, Roberts, and Cardozo wished to follow precedent and dismiss. Brandeis, speaking for his three colleagues, declared: "I do not disagree with the conclusional question announced by the Chief Justice; but, in my opinion, the judgment of the Circuit Court of Appeals should be affirmed without passing upon it."[265] He then reviewed the cannons of jurisdiction which the Court over the years had established for its own guidance and found that in the present case there was no reason for review."[266] While the Court had in the past entertained stockholders' suits, never had a challenge by non-voting "preferred" stockholders been upheld.

Justice McReynolds dissented with warnings of attendant evil.[267]

The four, who joined the Chief Justice in the majority opinion, accepted the right to sue and went on to the question of the validity of the power of the United States to build a dam on a navigable waterway, which was upheld, and to sell the electric power created by the dam. Citing Article IV, section 3 of the federal Constitution, the Chief Justice found that the sale was well within the meaning of that section of the organic law, but the matter of transporting the product to a market also had to be settled. On that point Hughes stated:

> We know of no constitutional ground upon which the Federal Government can be denied the right to seek a wider market. We support that in the early days of mining in the West, if the Government had undertaken to operate a silver mine on its domain, it could have acquired the mules and horses and equipment to carry its silver to market. And the transmission lines for electric energy are but a facility for conveying to market that particular sort of property, and the acquisition of these lines raises no different constitutional question, unless in some way there is an invasion of the rights reserved to the State or to the people. We find no basis for concluding that the limited undertaking with the Alabama Power Company amounts to such an invasion.[268]

The TVA decision was the only important domestic victory for the White House during 1936, but, as Professor Swisher points out, it was, in reality, "an embarrassment for the administration":

> It indicated that the Court had not set out maliciously to batter every major feature of the New-Deal program, and that if New-Deal

> legislation could be brought within the traditional lines of
> constitutional interpretation, it might be upheld by the Court.
> . . . [It] conveyed the suggestion that it was the program and not the
> Court that was wrong.[269]

This view was echoed by many of the editorials of the day. "Not the least
of its excellences," said the *New York Times* of the opinion, "is that it
may help to dispel the foolish notion that the Court is composed of nine
old men bent on imposing their will on Congress and writing their private
prejudices into the Constitution."[270] The *Cleveland Plain Dealer* noted
that a "Yardstick" had been "saved,"[271] but the equally liberal *Philadelphia Record* sulked; "when it came to a consideration of the Court's
jurisdiction in the matter, four out of nine denied it had any, among them
the conservative Justice Roberts."[272]

Ten months later, on the Monday before the Christmas recess, the
Court gave a present to the President in the form of the far-reaching
opinion in *United States v. Curtiss-Wright Export Corporation,*[273] Justice
Sutherland in an outstanding opinion declaring for a seven-to-one Court
that

> . . .the investment of the federal government with the powers of
> external sovereignty did not depend upon the affirmative grants of the
> Constitution. . . . As a member of the family of nations, the right and
> power of the United States in that field are equal to the right and
> power of the other members of the international family. . . . Not
> only. . .is the federal power over external affairs in origin and essential
> character different from that over internal affairs, but the partici-
> pation in the exercise of the power is significantly limited. In this vast
> external realm, with its important, complicated, delicate and manifold
> problems, the President alone has the power to speak or listen as a
> representative of the nation. He *makes* treaties with the advice and
> consent of the Senate; but he alone negotiates. In the field of
> negotiation the Senate cannot intrude; and Congress itself is powerless
> to invade it.[275]

The Court also upheld the practice of granting of fact-finding power to the
President of foreign affairs legislation through a joint resolution,[276] and so
the Presidential embargo on the sale of arms to the warring nations of Latin
America was upheld.

With the end of 1936 the attack on the New Deal and its attempt to
control the national economy also came to an end. Looking back over the
1933 to 1936 period in the area of federal taxation it may be noted that

the Court had ruled against the government in fifteen of twenty cases. In the area of the use of the interstate commerce power the Justices had upheld the government in twenty-five of thirty-eight cases. It must be repeated, however, that each case must be scrutinized, for among the thirteen vetoes were the major New Deal programs. In the other areas of federal power (spending, money and bankruptcy) the record was even, nine in favor and the same number against the exercise of the federal power.

Roberts' votes during this period continued to follow the line traced out by the Court itself. In the area of taxation, the Pennsylvania jurist dissented twice, once for the Government and once against it. In questions involving the interstate commerce power, there was complete correlation between the Justice's position and that of the Court as a whole. While in the cases involving the other powers of the federal government considered above, he dissented from two cases which were adverse to the government.[277]

During this period, Roberts voted ten times against New Deal legislation as compared with Hughes, eight; Stone and Brandeis, six; Cardozo, five. In only two cases would a change in Roberts' vote have affected the outcome, *Alton* and *Carter,* and possibly in a third, *Butler,* if the rumors about Hughes' vote are true.[278] This is evident from the fact that five of the twelve New Deal decisions were unanimous, and in two others there was only one dissent.[279]

State Cases and Comment

While state laws were not directly a part of the New Deal program, many of those which were passed during this period had economic recovery as a motivating force. Therefore, the Court's attitude toward governmental control on the federal level on occasion carried over to state enactments as well, especially toward the end of the 1933 to 1936 period.

"Prior to 1938," wrote Edward Barrett, Jr., "the United States Supreme Court's decisions dealing with both state regulation and state taxation of interstate commerce. . .were phrased in terms of a purely formal test: direct burdens on interstate commerce were forbidden, indirect or remote restraints were permitted."[280] Indeed, for the most part, the Court upheld state taxation of the incidents of interstate commerce. Included in the favorable decisions was *Minnesota v. Blasius,*[281] in which the validity of a tax on cattle held within the state for consignment after being transported in interstate commerce was upheld. The Court stated the rule covering such taxation;[282] it was basically, the test stated by Barrett in the quotation above. Only taxation of tank cars that spent most of the time outside of the taxing state, of interstate telephone equipment used in intrastate service, of carriers engaged solely in interstate commerce, and of the gross receipts of a radio station were voided.[283] But the Court continued during this first New Deal term to restrict governmental immunity from state taxation. In only two of five cases did the Court strike down the state tax.[284]

While state graduated taxes were upheld against the challenge of two petroleum companies,[285] they were voided in *Stewart Dry Goods v. Lewis*[286] and, on the strength of Roberts' opinion in that case, also in *Valentine v. Great A. & P. Tea Company.*[287]

A rational basis was found for a discriminatory tax in four cases but in two others, *Concordia Fire Insurance Co. v. Illinois*[288] and *Colgate v. Harvey*,[289] the levy was struck down. One observer estimates that this latter case and *Butler* were "two of the most power crippling decisions in our history."[290] The Court, through Justice Sutherland, invoked the "privileges and immunities" clause of the Fourteenth Amendment, unused for half a century, to void a state tax on income from sources outside the state, while exempting similar sources in the state. Benjamin Wright points out that there were no precedents for such a ruling and fifty precedents against it;[291] traditionally, the clause invoked had been used to protect those rights associated with national citizenship. Justice Sutherland's biographer sees the use of the "privileges and immunities" clause as an attempt to win Justice Roberts back to the conservative group after his rejection of the "public interest" test in the *Nebbia* decision.[292]

In the area of regulatory taxation, the Justice upheld one tax statute and voided one. In *Glenn v. Field Packing Co.*[293] an injunction against the tax on oleomargarine was upheld because the tax in question was violative of the state constitution. However, in *Magnano Co. v. Hamilton*,[294] the following year, the Court upheld a Washington tax on the same product which had the effect of making butter competitive. In light of the *Butler* decision two years later, Justice Sutherland's words seem contradictory:

> ...A tax designed to be expended to a public purpose does not cease to be one levied for that purpose because it has the effect of imposing a burden upon one class of business enterprises in such a way to benefit another class. ... From the beginning of our government, the

courts have sustained taxes although imposed with the collateral intent of effecting ulterior ends which, considered apart, were beyond the constitutional power of the lawmakers to realize by legislation directly addressed to their accomplishment.[295]

The New York *Herald-Tribune* noted the implications of the decision: "The legislatures are left with wide latitude in imposing taxes to prohibit industrial or other activity in some directions and encourage it in others."[296]

In one other regulatory tax case, *Grosjean v. American Press Co.*,[297] the Court found that a levy placed only on newspapers having more than a weekly circulation of twenty thousand violated the First Amendment freedom of the press as applied to the states through the Fourteenth Amendment. "Of these papers so taxed," notes Paul Bartholomew, "only one was not openly opposed to Senator Huey P. Long, under whose influence the law had been passed."[298] Justice Sutherland, for a united Court, admonished the press:

It is not intended by anything we have said to suggest that the owners of newspapers are immune from any of the ordinary forms of taxation for the support of the government. But this is not an ordinary form of tax, but one single in kind, with a long history of hostile misuse against the freedom of press.[229]

General regulation of business was supported in six cases; in a *per curiam* decision[300] the Justices stated a principle of long-range influence in questions of jurisdiction:

...Where it does not appear that the complainant is deprived of its license or is prevented by the regulation from prosecuting its business, the question is not the value or net worth of the business but the value of the right to be free from the regulation, and this may be measured by the loss, if any, that would follow the enforcement of the rule prescribed.[301]

Though continuing to rule in rate cases on the basis of a "fair return" to the investors, the Court seemed to define the limits of fluctuation, for in *West Ohio Gas Co. v. Public Utility Commission of Ohio*,[302] rates which returned four-and-a-half percent income were ruled confiscatory, while in *Clark's Ferry-Bridge Co. v. Public Service Commission of Pennsylvania*[303] seven percent was found to be sufficient profit on the investment. The "fair return on fair value" principle had developed in 1898 from *Smyth v. Ames*[304] and, as Professor Swisher notes:

[It was] used to mark the limit of the power to regulate prices when the government, whether state or federal, possessed the power in some degree. It gave rise to an enormous amount of litigation because of the indefiniteness of both "fair return" and "fair value," with use in new cases of the body of precedent developed earlier cases.[305]

In ten of fourteen cases, state control of rate regulation or the method of dermination was upheld by the Court during this period. One of the more notable cases was *West v. Chesapeake and Potomac Telephone Co.*[306] Justice Roberts speaking for five of his brethren declared void both the method of valuation and the order fixing telephone rates. It was one of the last times, if not *the* last time, in which economic due process would be employed against rate regulation by a state, for the use of this legal concept was coming rapidly to an end. And as Robert McCloskey points out, the amazing aspect of the repudiation was not that the Court abandoned "the inflexible negation of the old Majority," but that it should move "to the all out tolerance [of legislative control] of the new."[307]

In two decisions the Justices ruled that the state may exclude convict-made goods from its markets.[308] In the *Whitfield* case the federal Hawes-Cooper Act, which permitted the prohibition of sale of convict-made goods by the states in the "original package" entering the state in interstate commerce, was upheld.

On four occasions the Justices also supported state control of interstate carriers using its highways, and permitted a charge for the use,[309] but in the area of railroad control, four decisions were handed down voiding the state activity. In *Nashville, Chattanooga, & St. Louis Railroad v. Walters*[310] the attempt by the state to force the railroad to pay for the elimination of a grade crossing was found to violate the due process clause of the Fourteenth Amendment. Fifteen months later the judge who had originally ruled in the case wrote to F.D.R. that though he had at first decided against the state, he felt that the time had come for the courts to take a new view and to "progress with the times."[311]

In the six instances between 1933 and 1936 where the Court ruled on state limitations placed on contracts, all but two were upheld. One notable case was *Semler v. Oregon State Board of Dental Examiners;*[312] the Justices went so far as to approve legislation which in effect would nullify existing advertising contracts.

Some of the most controversial legislation passed during this period affected mortgage foreclosures and bankruptcy control. In attempting to relieve the hardships resulting from the economic chaos of the first half of the 1930's, the states employed their police power to effectuate emergency legislation. Professor Swisher tells us that "the concept [of the police power] continued after the adoption of the Fourteenth Amendment to define areas where the states might regulate in spite of the inhibitions of the due process clause, and particularly with respect to the regulation of the use of property."[313] And when the history of such legislation before the Court during the New Deal is reviewed, what T.R. Powell wrote in 1931 is appropriately applied to the 1933 to 1936 period:

> Whatever the theory, the fact is that the Supreme Court of the United States can pass on the reasonableness of the police measures of every state and city in the land. This is not to say that the judicial test of constitutional unreasonableness coincides with what the judges would not vote for if they were acting formally as a legislature. . . . Yet the point at which they call a halt as the limit of constitutional power is determined by them and not the Constitution.[314]

The outstanding case in this area was *Home Building & Loan Association v. Blaisdell*,[315] characterized by one commentator as the first indication that the Court intended to adapt the Constitution to a managed economy.[316] When economic conditions in Minnesota were in danger of being undermined by wholesale foreclosures or threats of foreclosure, the state moved in and through legislation permitted the courts to suspend action on a mortgage, provided that the holder was reimbursed during the period of suspension. A challenge was made to the law on the basis of the prohibition in Article I, section 10 of the Federal Constitition. "No State shall. . . pass any. . .Law impairing the Obligation of Contracts . . . ."[317] Fundamentally, the issue was "whether the Court's mandate to interpret the Constitution embraces the power and duty of adapting it to changing circumstances."[318]

The Chief Justice, speaking for the five member majority, decided:

> 1. An emergency existed in Minnesota which furnished a proper occasion for the exercise of the reserved power of the State to protect the vital interests of the community. . . .
> 2. The legislation was addressed to a legitimate end . . . .
> 3. . . . .
> 4. The conditions upon which the period of redemption is extended do not appear to be unreasonable. . . .
> 5. The legislation is temporary in operation. It is limited to the exigency which called it forth.
> We are of the opinion that the Minnesota statute as here applied does not violate the contract clause of the Federal Constitution.[319]

The dissenters through Justice Sutherland were unable to agree with the majority that there was a difference between the statute under review and one which would deprive the creditor of his property. The Justice continued:

> I quite agree with the opinion of the court that whether the legislation under review is wise or unwise is a matter with which we have nothing to do. Whether it is likely to work well or work ill presents a question entirely irrelevant to the issue. The only legitimate inquiry we can make is whether it is constitutional. If it is not, its virtues cannot save it; if it is, its faults cannot be invoked to accomplish its destruction[320]

Though there was only a state law involved, the members of the administration viewed the decision as a good omen for its own "emergency" legislation. As to the closeness of the vote, Arthur Krock noted that "many of the...lawyers [who would comment], promised anonymity, said that numerous five-to-four decisions should not necessarily taken as indicating a court division so close that the balance might swing any day to the side of inflexible legalism."[321] These authorities were soon to be proved wrong. The confusion about just what members of the Court were liable to fluctuate is obvious from a comment in *Newsweek* on the decision. "The decision shows Chief Justice Hughes and Stone, the Supreme Court's unpredictables, were lined up with the progressive Justices Brandeis, Cardozo and Roberts...."[322] And the New York *Herald-Tribune* advised its readers that "great political significance was attached with the fact that Chief Justice Charles Evans Hughes joined the so-called liberal group of the Court and handed down the majority decision...."[323] The *Washington Post* declared that the long range results of the decision extended beyond the borders of the state.[324] The *New York Times*, after claiming to be unable to find any lines in the decision to define an emergency, finally, acquiesced and noted that, "for the present, at any rate, the country will be disposed to say: *Roma dixit causa finita est.*"[325]

The Court's subsequent rulings on similar laws regarding mortgage and bankruptcy issues were not so favorable. In *Worthen Co. v. Thomas*[326] the Justices unanimously voided an Arkansas statute which limited action in insurance claim suits, and in *Worthen Co. v. Kavanaugh*[327] another statute of the same state which reduced the remedies in foreclosure proceedings was struck down. On the former case, *Newsweek* commented on June 2, 1934, "the third 'emergency' law to be reviewed by the Court, it was the first to be upset, and the only one so far on which the whole Court agreed."[328] In the area of building and loan associations, Justice Roberts speaking for a united Court[329] declared:

> Though the obligations of contracts must yield to a proper exercise of the police power, and vested rights cannot inhibit the proper exertion of the power, it must be exercised for an end which is in fact public and the means adopted must be reasonably adapted to the accomplishment of that end and must not be arbitrary or oppressive.[330]

And therefore, because it lacked these conditions, the state statute was void.

Though the Justices, through Roberts again, upheld state bankruptcy legislation against the challenge that it violated the property rights guaranteed by the Fourteenth Amendment,[331] they refused to allow the state to permit one of its agencies to seek relief through its bankruptcy laws.[332] In the former case, Roberts, answering a challenge that the state had limited the right to sue, declared "all that [the appellant] is guaranteed by the Fourteenth Amendment is the preservation of his substantive right to redress by some effective procedure."[333] In the latter suit, *Ashton v. Cameron County Water Improvement District#1,* the Court voided an amendment to the federal Bankruptcy Act which permitted the states to appeal to federal courts of bankruptcy for a readjustment of the obligations of their political sub-divisions.

Between 1933 and 1936 the high tribunal was asked to rule on state regulation of prices on eight occasions. In five of these the statutes were upheld. In a landmark case in 1934 the Justices by a five-to-four division upheld the use of the police power of the state to set the minimum cost of milk sold in New York.[334] "When Leo Nebbia sold two quarts of milk and a five-cent loaf of bread for the price fixed by the Milk Control Board for the milk alone, little did he know how many tons of white paper would be used in discussing his transaction."[335]

While the press attempted to make the opinion seem spectacular, it should not have been considered so, for there was a long line of precedents stretching back to *Munn v. Illinois*[336] which would support the concept of price (or rate) fixing by state legislation. For in determining the rates to be charged by warehouses, the legislature was influencing the price of the article stored. However, the Munn decision had had a rough journey through the years; its opposition, *laissez-faire,* had a well organized army in the form of the American Bar Association, which had been founded one year after *Munn* in order to fight the evil effects of the "public interest" doctrine.[337] However, from *Munn* to *Nebbia*, the dominant view of the Court was that a "business affected with the public interest" could be regulated by the state. In the *Wolff Packing Co.* case[338] ten years before, Chief Justice Taft had classified the businesses which could be considered in the "public interest" category. In *Nebbia*, however, a new concept of the power of the state to regulate prices charged by "private" businesses was announced. Corwin describes the new doctrine "as reasserting" the necessary predominance of the public interest over all private rights of property and contract if government is to remain a going concern."[339]

Indeed, the decision was not an easy one for Justice Roberts to make, for we are told that he paced the floor on the night before the vote.[340] But the result of the Justice's soul-searching was "the most liberal opinion of his whole judicial career."[341]

Again, the opinion begins with a clear statement of what is before the Court: "the question for decision is whether the Federal Constitution prohibits a state from so fixing the selling price of milk."[342] He then considers some practical problems of the milk business:

> Milk is an essential item of diet. It cannot long be stored. . . . Failure of producers to receive a reasonable return for their labor and investment over an extended period threaten a relaxation of vigilance against contamination. . . The fluid milk industry is affected by factors of instability peculiar to itself which call for special methods of control.[343]

To Nebbia's challenge of violation of equal protection, Roberts stated that "there is therefore no showing that the order placed him at a disadvantage, or in fact affected him adversely, and this alone is fatal to the claim of denial of equal protection."[344] Arriving at the heart of the opinion, Roberts plunged into the charge that the statute violated substantive due process of law of the 14th Amendment. There follows a discussion of the right to property under our system of government:

> . . .The use of property and the making of contracts are normally matters of private and not of public concern. The general rule is that both shall be free of governmental interference. But neither property rights nor contract rights are absolute; for government cannot exist if the citizen may at will use his property to the detriment of his fellows, or exercise his freedom of contract to work them harm.

Equally fundamental with the private right is that of the public to regulate it in the common interest.[345]

Then quoting Chief Justice Taney, Roberts went on to define the police power of the state as "nothing more or less than the powers of government inherent in every sovereignty to the extent of its dominions."[346] He continues: "thus has this court from the early days affirmed that the power to promote the general welfare is inherent in government."[347] And that to this end "the Court has repeatedly sustained curtailment of enjoyment of private property, in the public interest. The owner's rights may be subordinated to the needs of other private owners whose pursuits are vital to the paramount interests of the community."[348] Roberts admits that "the dairy industry is not, in the accepted sense of the phrase, a public utility." However the Justice continued:

> But if, as must be conceded, the industry is subject to regulation in the public interest, what constitutional principle bars the state from correcting existing maladjustments by legislation touching prices? We think there is no such principle. The due process clause makes no mention of sales or of prices any more than it speaks of business or contracts or buildings or other incidents of property. *The thought seems nevertheless to have persisted that there is something peculiarly sacrosanct about the price one may charge for what he makes or sells,* and that, however able to regulate other elements of manufacture or trade, with incidental effect upon price, the state is incapable of directly controlling the price itself. This view was negatived many years ago.[349] (Italics supplied.)

It is clear, then, that Roberts' reasoning was not based on the "public interest" doctrine which he takes pains to detail and reject, concluding with the comment that "it is clear that there is no closed class or category of business affected with a public interest, and the function of courts in the application of the Fifth and Fourteenth Amendments" in each case will be decided on its own merits.[350] Mr. Justice Roberts summarized his argument briefly:

> The Constitution does not secure to anyone liberty to conduct his business in such fashion as to inflict injury upon the public at large, or upon any substantial group of people. Price control, like any other form of regulation, is unconstitutional only if arbitrary, discriminatory, or demonstrably irrelevant to the policy the legislature is free to adopt, and hence an unnecessary and unwarranted interference with individual liberty.[351]

Justice McReynolds dissented and was joined by three of his brethren. He noted that the view taken by the Court puts "an end to liberty under the Constitution."[352] What worried the members of the administration was a statement made by the dissenter as *dictum:* "this court must have regard to the wisdom of the enactment."[353]

In general, the *Nebbia* decision was received as a good omen by the New Dealers, because, unlike the Minnesota Moratorium Law, this statute had not been based on emergency conditions. The administration was especially grateful for this judicial peg upon which to hang price-fixing in interstate commerce.[354] Indeed, the Chief Justice did indicate this in separate opinion in the *Guffey* case that *Nebbia* should have been invoked to uphold the price-fixing portions of the act.

Again, in 1934, nine members of the Court ruled in favor of limits placed on the retail price of milk,[355] ruling that "the 14th Amendment does not protect a business against the hazards of competition."[356] But in *Baldwin v. Seelig, Inc.*[357] Justice Cardozo for a unanimous Court voided an attempt to regulate the out-of-state wholesale purchase price of milk as an unconstitutional burden on interstate commerce. Arthur Krock disagreed:

> One of the arguments made for the injunction was that after all, the dry states with the consent of the Supreme Court in upholding the Webb-Kenyon law exclude liquor. . .from wet territory. It appeared to this observer that Justice Cardozo had a little trouble here in answering an argument based on complaisant rulings during the 1920's on laws growing out of the prohibition crusade, rulings which earlier courts would probably not have made.[358]

In another action the Justices set aside the dismissal of a suit against the implementation of a milk price regulation, because of alleged discrimination, as premature,[359] but two years later ruled on the merits of the case. In *Borden's Farm Products Co. v. TenEyck*[360] Justice Roberts for a five member majority ruled that a regulation requiring milk dealers who had "well advertised trade names" to charge one cent more than less-known brands was a reasonable distinction and not violative of the 14th Amendment; but in the next case, *Mayflower Farms, Inc. v. TenEyck,*[361] a six-to-three decision, Justice Roberts set aside the discrimination among the less-known brands on the basis of the date of their establishment, April 10, 1933, as arbitrary and unreasonable and contrary to the equal protection clause. Justice Cardozo struck out at the apparent inconsistency of Justice Roberts and the Chief Justice. "The judgment just announced is irreconcilable in principle with the judgement in Borden's case. . . announced a minute or so earlier." Cardozo concluded his attack by the declaration that "I have not seen the judicial scales so delicately poised and so accurately graduated as to balance and record the subtleties of all these rival equities and make them ponderable and legible beyond a reasonable doubt."[362] These two cases more than any others, perhaps, give us insight into the close workings of Mr. Justice Roberts' legal mind.

During this period the Justices also upheld the right of the state to determine the weight of bread[363] and the size of containers for the sale of farm products.[364]

Several workingmen's compensation laws appeared before the Court for review during these three and a half years. In only one incident did the high tribunal void such a law. In *Murray v. Eerrick Co.*[365] it was held that a state compensation law did not apply to a United States Navy Yard unless specifically extended by congressional action.

One week after the Court had destroyed the Guffey Coal Conservation Act the Justices handed down a ruling[366] which was to lose for the high bench the support of those groups who up to this time had supported most of the opinions during this period. It is, perhaps, the most controversial case during Roberts' term on the Court, and one which stirred most criticism because of his subsequent vote in *West Coast Hotel v. Parrish.*[367] Yet, as one authority has noted, had the *Morehead* case come to the Court a few years earlier, it probably would not have caused as much clamor; but because it came at the end of two terms which had been disastrous for the liberals, it took on special significance. It was, next to *Nebbia*, the greatest challenge to the non-emergency use of the police power of the states brought before the Court during the 1933-1936 time segment. Toward the end of April, 1936, the suit came to the United States Supreme Court from the Supreme Court of New York[368] in a *habeas corpus* proceeding against Morehead, Warden of King's County, New York, for the release of one Tipaldo, the proprietor of a laundry establishment, who had refused to implement the wage scale set by the commissioner as authorized by the 1933 New York Wage Law. It might be noted that the New York Laundry Employers' organization had submitted a brief in the New York Court in favor of the law which was regarded by the honest men in the industry as a solution to the constant turmoil over wage chiseling and cheating.[369]

Although the law was not directly of New Deal origin, it was based on a model bill prepared by Felix Frankfurter and Benjamin Cohen, which proposed to correct the errors Justice Sutherland had indicated in the *Adkins* law.[370] On April 12, 1933 the President had telegraphed the following to the governors of thirteen industrial states:

> May I call your attention to minimum wage law just passed by Legislature of New York. . . .This [statute] represents a great step forward against lowering of wages, which constitutes a serious form of unfair competition against other employers, reduces the purchasing power of the workers, and threatens the stability of industry. I hope that similar action can be taken by other states for the protection of the public interest.[371]

One of the main controversies about the case has been the question of whether the New York attorneys had asked for an overruling of the *Adkins*[372] precedent, or had they simply based their case on the possibility of distinguishing the New York statute from the District of Columbia act in the *Adkins* case. Justice Butler tells us in his majority opinion:

> The *Adkins* case, unless distinguishable, requires affirmance of the judgment below. The petition for the writ sought review upon the ground that this case is distinguishable from that one. No application has been made for reconsideration of the constitutional question there decided.[373]

And the Justice then indicated in a footnote that New York City and the state of Illinois submitted *amici curiae* briefs in support of a reconsideration of *Adkins*. Justice Roberts, in a memo give to Justice Frankfurter on November 9, 1945 and published by the latter after Roberts' death in 1955, wrote that "when my turn came to speak, I said I saw no reason to grant the writ unless the Court were prepared to re-examine and *overrule* the Adkins case." (Italics supplied.) Roberts continued: "Both in the petition for certiorari, in the brief on the merits and in oral argument, counsel for the State of New York took the position that it was unnecessary to overrule the *Adkins* case in order to sustain the position of the State of New York." The Justice indicated that the State attempted to distinguish the two laws and that to him "the argument seemed. . .to be disingenuous and born of timidity. I could find nothing in the record to substantiate the alleged distinction."[374] However, the *New York Times* reported that "Attorney General [John J.] Bennett [Jr.] maintained that the [New York] Court of Appeals decision invalidating the Wald Act had been made on the basis of the decision in the Adkins case and that in the petition to the Supreme Court for certiorari and a new appeal for reconsideration of the Adkins case had been stressed."[375] In a letter to the editor of the *New York Law Journal* on April 6, 1937, Bennett repeated his contention that the state had asked for an overruling of *Adkins*.[376] The solution to this apparent conflict may possibly be found in the fact that the Court and Justice Roberts were referring to the *Petition for Writ of Certiorari* (pp. 5, 8–9, 19–21) and the *Appellant's [sic] Brief on the Law* (pp. 32–49), while, possibly, the New York Attorney General's position is based on the *Amicus Curiae Brief in Support of the Writ of Certiorari* filed by the Corporation Counsel of the City of New York and referred to by Butler in his footnote on page 604 in the opinion.

The criticism of the New York lawyers for failing to make the repudiation of *Adkins* the key to their argument has been repeated by reputable authorities.[377] Roberts' position can be justified, for, as Charles Curtis writes:

> Roberts had done no more by joining with the ex-majority than to follow it as a precedent that was binding on him. No more, indeed, that Holmes, himself, had done, when he accepted Adkins in two cases[378] that had come up from Arizona and Arkansas shortly afterwards.[379]

And, finally, the strength of Roberts' reasoning was recognized by the future Justice Robert H. Jackson when he wrote in a discussion of *Tompkins v. Erie R.R.*[380] that *Morehead* had made matters, not brought up in the arguments, not reviewable by the Court.[381]

Roberts later told Merlo Pusey, Associate Editor of *The Washington Post*:

> I was rather neutral in [*Morehead*]. When the case came before the judicial conference, we discussed it thoroughly and decided simply to let the old precedent stand. New York had come down to the Court without challenging the old precedent, *Adkins v. Children's Hospital*. I thought that was a dishonest argument. I wasn't going to vote...to indicate there was any distinction. I agreed to stand on what was done before.[382]

Originally, Justice Butler rested his decision on the fact that *Adkins* was indistinguishable, as Roberts had directed him:

> I stated to him that I would concur in any opinion which was based on the fact that the State had not asked us to reexamine or overrule *Adkins* and that, as we found no material difference in the facts of the two cases, we should therefore follow the *Adkins* case. The case

was originally so written by Justice Butler, but after a dissent had been circulated, he added matter to his opinion, seeking to sustain the *Adkins* case in principle.[383]

Roberts' reference was to Stone's attack on the refusal of the majority to come to grips with the issues, which attack had infuriated Butler. It is at this point that Roberts was most open to criticism, as he himself admitted. "My proper course would have been to concur specially on the narrow ground I had taken. I did not do so. But at conference in the Court I said that I did not propose to review and re-examine the *Adkins* case until a case should come to the Court requiring that this should be done."[384] Frankfurter comments that "as a matter of history it is regrettable that Roberts' unconcern for his own record led him to abstain from stating his position." And the late jurist continued: "the occasions are not infrequent when the disfavor of separate opinion, on the part of the bar and to the extent that it prevails within the Court, should not be heeded. Such a situation was certainly presented when special circumstances made Roberts agree with a result but basically disagree with the opinion which announced it."[385] Dean Griswold agreed with Frankfurter but added this qualification: that in view of the bar's opposition to separate opinions, "it is hard to be too critical. ... [But] he should have foreseen the widespread public interest in the decision, and the misunderstanding which would result from his unqualified concurrence in the Butler opinion."[386] Finally, Arthur Schlesinger noted:

> One can with effort understand why, if he really wanted to reverse Adkins, technical scruples might still keep him from joining Stone in open reversal or Hughes in reversal by distinction. But one cannot understand why these same scruples permitted him to join Butler in a vehement reaffirmation of the decision he believed to be so wrong at a juncture so critical to the position of the Court. *The hopeless confusion of this entirely honest man suggests the tension of loyalties among the nine justices.* It may well be that, at the crucial moment in 1936, Roberts, having identified himself emotionally with the bloc of conservatives, could not bear to desert them. *The result of his failure to declare what he really believed was greatly to increase the Court's jeopardy.*[387] (Italics supplied.)

The Chief Justice, joined by Brandeis, Stone and Cardozo, took the middle ground by agreeing that the New York statute had corrected the errors pointed out by Justice Sutherland in his *Adkins* opinion. Hughes declared:

The constitutionality of a minimum wage statute like the New York act has not heretofore been passed upon by this Court. ... New York and other states have been careful to adopt a different and improved standard, in order to meet the objection aimed at earlier statutes, by requiring a fair equivalence of wage and service.[388]

Stone, however, added his separate views in which Brandeis and Cardozo concurred. As was noted above, he would have the Court come to grips with the issues. "While I agree with all that the Chief Justice has said," Stone wrote, "I would not make the difference between the present statute and that involved in the *Adkins* case the sole basis of decision."[389] Directing his pen at Justice Butler, he continued:

> There is grim irony in speaking of the freedom of contract of those who, because of their economic necessities, give their services for less than is needful to keep body and soul together. But if this is freedom of contract no one has ever denied that it is freedom which may be restrained, notwithstanding the Fourteenth Amendment, by a statute passed in the public interest.[390]

Then pointing his finger at Justice Roberts he concluded:

> We should follow our decision in the *Nebbia* case and leave the selection and the method of the solution of the problems to which the statute is addressed where it seems to me the Constitution has left them, to the legislative branch of the government.[391]

The reaction to the decision was immediate and vociferous. On the part of the press for the first time the support of the fourth estate was lost to the Court. One survey shows that of the three hundred and forty-four editorials on the decision only ten—mostly from textile towns—approved the Tipaldo decision. Nearly sixty papers, including some of the conservative organs, called for the submission of a constitutional amendment.[392] The *Washington Post* called it, "an unfortunate decision" which would result in a "reaction against the Court itself,"[393] and The *New York Times* objected to the decision for three reasons: the one-vote margin; the law was carefully drawn and admirably administered; and the decision leaves the whole question of women in industry vis-à-vis their protection by the state in the air.[394] The *Cleveland Plain Dealer* lashed out that "years of effort to protect women and children from labor exploitation became a labor of futility in light of yesterday's decision. . .".[395] The *Philadelphia Records, caught the real implications* when it delcared that "like the Dred Scott decision on chattel slavery, the Supreme Court's decision on state wages brings the American People face to face with an irrepressible conflict. If this new conflict is not to culminate like the other in civil war, the power of the Court must be curbed";[396] and the following day the same paper declared that "black robes do make gods of men. Is that not crystal clear to every American in this wage decision?"[397] In one of the few favorable editorials, the Philadelphia *Evening Bulletin* reminded its readers that "Mr. Justice Roberts was with the majority again, marking himself essentially as a conservative in his interpreation of the spirit and purposes of the Constitution."[398]

At his press conference on June 2, 1936 the President, commenting on the decision, stated:

> It seems fairly clear, as a result of this decision and former decisions, using this question of minimum wages as an example that the "no-man's-land" where no government—state or federal—can function is being more clearly defined. A state cannot do it and the Federal Government cannot do it.[399]

The political implications of the decision were widespread. Justice Stone commented that "it is rather amusing to have the Republicans, as well as Democrats expressing doubts about the wisdom of the Minimum Wage decision."[400] As the Beards noted: "For many years Rupublicans, as well as Democrats, spurred on by women who championed the idea of improving the weak economic position of their sex by law, had sponsored such legislation...."[401] And the Republican Convention, which convened eight days after the decision was announced, inserted a minimum wage plank into their platform—"We pledge ourselves to:

> Support the adoption of State laws and interstate compacts to abolish sweatshops and child labor, and to protect women and children with respect to maximum hours, minimum wages and working conditions. *We believe that this can be done within the Constitution as it now stands.*[402] (Italics supplied.)

Time seemed to summarize best the feeling of the majority of the nation: "...The Supreme Court this week handed down one more five-to-four decision against 'social justice.' "[403]

A decision, which to some observers seemed an indication of a change of heart by the Court, or at least the beginning of one, was handed down, *per curiam*, on November 23, 1936. In *Chamberlain v. Andrews*[404] the Justices, in a four-to-four split, made possible because of Justice Stone's absence due to illness, upheld the New York Unemployment Insurance

Law. It was clear that Roberts had joined the minority in the *Morehead* case to make the four votes to support,[405] and so the guessing game began as to what Roberts would do in the future and what had caused him to change. The picture was further confused because the Court had refused on October 12, 1936 to rehear *Morehead.*[406] So as the Court entered 1937, its most spectacular year of the century, if not of the whole history of the Republic, the nation wondered if Mr. Dooley's comment was still valid: "No matther whether th' constitution follows th' flag or not, th' supreme court follow th' iliction returns."[407]

The Court's scorecard on state legislation during the 1933 to 1936 period showed seventy-seven favorable decisions and thirty-nine invalidation, which broken down into categories reveals these things: tax laws, twenty-two in favor, fifteen against; regulation of business and rates, thirty-two in favor, seven against; regulation of health, welfare, and safety, twenty-one in favor, fourteen against. Roberts' only deviation from this record was one dissent in the area of rate regulation.[408]

Totaling the high bench's rulings on the use of federal or state economic controls, we find that the government was upheld one hundred and sixteen times and rejected seventy-three times. In sum, governmental activity was upheld sixty-two percent of the time between 1933 to 1936, as compared with seventy percent in the period between 1930 to 1933. Roberts did not significantly vary from this percentage. It must be stressed in reading these figures that among those statutes or administrative activities voided were the most important New Deal and New-Deal-inspired legislation.

Notes

[1] *Documents of American History*, ed. H.S. Commanger (6th Ed., New York 1958) pp. 417-419.
[2] D. Perkins, *The New Age of Franklin Roosevelt* (Chicago, 1957), p. 2.
[3] *Ibid.*
[4] *Lions under the Throne*, p. 94.
[5] Perkins, p. 5.
[6] *Holmes-Laski Letters*, p. 1420.
[7] Mason, *Stone*, pp.344-45.
[8] "The Child Labor Law, the Tenth Amendment and the Commerce Clause," *Southern Law Quarterly*, 111 (1918), 213.
[9] Pusey, *Hughes*, p. 731.

[10] Mason, *Stone*, p. 345.

[11] U.S., Congress, House, *Inaugural Addresses of the Presidents of the United States,* 82d Congress, 2d Session 1952, House Docket 540, p. 227.

[12] *Ibid.,* p. 228.

[13] R.A. Wormser, *The Story of the Law* (New York, 1962), p. 441.

[14] "Government's Responsibility for Economic Security," *Annals of American Academy of Political & Social Science,* CCVI (1939), p. 81.

[15] *Twilight of the Supreme Court* (New Haven, 1934), p. 46.

[16] Vol. XXII (1937), pp. 575-76. Notes.

[17] Jackson, *Struggle for Judicial Supremacy,* p. 74.

[18] 285 U.S. 495 (1922).

[19] *The Supreme Court on Trial* (New York, 1963), pp. 158-59.

[20] W.E. Leuchtenburg, *Franklin D. Roosevelt and the New Deal,* (New York, 1963), pp. 42-43.

[21] Jackson, p. 77.

[22] "Business of the Supreme Court, October Term, 1933," *Harvard Law Review,* XLVIII (1935), 279.

[23] Mason, *Stone,* pp. 358-59.

[24] *American Constitutional Development,* p. 922.

[25] Jackson, pp. 77-78.

[26] *The American Supreme Court* (Chicago, 1960), p. 163.

[27] *America in Midpassage* (New York, 1939), p. 258.

[28] 291 U.S. 339.

[29] 292 U.S. 571 (1934).

[30] Rodell, *Nine Men,* p. 223.

[31] 292 U.S. 360 (1934).

[32] 293 U.S. 204 (1934).

[33] 299 U.S. 92 (1936).

[34] *Macray v. United States,* 195/27 (1904); *Doremus v. United States, 249 U.S. 86 (1919); Hampton, Jr, & Co. v. United States,* 276 U.S. 394 (1928); *University of Illinois v. United States,* 289 U.S. 48 (1933).

[35] 219 U.S. 219 (1922).

[36] 296 U.S. 397 (1935).

[37] Trapp, *The Constitutional Doctrines of Owen J Roberts* (unpublished) p. 85.

[38] 296 U.S. 299 (1935).

[39] *United States v. Butler,* 297 U.S. 1 (1936).

[40] 296 U.S. 87 at 294.

[41] *Ibid.,* pp. 298-99.

[42] *Panama Refining Co. v. Ryan,* 293 U.S. 388 (1935).

[43] *Schechter Polutry Corp. v. United States,* 295 U.S. 495 (1935).

[44] *Railroad Retirement Board v. Alton R. Co.* 295 U.S. 330 (1935).

[45] A.T. Mason, *The Supreme Court: Vehicle of Revealed Truth or Power Group, 1930-1937,* (Boston, 1953), p. 29.

[46] *The Public Papers & Addresses of Franklin D. Roosevelt,* 137 vol., Compiled and collated by Samuel I. Rosenman (New York, 1941), LV. (Cited hereafter as *FDR Papers*).

[47] January 7, 1936, p. 10.

[48] *The Story of the Supreme Court* (Indianapolis, 1938), p. 304.

[49] Pusey, p. 743.

[50] Franklin Delano Roosevelt Library (hereafter cited as *Roosevelt Library)* Official File, 1-K, Agricultural Dept., A.A.A., 1935-36. Memo from Chester Davis to Roosevelt, July 13, 1935.

[51] *Ibid.,* Memo to Secretary of Agriculture and Chester Davis.

[52] *Ibid.,* Martin Dies to Roosevelt, July 17, 1935.

[53] *Ibid.,* Correspondence Roosevelt with Cummings, Nov. 18 to 22, 1935.

[54] *Ibid.,* Stanley Reed to Roosevelt.

[55] December 21, 1935, VI, p. 30.

[56] *Ibid.,* p. 30-31.

[57] S.J. Konefsky, *Chief Justice Stone and the Supreme Court* (New York, 1945), p. 114.

[58] Schlesinger, *The Age of Roosevelt,* III, 471.

[59] Pusey, p. 745.

[60] Mason, *Stone,* p. 414.

[61] Pearson and Allen, p. 44.

[62] Pusey, p. 744.

[63] *Stone,* p. 414.

[64] *Nebbia v. New York,* 291 U.S. 502 (1934).

[65] "The Business of the Supreme Court as conducted by Chief Justice Hughes," *Harvard Law Review,* LXIII (1949), 18.

[66] Rodell, p. 236.

[67] C. & M. Beard, *America in Midpassage,* pp. 270-71.

[68] E. Griswold, "Owen J. Roberts as a Judge," p. 345

[69] *Ibid.*

[70] *Newsweek,* VI, October 12, 1935, p. 20.

[71] 297 U.S. 44.

[72] 297 U.S. 1, 53.

[73] 262 U.S. 447 (1923).

[74] Federal Maternity Act.

[75] Konefsky, p. 102.

[76] Mason, *Stone,* pp. 415-16.

[77] Schlesinger, III, 471.

[78] 297 U.S. 1, 59.

[79] *Ibid.,* 58.

[80] *Ibid.,* 61.

[81] *Ibid.*

[82] See T.R. Powell, "From Philadelphia to Philadelphia," *American Political Science Review* XXXII (1938), 22, for an analysis.

[83] Abraham, *The Judicial Process,* p. 285.

[84] 397 U.S. 1 at 62-63.

[85] V.D. Nicholas, "The Federal Spending Power," *Temple Law Quarterly,* IX (1934), 22.

[86] *Ibid.,* 66.

[87] 297 U.S. 1, 66.

[88] *Ibid.,* 67.

[89] *Ibid.,* 68

[90] *Stone*, p. 410 n.
[91] 282 U.S. 716-733.
[92] *Constitutional Revolution*, Ltd. (Clermont, Cal., 1946), pp 37-38.
[93] 297 U.S. 1, 70-75.
[94] Mason, *Stone*, p. 415.
[95] 297 U.S. 1, 77.
[96] *Ibid.*, 70.
[97] *Ibid.*, 61.
[98] *Charles Evans Hughes & American Democratic Statesmanship* (Boston, 1956), pp. 176-77.
[99] Burns, pp. 232-33.
[100] *F.D.R. Papers*, 1936 vol., p. 44.
[101] Schlesinger, III, 488.
[102] *New York Herald-Tribune*, January 7, 1936, p. 9, Summary of editorials.
[103] January 7, 1936, p. 18.
[104] January 7, 1936, editorial page.
[105] January 7, 1936, p. 12.
[106] January 8, 1936, p. 18.
[107] *Roosevelt Library*, Official File 10-J, January 25, 1936.
[108] *Rickert Rice Mills v. Fontenot* 297 U.S. 110 (1936).
[109] 290 U.S. 247 (1933).
[110] 292 U.S. 53 (1934).
[111] 295 U.S. 555.
[112] *Ibid.*, 589.
[113] *Ibid.*, 602.
[114] *Schechter Poultry Corp. v. United States*, 295 U.S. 495.
[115] *Rathbun v. United States*, 295 U.S. 602.
[116] *Hopkins Savings & Loan Assn. v. Cleary*, 296 U.S. 315 (1935).
[117] *Norman v. B. & O. Rd.*, 294 U.S. 240; *Nortz v. United States*, 294 U.S. 317.
[118] *Perry v. United States*, 294 U.S. 330.
[119] *Ibid.*, 381.
[120] Leuchtenburg, *Franklin D. Roosevelt and The New Deal*, p. 144.
[121] *Ibid.*
[122] "Note," Tennessee Law Review XVII (1945), 768 ff.
[123] 258 U.S. 495 (1922).
[124] *St. Jos. Stockyards v. United States*, 297 U.S. 38; *Archer v. United States*, 298 U.S. 429; *United States v. Corrick*, 298 U.S. 435.
[125] 298 U.S. 468 (1936).
[126] *Atchison, Topeka & Sante Fe Ry. v. United States*, 295 U.S. 193 (1935).
[127] 234 U.S. 342 (1914).
[128] *United States v. Louisiana*, 290 U.S. 70 (1933); *Florida v. United States*, 292 U.S. 1 (1934); *Illinois Commerce Commission v. United States*, 292 U.S. 474 (1934).
[129] *The Court & The Constitution*, p. 43.
[130] 295 U.S. 602 (1935).
[131] E.M. Eriksson, *Supreme Court and the New Deal* (Los Angeles, 1941), p. 116.

[132] *Myers v. United States,* 272 U.S. 52 (1926).

[133] Schlesinger, III, 279-280.

[134] 291 U.S. 587 (1934).

[135] Mason,*Stone,* p. 230 n.

[136] 298 U.S. 1 (1936).

[137] 298 U.S. 9-10.

[138] 298 U.S. 1.

[139] *Ibid.,* 28.

[140] *Ibid.,* 27.

[141] *Ibid.,* 29.

[142] *Ibid.,* 30.

[143] *F.D.R. Papers,* 137 vol., LVII.

[144] 591 U.S. 293 (1934).

[145] 196 U.S. 375 (1905). See C.H. Pritchett, *The American Constitution* (New York, 1959), pp. 239-40.

[146] *Indiana Farmer's Guide Publishing Co. v. Prairie Farmer Publishing Co.,* 293 U.S. 268 (1934).

[147] 297 U.S. 553 (1936).

[148] "The Commerce Clause and the National Economy, 1933-1946," *Harvard Law Review* LIX (1946), p. 651.

[149] 297 U.S. 124 (1936).

[150] *Story of the Supreme Court* (Indianapolis, 1938), p. 298.

[151] *Congress and the Court* (Chicago, 1962), p. 55.

[152] Mason, *Stone,* p. 393.

[153] The*Herald-Tribune* (New York), May 7, 1935, p. 9.

[154] 295 U.S. 330, 362 (1935).

[155] *Ibid.,* 350.

[156] *Ibid.*

[157] Schlesinger, III, 275.

[158] 295 U.S. 330 at 374-75, 392.

[159] Rodell, p. 30-31.

[160] *Texas & N.O. Ry. v. Brotherhood of Ry. & SS. Clerks,* 281 U.S. 548.

[161] Mason, *Stone,* p. 382; Rodell, pp. 232-33.

[162] *Roosevelt Library,* Official File 1095, June 6, 1935.

[163] *Ibid.,* June 4, 1935.

[164] Swisher, *American Constitutional Development,* p. 940.

[165] The *Herald-Tribune* (New York), May 8, 1935, p. 16; *The Washington Post* May 7, 1935, p. 8.

[166] *Philadelphia Record,* May 9, 1935, p. 10.

[167] *Ibid.* See Figure 1 - Jerry Doyle, "Mighty Casey Had Struck Out."

[168] B. Wright, *Growth of American Constitutional Law* (New York, 1942), p. 180.

[169] Schlesinger, III, 447.

[170] S.B. Pettengill & P.C. Bartholomew, *For Americans Only* (New York, 1944), p. 22.

[171] Pearson and Allen, p. 250.

[172] 293 U.S. 388 (1935).

[173] *Ibid.*, 390-91.
[174] Pusey, p. 734.
[175] Jackson, p. 90.
[176] Pusey, *loc. cit.*
[177] *Ibid.*
[178] Curtis, p. 116; Curtis also maintains it is the only real use of the "delegation" question to void a law, though it was used also in *Schechter*; Pearson & Allen, p. 253.
[179] 8293 U.S. 388, 415.
[180] *Ibid.*, 436.
[181] *Holmes-Laski Letters*, January 29, 1935, p. 1479.
[182] January 9, 1935, editorial page.
[183] January 9, 1935, p. 8.
[184] January 9, 1935, p. 12.
[185] S. 1190, 76th Congress, 1st Session; 49 Stat. 30 (1935).
[186] 307 U.S. 214 (1939).
[187] 295 U.S. 174.
[188] *Ibid.*, 192.
[189] Schlesinger, III, 216. Crawford had lost ten of seventeen cases in his first five months and was blamed for many of the New Deal setbacks.
[190] *United States v. Belcher*, 294 U.S. 736 (1935),
[191] C.B. Swisher, "Supreme Court in Transition," *Journal of Politics* 1 (1939), 353.
[192] April 3, 1935, p 18.
[193] *Roosevelt Library*, Correspondence of Richberg and Corcoran with Roosevelt, April 3-6, 1935, Official File 200-M; Schlesinger, p. 278.
[194] Pearson and Allen, 257-58.
[195] *Roosevelt Library*, Correspondence of Solicitor General with F.D.R., April, 1935, President's File, 666-Codes.
[196] 294 U.S. 732 (1935).
[197] *Schechter Brothers Poultry Corporation v. United States*, 295 U.S. 495 (1935).
[198] Jackson, p. 112.
[199] "Some Probable Repercussions of 'NIRA' on our Constitutional System," *Annals of A.A.P.S.S.* CLXXII (1934), 142. The author used "Nira" as a single noun.
[200] Wormser, *The Story of the Law*, p. 446.
[201] *The Court and The Constitution*, p. 46.
[202] C.E. Hughes Papers, Library of Congress, Manuscript Division, Box 157.
[203] 295 U.S. 495, 543.
[204] *Ibid.*, 546.
[205] *Ibid.*, 550.
[206] *Ibid.*, 528.
[207] 295 U.S. 459, 529.
[208] Interview with Judge Charles Fahy, April 8, 1934.
[209] 295 U.S. 495, 553.
[210] Pusey, p. 741.
[211] Schlesinger, III, 280.
[212] E. Eriksson, p. 45.

[213] Pusey, p. 743

[214] F.D.R. Papers, 1935 vol., 205.

[215] Ibid., p. 221.

[216] "The Great Constitutional War," Virginia Quarterly Review XVIII (1942), 537.

[217] W. Hurst, "Review and The Distribution of National Power," Supreme Court and Supreme Law ed. E. Cahn (Bloomington, 1954), p. 147.

[218] F.D.R. Library, Pres. Personal File, 20, Correspondence HLS with FDR, June 4 & 10, 1935.

[219] May 28, 1935, p. 24.

[220] May 28, 1935, p. 1.

[221] May 29, 1935, p. 10.

[222] The New York Times, May 29, 1937, p. 24.

[223] The New York Times, May 28, 1935, p. 24.

[224] Stern, p. 664.

[225] Stern, p. 666.

[226] F.D.R. Papers, 1935 vol., 297-98, July 6, 1935.

[227] The Herald-Tribune, New York, May 19, 1936, p. 26.

[228] Schlesinger, III, 336.

[229] C. Curtis, p. 28.

[230] The other members were his father and an employee, Carter's parents were the majority stockholders, and his wife and himself held the remaining stock.

[231] Stern, pp. 667-71. Mr. Stern was on brief for the government as a member of the Dept. of Justice at this time.

[232] 298 U.S. 277.

[233] The Washington Star, May 19, 1936, p. A 10.

[234] 298 U.S. 238.

[235] May 19, 1936, p. 1.

[236] 298 U.S. 238, 289.

[237] Ibid., 291-297.

[238] Ibid., 303.

[239] Ibid., 308-9.

[240] J. Roberts, The Court and The Constitution, p. 49.

[441] 298 U.S. 238, 312.

[242] Ibid.

[243] Ibid., 313.

[244] Stern, 316.

[245] Ibid., pp. 317-319.

[246] Ibid.

[247] Ibid., 331.

[248] Ibid., 341.

[249] In Butler, however, the Court did rule on the challenged tax as well, even though the burden of the opinion and the basis for striking down the Act was the use of the spending power. See Stone, Hughes, p. 407.

[250] May 25, 1935, p. 13.

[251] May 19, 1936, p. 8.

[252] May 19, 1936, p. 6.

[253] May 19, 1936, p. 8.
[254] May 19, 1936, p. 12.
[255] May 19, 1936, p. 1.
[256] May 19, 1936, p. 8.
[257] *C.E. Hughes Papers,* file 157, transcript of Mac Parker's comment on *Record* editorial of May 19, 1936 on his program on Station KYW, Philadelphia, Pennsylvania, May 20, 1936, 8 P.M.
[258] *Burns,* p. 233.
[259] *Ashwander v. T.V.A.,* 297 U.S. 288 (1936).
[260] "Business of the Supreme Court," *Harvard Law Review* LI (1938), 627.
[261] Swisher, *American Constitutional Development,* pp. 862-68.
[262] *Stone,* p. 418.
[263] *Ibid.*
[264] "In Washington,"The *New York Times,* February 18, 1936, p. 22.
[265] 297 U.S. 288. 341.
[266] *Ibid.,* 346-48.
[267] *Ibid.,*372.
[268] *Ibid.,* 339.
[269] Swisher, *American Constitutional Development,* p. 938.
[270] February 18, 1936, p. 22: see also on the same date, *Washington Post,* p. 8, *Washington Evening Star,* p. A 10, Baltimore *Sun,* p. 10.
[271] February 18, 1936, p. 6.
[272] February 18, 1936, p. 10.
[273] 299 U.S. 304 (1936).
[274] Justice Stone did not participate in Court business from October 12, 1936 to February 1, 1937 due to illness. A.T. Mason, "Harlan Fiske Stone and FDR's Court Plan," *Yale Law Journal,* LXI (1952), pp. 793-95.
[275] 299 U.S. 304, 318-19.
[276] *Ibid.,* 322.
[277] *American Surety Co. v. Westinghouse Corporation,* 296 U.S. 133 (1935); *Becker Steel Co. v. Cummings,* 296 U.S. 74 (1935).
[278] Gossip had it that Hughes voted with the majority to avoid another five-to-four decision. Hughes' biographer vigorously denies such a rumor. See Pusey, II p. 744.
[279] *New York Times,* May 30, 1937, Section IV, p. 7, chart.
[280] "'Substance' vs. 'form' in the Application of the Commerce Clause to State Taxation," *University of Pennsylvania Law Review* CI (1953), 740.
[281] 290 U.S. 1 (1933).
[282] *Ibid.,* 8.
[283] *Johnson Oil Refining Co. v. Oklahoma,* 290 U.S. 158 (1933); *Conney v. Mountain States Tel & Tel Co.,* 294 U.S. 384 (1935); *Bingaman v. Golden Eagle Western Lines,* 297 U.S. 626 (1936); *Fisher's Bend Station v. State Tax Commission,* 297 U.S. 650 (1936).
[284] Government Bonds-*Schuylkill Trust Co. v. Pennsylvania,* 296 U.S. 113 (1935); Gasoline sold to Navy-*Groves v. Texas,* 298 U.S. 393 (1936).
[285] *Fox v. Standard Oil,* 294 U.S. 87 (1935); *Gulf Refining Co. v. Fox,* 297 U.S. 137 (1936).

[286] 294 U.S. 550 (1935).
[287] 299 U.S. 32 (1936).
[288] 292 U.S. 535 (1934).
[298] 296 U.S. 404 (1935).
[290] A.T. Mason, *Supreme Court: Vehicle of Revealed Truth or Power Group,*
1930-1937 (Boston, 1953), p. 37.
[291] Wright, pp. 197-98.
[292] Pascal, p. 175.
[293] 290 U.S. 177 (1933).
[294] 292 U.S. 40 (1934).
[295] *Ibid.,* 43, 47.
[296] April 3, 1934, p. 10.
[297] 297 U.S. 233 (1936).
[298] *Leading Cases on the Constitution* (4th edition, Paterson, N.J., 1962), p.
106.
[299] 297 U.S. 233 at 250.
[300] *Kroger Grocery & Baking Co. v. Lutz,* 299 U.S. 300 (1936).
[301] *Ibid.,* 301.
[302] 294 U.S. 63 and 294 U.S. 79 (1935).
[303] 291 U.S. 227 (1934).
[304] 169 U.S. 466.
[305] *The Supreme Court in Modern Role* (New York, 1958), p. 173.
[306] 295 U.S. 662 (1935).
[307] "Economic Due Process and The Supreme Court, An Exhumation and
Rebuttal," *The Supreme Court Review: 1962* (Chicago, 1962), pp. 36-37.
[308] *Alabama v. Arizona et al.,* 291 U.S. 268 (1934); *Whitfield v. Ohio,* 297 U.S.
431 (1936).
[309] *Aero Mayflower Transit Co. v. Georgia Public Service Commission,* 295 U.S.
285 (1935).
[310] 294 U.S. 405 (1935).
[311] *Roosevelt Library,* Official File 41 A, Miscellaneous Judiciary, Supreme
Court 1936-44, R.C.B. Howell to F.D.R., June 24, 1936.
[312] 294 U.S. 608 (1935).
[313] Swisher, *Supreme Court in a Modern Role,* p. 172.
[314] "Supreme Court & State Police Power, 1922-1930," *Virginia Law Review*
VIII (1931), 529.
[315] 290 U.S. 398 (1934).
[316] D. Alfange, *Supreme Court & National Will* (New York, 1937), p. 115.
[317] U.S. Congress, House of Representatives, 87th Congress, 1st Session House
Document 206 (1961), p. 5.
[318] Corwin, *Twilight of the Supreme Court,* p. 117.
[319] 290 U.S. 398, 447.
[320] *Ibid.,* 483.
[321] "In Washington," The *New York Times,* January 10, 1934, p. 20.
[322] "Law," January 13, 1934, p. 29.
[323] January 9, 1934, p. 1.
[324] January 10, 1934, editorial page.

[325] January 10, 1934, p. 20.
[326] 292 U.S. 426 (1934).
[327] 295 U.S. 56 (1935).
[328] *Newsweek*, p. 31.
[329] *Treigle v. Acme Homestead Association* 297 U.S. 189 (1936).
[330] *Ibid.*, 197.
[331] *Gibbes v. Zimmermaan*, 290 U.S. 326 (1933).
[332] 298 U.S. 513 (1936).
[333] 290 U.S. 326 at 332.
[334] *Nebbia v. New York*, 291 U.S. 503 (1934).
[335] E.H. Wilson, "Property Affected with a Public Interest," *Southern California Law Review* IX (19), 1.
[336] 94 U.S. 113 (1877).
[337] E.S. Corwin, *Liberty vs. Government* (Baton Rouge, 1948), pp. 137-38. For a different view of the part the *Munn* decision played in the founding of the A.B.A. see Norbert Brackman, *The History of the American Bar Association*, unpublished doctoral dissertation, Catholic University of America, 1963.
[338] *Wolff Packing Co. v. Court of Industrial Relations*, 262 U.S. 522 (1924).
[339] *Twilight*, p. 99.
[340] Corwin, *Constitutional Revolution, Ltd.*, pp. 75-76; Pusey, p. 700.
[341] Rodell, p. 230.
[342] 391 U.S. 502 @ 515.
[343] *Ibid.*, 516-17.
[344] *Ibid.*, 521.
[345] *Ibid.*, 523.
[346] *Ibid.*, 524
[347] *Ibid.*
[348] *Ibid.*, 525.
[349] *Ibid.*, 531-32.
[350] *Ibid.*, 536.
[351] *Ibid.* 539.
[352] *Ibid.*, 555.
[353] *Ibid.*, 556.
[354] Pearson & Allen, p. 157.
[355] *Hegeman Farm's Corporation v. Baldwin*, 293 U.S. 163.
[356] *Ibid.*, 170.
[357] 294 U.S. 511 (1935).
[358] "In Washington," *New York Times* March 5, 1935, p. 18.
[359] *Borden's Farm Products Corporation v. Baldwin*, 293 U.S. 194 (1934).
[360] 297 U.S. 251 (1936).
[361] 297 U.S. 266 (1936)
[362] *Ibid.*, 274, 278.
[363] *Peterson Baking Co. v. Bryan*, 290 U.S. 570 (1934).
[364] *Pacific Box and Basket Co. v. White*, U.S. 176 (1935).
[365] 291 U.S. 315 (1934).
[366] *Morehead v. New York ex rel. Tipaldo*, 298 U.S. 587 (1936).
[367] 300 U.S. 379 (1937).

[368] The Court of Appeals, New York's highest tribunal, had remitted the case to the lower court after ruling that the law was void under the *Adkins* rule. 298 U.S. 587, 603.

[369] The *Washington Evening Star*, June 2, 1936, p. A 10.

[370] Schlesinger, III, 479.

[371] *F.D.R. Papers*, 1933 vol., p. 133.

[372] *Adkins v. Children's Hospital*, 261 U.S. 525 (1923).

[373] 298 U.S. 587, 604.

[374] F. Frankfurter, "Mr. Justice Roberts," *University of Pennsylvania Law Review* CIV (1955), 314.

[375] March 31, 1937, p. 10 col. 3.

[376] *United States Law Review* LXXI (1937), 183.

[377] Griswold, p. 341; M.J. Pusey, *The Supreme Court Crisis* (New York, 1937), p. 49.

[378] *Murphy v. Sardell*, 269 U.S. 530 (1925); *Donham v. West-Nelson Mfg. Co.*, 273 U.S. 657 (1927).

[379] Curtis, p. 163.

[380] 304 U.S. 64 (1938).

[381] Jackson, p. 282.

[382] Author's interview with Merlo Pusey, The Washington Post Building, March 14, 1963.

[383] Frankfurter, *Mr. Justice Roberts*, pp. 314-15.

[384] Frankfurter, *Mr. Justice Roberts*, p. 315.

[385] *Ibid.*, pp. 315-16.

[386] Griswold, p. 342.

[387] Schlesinger, III, 480.

[388] 298 U.S. 587, 622-23.

[389] *Ibid.*, 631.

[390] *Ibid.*, 632.

[391] *Ibid.*, 636.

[392] Schlesinger, III, 489.

[393] June 2, 1936, p. 8.

[394] June 2, 1936, p. 26.

[395] June 2, 1936, p. 8.

[396] June 2, 1936, p. 12.

[397] June 3, 1936, p. 10.

[398] June 2, 1936, p. 8.

[399] *F.D.R. Papers*, 1936 vol., 191-92.

[400] Mason, *Stone*, p. 425.

[401] Charles and Mary Beard, p. 285.

[402] The *New York Times*, June 12, 1936; *Documents of American History*, ed. H.S. Commager (New York, 1949), II, 535

[403] June 8, 1936, p. 11.

[404] 299 U.S. 515.

[405] Frankfurter, *Mr. Justice Roberts*, p. 316; *Time*, November 30, 1936. p. 14.

[406] 299 U.S. 619.

[407] F.P. Dunne, *Mr. Dooley on Ivrything and Ivrybody* (New York, 1963), p. 160.

[408] *Atlantic Coast Line Co. v. Florida*, 295 U.S. 301 (19355).

Chapter III

A Switch in Time, 1937[1]

What occurred within the Court during the second half of the
October, 1936 term has been variously described as a "revolution,"
"evolution," and "renaissance." The future justice, Robert H. Jackson,
wrote in 1941 that "it has been in the nature of a Constitutional
Renaissance – a rediscovery of the Constitution itself."[2] Erwin N.
Griswold declared that Roberts "helped to show to those who cared to
look that we did not go through a constitutional revolution in 1937 but
through a gradual constitutional development extending over many years."[3]
However, Edward S. Corwin noted in his *Constitutional Revolution, Ltd.*:
"It would be relevant at this point to speculate as to the causes which
brought about the remarkable reversal of the Court's attitude toward the
New Deal early in 1937 ... On the other hand, it seems at least equally
logical to show ... that a revolution *did* take place and in what respects
it *was* a revolution."[4] Whatever the change may be called, and a review of
the commentators leads one to exclaim with Shakespeare "What's in a
name?", beginning in 1937 there came to the high bench a new approach
to the economic powers of government.

The real surprise resulted from the fact that the change occurred
before a single new member had been named to the Court. It is conceded
by all observers, and is a matter of record, that the change was made
possible by the "conversion of 'odd men' Roberts and Hughes."[5] However,
at least one commentator was quick to point out that "the more liberal
construction given the commerce clause has been commonly ascribed to a
change of opinion on the part of Justice Roberts. This assumption is not
altogether correct,"[6] for, as the same author points out, the Court had
been unanimous on numerous occasions in *voiding* legislation during the
1933 to 1936 period.

The beginning came in March with a railroad labor decision[7] on the
federal level and the reversal of the *Morehead* decision of the previous June
in *West Coast Hotel v. Parrish*[8] on the state level. The climax came during

the months of April and May. "The capitulation of the Court to the New Deal was somewhat uncertainly signalized in its decision of March 29, 1937 in *West Coast Hotel Co. v. Parrish.*[9]   But the "decisions in 301 U.S. formed the heart of the constitutional revolution of 1937."[10]

Just what change took place within Justice Roberts will be detailed further on, but before beginning the analysis of the cases involved in the "switch," we might note Justice Cardozo's words on the struggle which goes on within a judge's mind between his duty to precedent and his duty to social welfare, much like that which must have gone on within Justice Roberts:

> The social interest served by symmetry or certainty must then be balanced against the social interest served by equity and fairness or other elements of social welfare. These may enjoin upon the judge the duty of drawing the line at another angle, of staking the path along new courses, of marking a new point of departure from which others who come after him will set out upon their journey.[11]

Federal Cases and Comment

In the area of the interstate commerce power the Justices upheld the government in ten of eleven cases. The first decision announced after the new year was *Kentucky Whip and Collar Co. v. Illinois Central R.*[12] As if to stress that the Court had been willing in the past to recognize that the commerce power could be used for prevention as well as promotion of commerce, the Chief Justice listed the federal statutes which had been upheld by the Court to exclude articles from interstate commerce.[13] To this list the Court now added the transportation of convict-made goods into those states where their sale had been prohibited by the state, as authorized by the Ashurst-Sumners Act of 1935, which was a corollary of the Hawes-Cooper Act of 1929, upheld in *Whitfield v. Ohio,* the previous March. Chief Justice Hughes declared for a unanimous Court, the commerce power " 'is complete in itself, may be exercised to its upmost extent, and acknowledges no limitations other than are prescribed in the constitution.'. . . The question is whether this rule goes beyond the authority to 'regulate.' "[14] The implications of the Court's answer were obvious, for although, as Robert H. Jackson put it, the *Child Labor* case[15] "was laid aside as inapplicable," but not overruled,[16] the Justices had now intimated that they were willing to take a second look at that precedent. The New York *Herald-Tribune* speculated:

Whether the Supreme Court decision in the Convict-labor case will bear all the weight which the Congressional advocates of labor legislation seek to put upon it is open to question, but it does seem to disclose some rather wide vistas. The Court now unanimously lays down the principle that where the state has the constitutional right to restrict or prohibit a traffic in its internal trade, Congress may use its power over interstate commerce so as to prevent that commerce from being used to impede the carrying out of state policy.[17]

On March 29th, the same day that the *West Coast Hotel* decision was announced, the first clear manifestation of a new view of federal power was handed down in *Virginia Railway Co. v. System Federation #40, American Federation of Labor.*[18] As previously noted, prior to 1937 the Court was reluctant to extend federal railroad legislation to non-operating employees. However, in 1930 the Justices had upheld the Railway Labor Act of 1926 to permit clerical employees to bargain collectively through a non-company union.[19] Congress had amended that act in 1934 to broaden its coverage,[20] and both the federal district Court[21] and the Court of Appeals[22] in an opinion written by Judge John J. Parker, [whose rejection, it will be recalled, had opened the way to Roberts' nomination to the Supreme Court in 1930] upheld the law and its application. The railroad appealed and on February 11, 1937 Attorney General Homer S. Cummings wrote to the President that "the arguments in the six cases involving the Railroad Labor Act, and the Wagner Bill, have been completed and the matter now rests in the bosom of the Court."[23] *Time* noted that the law had been "accepted by most railroads without legal quibble; it has helped make the railway industry a national model of pacific labor relations."[24] The article further pointed out that the company wanted to negotiate with the company union, while most of the shop employees had voted to be represented by a unit of the American Federation of Labor.

Justice Stone wrote the opinion but was not pleased with the final product for reasons which he indicated in a letter to his sons; "it was fairly good as written, but it was mangled somewhat in order to meet the wishes of some of the other judges. It finally won concurrence of the entire Court."[25] Swisher believes that because it was unanimous, it was only a very small step on the part of the Court.[26]

In answer to the charge that the "back shop" men were not involved in interstate commerce, Justice Stone stated:

The power of Congress over interstate commerce extends to such regulations of the relations of rail carriers to their employees as are reasonably calculated to prevent the interruption of interstate commerce by strikes and their attendant disorders. ... The repair

> work is upon the equipment used by the petitioner in its trans-
> portation service, 97% of which is interstate. . . . The activities in
> which these employees are engaged have such a relation to the other
> confessedly interstate activities of the petitioner that they are to be
> regarded as part of them. All taken together fall within the power of
> Congress over interstate commerce.[27]

Against the contention that the law violated due process because of
enforced negotiations, Stone replied:

> The provisions of the Railway Labor Act . . . do not require petitioner
> to enter into any agreement with its employees, and they do not
> prohibit its entering into such contract of employment as it chooses,
> with its individual employees. . . . If the compulsory settlement of
> some differences, by arbitration, may be within the limits of due
> process, see *Hardware Dealers Mutual Fire Ins. Co. v. Glidden Co.*,
> 284 U.S. 151, it seems plain that the command of the statute to
> negotiate for the settlement of labor disputes, given in the appropriate
> exercise of the commerce power, cannot be said to be so arbitrary or
> unreasonable as to infringe due process.[28]

Miss Virginia Wood in her study of *Due Process of Law* stated that this is
the first time the right to bargain collectively was ruled not to violate the
substantive "due process" limitation on legislative activity.[29]

Two weeks after the *Virginia Railway* case was decided, the Court
announced the long awaited decision on the National Labor Relations Act.
The National Labor Relations Board began its existence under the National
Recovery Administration as the National Labor Board. Under Chairman
Lloyd K. Garrison and his successor, Francis Biddle, the board had fought
with Hugh S. Johnson and Donald Richberg over the jurisdiction which the
former body would exercise, and Roosevelt had upheld the NRA adminis-
trators. The President ordered Biddle to stay out of cases where labor
relations machinery existed under the codes, which led Heywood Broun to
declare that "labor's public enemy number one is Franklin D.
Roosevelt."[30]

Meanwhile, Senator Robert F. Wagner attempted to set up machinery
for the settlement of labor strife which was plaguing the nation. He was
almost alone in this crusade. The administration was opposed to such
legislation, and Roosevelt successfully sidetracked the bill in 1934, but with
the dissolution of NRA as a result of the *Schechter* decision, he
reconsidered and added his support to the Wagner bill, which became law
on July 5, 1935.[31] Contrary to the popular view, this was the first time, as
Professor Burns points out, that "Roosevelt and labor became partners."[32]

An additional stimulant to the President's change of heart, and perhaps to that of the Court two years later, was the increased incidence of strikes, which were becoming increasingly violent. Six hundred and fourteen strikes began in March, 1937, and the top number in progress, nine hundred and forty, was recorded in June of the same year. March was the peak month for sit-down strikes as well.[33] And these incidents had been on the increase since early 1935.

The Wagner Law was considered by many commentators to be unquestionably unconstitutional. Earl F. Reed, counsel for Weirton Steel Co. and chairman of the Liberty League Committee, told one reporter, "I feel perfectly free to advise a client not to be bound by a law that I consider unconstitutional." And Arthur Schlesinger, Jr., historian of the New Deal, conceded that "by principles already handed down, the Wagner Act would surely fall . . . ."[34] However, the general counsel for the NLRB at this time, Charles Fahy, felt in 1963 that "the Wagner Act should have been sustained on the basis of precedents, . . . and I am not inclined to attribute the fact that it was sustained to anything but that it was believed to be constitutional. In fact, I thought it might be sustained by a vote other than Roberts'."[35]

The basic philosophy of the act was the supposition that "the welfare of the nation as a whole would be advanced if workers and employers would be able to bargain on an equal basis on such items as wages and working conditions."[36] Yet, "probably no act of the New Deal," wrote Jackson, "was more widely misunderstood or more actively misrepresented than the National Labor Relations Act."[37] The opposition of the Liberty League Lawyers' Committee was expressed in a statement on September 19, 1935. The act "constitutes a complete departure from our constitutional and traditional theories of government."[38] David Lawrence declared in his column of May 28, 1935 that "the Wagner Bill, as passed by the Senate, is obviously invalid. The common law protects the right of collective bargaining, but the federal power cannot extend to compulsion or coercion over employers."[39]

The board's first case came in The Pennsylvania Greyhound Line,[40] an interstate bus system, but it did not reach the Supreme Court until 1938.[41] In the first cases to reach the high court, the lower courts had voided the law in three instances[42] and sustained it in two.[43] The Chief Justice wrote the opinions in the first group, and Justice Roberts authored those in the second. Mason holds that Cardozo should have been allowed the privilege of marking the new trail, but that the two swing men demanded the honor as the price for their vote.[44]

Though Roberts read his opinions first, due to the custom of printing opinions in the official reports in the order of seniority of the Justices who authored them, the *Jones and Laughlin* opinion appears first in the *United States Reports*, and, indeed, the principles and rulings governing the remaining cases are found in that opinion.

After stating the details of procedure, the Chief Justice noted:

> The facts as to the nature and scope of the business of the Jones & Laughlin Steel Corporation have been found by the Labor board and, so far as they are essential to the determination of this controversy, they are not in dispute here. The Labor Board has found . . . that the works in Pittsburgh and Aliquippa "might be likened to the heart of a self-contained, highly integrated body."[45]

The majority, while conceding that "that distinction between what is national and what is local in the activites of commerce is vital to the maintenance of our federal system," declared that "we think it clear that the National Labor Relations Act may be construed so as to operate within the sphere of constitutional authority."[46] This is supported by the fact that the act "purports to reach only what may be deemed to burden or obstruct that commerce and, thus qualified, it must be construed as contemplating the exercises of control within constitutional bounds."[47] In addition, "whether or not particular action does affect commerce in such a close and intimate fashion as to be subject to federal control, and hence to lie within the authority conferred upon the Board, is left by the statute to be determined as individual cases arise."[48] Arriving at the heart of the decision, the legal right to unionize, the Chief Justice states:

> . . . The statute goes no further than to safeguard the right of employees to self-organization and to select representatives of their own choosing for collecting bargaining or other mutual protection without restraint or coercion by their employer.
>
> That is a fundamental right. Employees have as clear a right to organize and select their representatives for lawful purposes as the respondent has to organize its business and select its own officers and agents. . . . [We have said in the past] that Congress was not required to ignore this right but could safeguard it. Congress could seek to make appropriate collective action of employees an instrument of peace rather than strife.[49]

Rejecting the "stream of commerce" principle, the Court ruled:

> The congressional authority to protect interstate commerce from burdens and obstructions is not limited to transactions which can be deemed to be an essential part of a "flow" of interstate or foreign commerce. Burdens and obstructions may be due to injurious action springing from other sources. The fundamental principle is that the

power to regulate commerce is the power to enact "all appropriate legislation" for "its protection and advancement" ...[50]

The Chief Justice then distinguishes *Schechter and Carter* and finds that "these cases are not controlling here."[51] This part of the opinion concludes with the firm statement:

> Instead of being beyond the pale, we think that it [the steel company] presents in a most striking way the close and intimate relation which a manufacturing industry may have to interstate commerce, and we have no doubt that Congress has constitutional authority to safeguard the right of the respondent's employees to self-organization and freedom in the choice of representatives for collective bargaining.[52]

In the two other opinions which the Chief wrote, the main point was to establish the question of the effect of the business on interstate commerce. Once this was substantiated the principles of *Jones and Laughlin* were invoked.

Justice McReynolds delivered a single dissenting opinion in the three cases and spoke for his brethren, Van Devanter, Sutherland, and Butler. The Justice noted that "a more remote and indirect interference with interstate commerce or a more definite invasion of the power reserved to the states is difficult, if not impossible, to imagine."[53] Refuting the validity of the precedents cited by the majority, McReynolds continued:

> It is unreasonable and unprecedented to say that the commerce clause confers upon Congress power to govern relations between employers and employees in these local activities. ... In *Schechter's* case we condemned as unauthorized by the commerce clause assertion of federal power in respect of commodities which had come to rest after interstate transportation. And, in *Carter's* case, we held Congress lacked power to regulate labor relations in respect of commodities before interstate commerce has begun.[54]

The reaction of the press was mostly favorable. The *Cleveland Plain Dealer* exulted that "the New Deal victory was as sweeping as the defeat in the NRA case almost two years ago ...."[55] The Baltimore *Sun* declared that "this is the most liberal definition of interstate commerce that has come down from the Supreme Court in years."[56]

The *Chicago Daily News* declared that "the way to labor peace is open."[57] The New York *Herald-Tribune* titled its editorial, "A Great Decision," and the President was quick to point out in his press conference that that particular paper had taken the opposite view of the law when it was passed two years before.[58] Not a few papers qualified their applause with a call for amendments to the law to correct its inequities.[59]

In the first of Justice Roberts' opinions that day, the *Associated Press* case, a different issue was injected, that of freedom of the press, as the Justice noted: "in this case we are to decide whether the National Labor Relations Act ... abridges the freedom of the press guaranteed by the First Amendment ...."[60] After finding that the class of employees whose inclusion under the act was being challenged was truly within the statute, Roberts declared that the National Labor Relations Act did not limit the freedom of the press, or of speech, invoked by the petitioner.[61] And the Justice stated the principle upon which that judgment was based:

> The business of the Associated Press is not immune form regulation because it is an agency of the press. The publisher of a newspaper has no special immunity from the application of general laws. He has no special privilege to invade the rights and liberties of others. He must answer for libel. He may be punished for contempt of court. He is subject to the anti-trust laws. Like others he must pay equitable and nondiscriminatory taxes on his business. *The regulation here in question has no relation whatever to the impartial distribution of news.*[62] [Italics supplied]

Justice Sutherland, for the dissenters, held that "due regard for the constitutional guaranty requires that the publisher or agency of the publisher of news shall be free from restraint in respect of employment in the editorial force." And in what, in retrospect, seems a basis for "right-to-work laws" he declared that "the right to belong to a labor union is entitled to the shield of the law, but no more so than the right not to belong. Neither can be prescribed. So much must be true, or we do not live in a free land."[63] And, in conclusion, Sutherland advised:

> Do the people of this land—in the providence of God, favored, as they sometimes boast, above all others in the plenitude of their liberties—desire to preserve those so carefully protected by the First Amendment. . .? If so, let them withstand all *beginnings* of encroachment. For the saddest epitaph which can be carved in memory of a vanished liberty is that it was lost because its possessors failed to stretch forth a saving hand while yet there was time.[64]

However, even the *Chicago Tribune* was unable to concur with the "four stalwarts,"[65] and it agreed with the majority:

> ... In the issue adequately presented to the Court, we believe the decision of the Court could hardly have been otherwise, and as the statement of principles involved it will have the assent of responsible newspapers. The freedom guaranteed by the First Amendment of the Constitution, as Mr. Justice Roberts points out, does not imply immunity from all regulation of press agencies.[66]

The last of the cases of the day involved an interstate bus company, and in light of the foregoing cases the conclusion was obvious, even to the dissenters in the first four cases, and so the Court unanimously upheld the application of the act to the Washington, Virginia, and Maryland Coach Company.

The White House was delighted. "Today is a very, very happy day ... ," the President told the press on the morning after the decisions were announced.[67] Further, he relayed what Edward Roddan had remarked about the decision:[68]

> He said, "Well, we have all been wondering about this 'No Man's Land.' We have been worrying about the future of the country as long as the 'No Man's Land' continued to exist. Well, in the last two days the 'No Man's Land' has been eliminated, but see what we have in place of it: We are now in 'Roberts' Land.' "[69]

Not a few commentators have noted that the NLRB cases overruled the *Carter* case, at least in effect, despite the Chief Justice's attempt to distinguish that case.[70] And Roberts, himself, stated in 1951 that "two years later the *Carter* case, with the line of decisions on which it relied, was so limited as to be virtually overruled."[71] The *Carter* case had been based on the traditional definition of "commerce" and on "the stream of commerce" doctrine, while the *Wagner* decision was founded on the effect or burden on interstate commerce.[72] This is, perhaps, a thin line to justify Roberts' switch but it is a legal distinction, and Roberts' lawyer-like mind might have felt such a distinction a justification of a change in vote. However, as will be detailed later, there were external pressures as well.

Legally speaking, the Court had restored the *Shreveport* doctrine to its full force;[73] but, in fact, what it had done, at least in the view of a former Solicitor General of the United States, was to transfer to Congress the determination of the border between federal and state responsibility for the regulation of labor relations.[74] In effect, the Madisonian concept of *dual federalism*, "the notion that entirely apart from the 10th Amendment the coexistence of the states and their powers is of itself a limitation upon the national power,"[75] had been destroyed, for as The *New York Times* noted: "For the first time in American History, industries organized on a national scale, though their products are locally manufactured, were held today by the Supreme Court to come specifically within the regulatory powers of Congress."[76]

In a different vein Arthur Krock pointed out a practical aspect of the decision: "... as far as Washington is concerned, the Supreme Court's conclusions today in the Wagner Cases were assayed exclusively on the scales of politics and not on the scales of law. Elsewhere in the United States it may be that the analyses were legal. Not here."[77]

The new liberalism carried over into the areas of the taxing and spending powers. In eight of nine cases from January to June of 1937 the federal power was upheld. The one negative vote was handed down in *Brush v. Commissioner.*[78] While the vote was seven to two to void a federal income tax on the chief engineer of a city owned water system as a burden on a state instrumentality, two of the seven, Stone and Cardozo, concurred in the decision only because the government counsel had failed to challenge the immunity principle and, therefore, "in the absence of such a challenge no opinion is expressed as to the need for revision of the doctrine of implied immunities declared in earlier decisions."[79] This reasoning is similar to that employed by Roberts in his private comments on the *Morehead* case. In this instance, however, perhaps in response to the criticism for taking such a position, Roberts dissented and was joined by Justice Brandeis. "The sole question here," Roberts declared,

> is whether one performing work or rendering a service of a type commonly done or rendered in ordinary commercial life for gain is exempt from the normal burden of a tax on that gain for the support of the national government because his compensation is paid by a state agency instead of a private employer. I think that imposition of a tax upon such gain where, as here, the tax falls equally upon all employed in like occupation, and where the supposed burden of the tax upon state government is indirect, remote, and imponderable, is not inconsistent with the principle of immunity inherent in the constitutional relation of state and nation.[80]

The Court also upheld the Silver Purchase Act and its accompanying tax on the transfer of silver.[81] Fred Rodell cites this case as the first indication of the change in the mind of the Court, despite the fact that at the time the decision went practically unnoticed.[82] In *Sonzinsky v. United States*[83] the Justices unanimously upheld the use of the taxing power to restrict the sale of firearms. Stone declared in his opinion:

> On its face it is only a taxing measure, and we are asked to say that the tax, by virtue of its deterrent effect on the activities taxed, operates as a regulation which is beyond the congressional power.
>
> Every tax is in some measure regulatory. To some extent it interposes an economic impediment to the activity taxed as compared with others not taxed. But a tax is not any the less a tax because it has a regulatory effect . . . .
>
> Inquiry into the hidden motives which may move Congress to exercise a power constitutionally conferred upon it is beyond the competency of the courts. . . . They will not undertake, by collateral

inquiry as to the measure of the regulatory effect of a tax, to ascribe to Congress an attempt, under the guise of taxation, to exercise another power denied by the Federal Constitution.[84]

Such language seems to be an indirect repudiation of the decision on the use of the taxing power in *Butler*. Indeed, as Professor Robert E. Cushman wrote in 1934 before the Agricultural Adjustment program was struck down, "It would be impossible for Congress to levy a tax which did not have social and economic consequences of a non-fiscal character."[85]

The Court also seemed to review its *Butler* views in *Cincinnati Soap Co. v. United States*.[86] Unanimously, the Justices ruled that a processing tax on Philippine coconut oil, which was in turn paid into the Philippines' Territorial treasury, was valid. "We think," stated Justice Sutherland, "the law may be sustained as an act in discharge of a high moral obligation, amounting to a 'debt' within the meaning of the Constitution as it always has been practically construed."[87] And he concluded with the declaration that "other queries directly or indirectly challenging the wisdom or necessity of the Congressional action are all matters, as we repeatedly have pointed out, with which the courts have nothing to do."[88]

In another postscript to the *Butler* decision, the Court ruled in *Anniston Manufacturing Co. v. Davis*[89] that Congress could abolish the right to sue for the return of the processing tax collected under the Agricultural Adjustment Act, provided an adequate remedy remained. The Court also ruled that if the taxpayer had shifted the burden to others he lost his right to a claim.

Finally, in the Social Security cases, the Justices in the majority accepted the principles which had been laid down in the *Butler* decision by Justice Roberts on the matter of spending for the general welfare.[90] The act had been an integral part of the New Deal program announced in the platform in 1932, but it was not, by any means, the property of one political party, as the *Chicago Tribune* indicated in its editorial of May 26, 1937.[91] In addition, the first chairman of the Social Security Board, John G. Winant, a Republican, in his letter of resignation reminded the President that three times as many Republicans in Congress had voted for the measure as voted against it.[92]

The chief model for the federal program was that already in operation in Wisconsin which had been developed by John R. Commons and revised by Harold R. Goves and Paul A. Raushenbush, who, incidentally, was Justice Brandeis's son-in-law. Subsequently, a different plan had been proposed in Ohio which was supported by Abraham Epstein, an authority on old age insurance, and Paul H. Douglas, a professor of economics at the

University of Chicago and, formerly, Senator from Illinois. The Wisconsin Plan was supported in Congress by Senator Wagner and Representative David J. Lewis of Maryland, while the Ohio Plan was sponsored by Senator Clarence C. Dill of Washington and Representative William P. Connery of Massachusetts. Eventually, in June of 1935, a compromise bill was passed.[93] The 1st Circuit Court of Appeals held both the unemployment compensation and old-age benefits provisions unconstitutional in *Helvering v. Davis.*[94] However, the 5th Circuit Court upheld the dismissal of a suit to recover the taxes collected from an employer in *Stewart Machine Co. v. Davis,*[95] while a three-judge Federal District Court in Alabama had held that state's Unemployment Compensation Act invalid.[96] On November 5, 1936 the Solicitor General requested an appointment with the President to discuss the question of expediting the Social Security cases.[97] Certiorari was granted in *Stewart Machine Co.* by the Court on March 29th[98] and on April 26th in *Helvering v. Davis.*[99] The *Carmichael* case came up on appeal.[100] The opinions in the federal cases[101] were written by Justice Cardozo and in the state case by Justice Stone.

In *Stewart Machine* Cardozo made a strong argument for unemployment compensation when he declared:

> During the years 1929 to 1936, when the country was passing through a cyclical depression, the numbers of the unemployed mounted to unprecedented heights. . . . Disaster to the breadwinner meant disaster to dependents. . . . There was need of help from the nation if the people were not to starve. It is too late today for the argument to be heard with tolerance that in a crisis so extreme the use of the moneys of the nation to relieve the unemployed and their dependents is a use for any purpose narrower than the promotion of the general welfare.[102]

He cited *United States v. Butler* as justification for his statement, although the Justice took pains to distinguish the ruling in that case from the present instance.[103] Against the charge of coercion by the federal government on the state, Cardozo stated:

> The statute does not call for a surrender by the states of powers essential to their quasi-sovereign existence. . . . Alabama is still free, without breach of an agreement, to change her system overnight. No officer or agency of the national Government can force a compensation law upon her or keep it in existence.[104]

It was this aspect which had caused the Agricultural Adjustment Act to fall and which was absent from the Social Security Act, as Solicitor General Reed pointed out in a national radio address on September 13, 1937.[105]

In the *Helvering* Case the Justice declared:

> The problem is plainly national in area and dimensions. Moreover, laws of the separate states cannot deal with it effectively. Congress, at least, had a basis for that belief. States and local governments are often lacking in the resources that are necessary to finance .an adequate program of security for the aged. . . . When money is spent to promote the general welfare, the concept of welfare or the opposite is shaped by Congress, not the states. So the concept be not arbitrary, the locality must yield.[106]

Although the Court split five to four in the former case, only McReynolds and Butler dissented in *Helvering v. Davis.* In this case, however, Justices Cardozo, Brandeis, Stone, and Roberts would have dismissed the suit for lack of standing, since Davis, a shareholder of the Edison Electric Illuminating Co. of Boston, could not show irreparable injury.[107]

In a third Social Security case ruled on that day, the Court was asked to decide the validity of the Albama Unemployment Compensation Act and to decide the question of the coercion in the federal depository under the federal act. Justice Stone spoke for the majority:

> It is inherent in the exercise of the power to tax that a state be free to select the subjects of taxation and to grant exemptions. Neither due process nor equal protection imposes upon a state any rigid rule of equality of taxation. . . . but the requirements of due process leave free scope for the exercise of a wide legislative discretion in determining what expenditures will serve the public interest. . . . Support of the poor has long been recognized as a public purpose. [And] . . . poverty is one, but not the only evil consequence of unemployment.[108]

Stone includes a lecture on taxes under our system of government, "the only benefit to which the taxpayer is constitutionally entitled is that derived from his enjoyment of the privileges of living in organized society, established and safeguarded by the devotion of taxes to public purposes."[109] In answer to the second challenge in the suit, that of the federal depository, Stone formulated what was, perhaps, the first definition of *cooperative federalism;*

> The United States and the State of Alabama are not alien governments. They coexist within the same territory. Unemployment within it is their common concern. Together the two statutes now before us embody a cooperative legislative effort by state and national governments, for carrying out a public purpose common to both, for neither could fully achieve without the cooperation of the other. The Constitution does not prohibit such cooperation.[110]

The Court seems to have reversed the position it took in the *Alton Railroad* case, as well as that in *Butler,* that money cannot be taken from one group for the benefit of another. Virginia Wood saw the *Carmichael* decision as "a new interpretation of [the Court's] role in the application of the due process of law clause to state social and economic legislation."[111] And Justice Roberts, reviewing this series of cases in 1951, noted that "when we add this type of federal legislation to that which Congress may enact under the commerce power, it becomes apparent that if Congress so determines, not only local business activities but local social and community services may be taken from the states and, in effect, assumed by the federal government."[112] Arthur Schlesinger maintains:

> For all the defects of the Act, it still meant a tremendous break with the inhibitions of the past. The federal government was at last charged with the obligation to provide its citizens a measure of protection from the hazards and vicissitudes of life. One hundred and ten years earlier, John Quincy Adams had declared that "the great object of the institution of civil government" was "the progressive improvement of the condition of the governed."[113]

Most of the newspapers looked favorably on the decision. The *New York Times* referred to the work of May 24, 1937 as "three great decisions and an opportunity,"[114] while the *Washington Herald* declared that "every intelligent person rejoiced that the Supreme Court finds it legal as well as laudable to carry out the Social Security program."[115] The Washington *Evening Star* found the decision to be the "climax of a trilogy" (*West Coast Hotel* and *Wagner*),[116] and the Baltimore *Sun* reminded its readers that "it was just two years ago this month that the Supreme Court dividing five-to-four ruled that the Railway Pensions Act was unconstitutional."[117] And, finally, the *Philadelphia Record* announced that "Justice Roberts' cook comes through" and continued, "the thirty million American workers protected by unemployment insurance law owe a debt of gratitude to Mr. Justice Roberts' cook. Apparently, the Justice enjoyed his breakfast the day he decided that unemployment insurance was constitutional."[118]

The Justices upheld, once more, the negation of the gold clauses in the Joint Resolution of June 1933, in *Holyoke Water Power Co. v. American Writing Paper Co.*[119] The four Justices who dissented in the first gold cases merely noted their negative vote.

In *Wright v. Vinton Branch of the Mountain Trust Bank of Roanoke,*[120] the Court unanimously upheld the second Frazier-Lemke Act. *Time* noted the difference between the first and second cases:

In May 1935 a Kentucky farmer named Radford lost his farm when
Mr. Justice Brandeis read a unanimous Court opinion nullifying the
[first] ... Act. That act permitted a farmer to declare himself
bankrupt and keep his farm by having it appraised at its current value,
paying this sum to his creditors within five years. This week a Virginia
farmer named Wright kept his farm when Mr. Justice Brandeis read a
unanimous Court opinion upholding the amended ... Act, ... which
permits a bankrupt farmer to keep his property only three years,
meanwhile paying his mortgagee a "reasonable rent." Difference
between the two laws, held the Court, was that the first deprived the
mortgagee of his property rights, while the second does not.[121]

In a similar case, *Kuehner v. Irving Trust Co.,*[122] Roberts spoke for a
unanimous Court, Brandeis and Stone not participating, in upholding that
section of the Federal Bankruptcy Act which limits a landlord's claim for
rent from a bankrupt lessee.

From January to June 1937, the Supreme Court ruled in twenty-one
cases dealing with federal economic power; in only two instances was the
use of this power voided—once regarding a tariff set by the Interstate
Commerce Commission for a railroad spur leased from the Army[123] and
once, as noted above, in *Brush v. Commissioner*, regarding the immunity of
state employees from federal taxation. Roberts' votes coincided with those
of the majority of the members of the Court in all its ruling except the
Brush case, and, it might be noted that, within two years the views
expressed in his dissent became the decision of the Court in *Graves v. New
York ex rel. O'Keefe.*[124]

State Cases and Comment

In the area of state taxation and rate and business regulation, the
Court was less liberal. In eight of twenty cases the activity of the state was
voided.

The Justices unanimously set aside a state commission order in
Thompson v. Consolidated Gas Utility Corp.,[125] which limited the daily
production of gas at the oil fields because such limitation constituted the
taking of private property for private use. According to one commentator,
this decision was "one of the last based on the old-line restrictive interpretation of due process as applied to property rights."[126] One month later,
the Court upheld a similar limitation where discrimination was not
manifested and, through Justice Brandeis, ruled that "the needs of
conservation are to be determined by the Legislature .... [And] no facts
have been found or established by the evidence, which would justify us in

pronouncing the action of the Legislature arbitrary."[127]

The Justices also upheld the annulment by the Missouri Public Service Commission of a rate contract between a utility and its customers[128] and, by a similar nine-to-nothing vote, upheld the power of Georgia to set tobacco warehouse rates.[129] But in *Ohio Bell Telephone Co. v. Public Utility Commission of Ohio*,[130] the nine Justices ruled that the commission had exceeded the constitutional limitation by requiring the company to refund excessive earnings without providing a fair hearing. In a *per curiam* decision, *Railroad Commission of California v. Pacific Gas and Electric Co.*,[131] the Court, dividing four-to-four, let stand the lower court's ruling that the commission could not refuse to hear evidence of reproductive costs when determining rates.[132] The Court of Appeals had cited as the basis for its decision Justice Roberts' opinion in *West v. Chesapeake and Potomac Telephone Co.* in 1935. Arthur Krock speculated that since Justice Sutherland did not participate, Roberts must have cast the fourth vote to uphold the lower court, since he had written the earlier decision.[133] Krock found that as a result of the decision, "from the viewpoint of the Administration, Justice Roberts stands by what it considers a bad and illiberal precedent of the Court's own making. It is sure Justice Sutherland approves, making a majority of five in such instances. On this basis the New Deal justifies the continuation of its struggle further to change the personnel of the Court."[134]

During the period, the Justices found that a legal distinction between a mutual and stock insurance company was discriminatory and therefore void.[135] Justice McReynolds declared that "it is idle to elaborate the differences between mutual and stock companies. These are manifest and admitted. But the statutory discrimination has no reasonable relation to these differences."[136] While Roberts for Brandeis, Stone and Cardozo dissenting, declared that "on its face, the statute is a proper exercise of the state's police power. . . . The presumption of constitutional validity must prevail unless the terms of the statute, or what we judicially know, or facts proved by the appellants, overthrow that presumption."[137]

In the area of taxation the Justices ruled seven times in favor and three times against the use of the power by the state. Continuing the extension of the immunity of federal instrumentalities to include individuals, the Court voided the application of a state income tax to the general counsel of the Panama [Canal] Railroad Company.[138] In a Roberts opinion the members of the Court also thought that a tax on an interstate railroad beyond the amount required for inspection and supervision was violative of both the commerce clause and the Fourteenth Amendment.[139]

And, finally, in *Ingels v. Morf*[140] the Court unanimously voided a "caravan" tax on the interstate transportation of vehicles for sale.

In an apparent reversal of *Colgate v. Harvey, sub rosa,* the Justices upheld a state tax on rent paid to its citizens from holdings outside the state.[141] In a further extension of the subjects of taxation, the Court ruled in *Henneford v. Silas Mason Co.*[142] that a chattels use tax on construction machinery purchased out-of-state was valid. The tax had been levied to "prevent an increase in interstate commerce at the expense of intrastate commerce as a result of the [recently levied] sales tax law. Recognizing the fact that the purpose was to maintain the status quo with respect to interstate commerce and not to injure it, the Supreme Court upheld the measure."[143] In addition, the Court further broadened the power of the state to place a graduated tax on chain stores by upholding a tax determined by the number of stores within the chain.[144]

In the eight cases in which the state's right to legislate for health, welfare, and safety was challenged, the Justices upheld the state in each instance. Half of the cases were decided by five-to-four votes, Van Devanter, McReynolds, Sutherland, and Butler in the minority each time.

The Court unanimously upheld the right of a city to require a weight certificate for load sales of coal, the state's classification of teachers for salary purposes, a state regulation that weight and ingredients be printed on the container, and that cosmetics be registered before sale within the state.[145]

The split votes came in *Highland Farm Dairy v. Agnew,*[146] in which the majority upheld the control of milk prices. Similarly, the Court supported in *Senn. v. Tile Layers' Protective Association*[147] the Wisconsin Labor Code that made peaceful picketing lawful and also prohibited the state courts from issuing injunctions against such demonstrations. Robert G. McCloskey saw in that decision "that the range of allowable legislative judgment was growing, but not that it was unlimited."[148] In this case the Court had upheld a law which was not appreciably different from one that had been voided in *Truax v. Corrigan* in 1921,[149] and Brandeis, who had dissented in the earlier case, wrote the opinion in the present instance.[150] In a third five-to-four decision, the Court upheld the Alabama Unemployment Compensation Act, which was discussed above.[151]

Chronologically, the first of the cases in which the new view of the Court toward state labor legislation was revealed was *West Coast Hotel v. Parrish.*[152] Felix Frankfurter once wrote "there is a lack of scientific method either sustaining or attacking [such] legislation. ... This is not the fault of the courts. It was characteristic of our legislative processes, as well as of the judicial proceedings which called them into question. It was true, substantially, of the social legislation of the 19th Century."[153] The confusion caused by the *Morehead-West Coast Hotel* reversal is a prime example of Frankfurter's contention. The usual basis for the voiding of state legislation in the field of wage control had been the legal concept of *substantive* due process of law. The stages by which this principle was incorporated into constitutional law have been described by John O'Connor:

> ... In the year 1877 in the case of *Davidson v. New Orleans*, 96 U.S. 97, we find a dictum to the effect that the due process clause was a limitation on the legislature of a substantive character affecting life, liberty and property. In the year 1887 in *Mugler v. Kansas*, 123 U.S. 623, the Court again expressed the opinion that this clause was a substantive limitation. But it was not until 1894 that a state police regulation was declared unconstitutional because it was inconsistent with due process of law as a substantive limitation. (See *Reagen v. Farmers' Loan and Trust Co.* 154 U.S. 362.)[154]

And the same author defines the term:

> The whole due process clause therefore means that the rights of liberty and property may not be limited except on the principles of natural law. Expressed in another way: according to the natural law there are fundamental rights of liberty and property whose limitations are determined by the reasonable interests of the commonweal.[155]

In the fourteen cases involving the question of wage legislation decided between 1899 and 1932, the Court voided the statute in only two, *Adkins v. Children's Hospital*[156] and *Connally v. General Construction Company*.[157]

The first general[158] minimum wage case was *Stettler v. O'Hara*,[159] and the Court split four-to-four, thereby upholding the state supreme court's validation of the law; Justice Brandeis did not participate because he had been a counsel in the earlier stages.[160] But six years later the Justices, by a five-to-three vote, Brandeis again not participating, ruled that a District of Columbia minimum wage law violated the due process clause of the Fifth Amendment. Justice Sutherland stated that liberty of contract was a part of the liberty of the individual guaranteed by the Constitution. Thomas Reed Powell disagreed with the Justice. "No such doctrine," Powell declared, "is stated in the Constitution. As a statement of fact, it is unsupported by the balance on the ledger of Supreme Court decisions, for the catalogue shows that the Court has sustained many more regulatory statutes than it has annulled."[161]

However, so sure did the striking down of the Washington law seem in view of the *Adkins-Morehead* precedents that the Massachusetts Legislature requested Congress to propose an amendment "to provide for the determination and establishment of minimum wages for women and children."[162]

The facts in the case were:

> Off and on from 1933 to 1935, the Cascadia Hotel of Wenatchee Wash. employed Mrs. Elsie Parrish as a chambermaid for $12 a week. Under Washington's Minimum Wage Law for women she should have got $14.50 for her 48-hour week. She demanded what the law said was coming to her. The hotel offered $17 in settlement. Elsie Parrish spurned it. She sued for $216.19.[163]

Justice Roberts described what occurred after the Washington Supreme Court upheld Mr. and Mrs. Parrish:

> August 17, 1936, an appeal was filed in *West Coast Hotels* [sic] *Company v. Parrish*, 300 U.S. 379. The Court as usual met to consider applications in the week of Monday, October 5, 1936 and concluded its work by Saturday, October 10. During the conferences the jurisdictional statement in the *Parrish* case was considered and the question arose whether the appeal should be dismissed (Evidently he meant should be reversed summarily, since the Washington Supreme Court had sustained the statute. – Frankfurter) on the authority of *Adkins* and *Morehead*. Four of those who had voted in the majority in the *Morehead* case voted to dismiss the appeal in the *Parrish* case. I stated that I would vote for the notation of probable jurisdiction. I am not sure that I gave my reason, but it was that in the appeal in the *Parrish* case the authority of *Adkins* was definitely assailed and the Court was asked to reconsider and overrule it. Thus, for the first time, I was confronted with the necessity of facing the soundness of the *Adkins* case. Those who were in the majority in the *Morehead* case expressed some surpise at my vote, and I heard one of the brethren ask another, "What is the matter with Roberts?"[164]

The question presented here was *procedurally* the same as that in *Morehead*—whether to uphold the highest court in the state in its view of its own law. In *Morehead* the New York court had ruled that there was no difference between the New York statute and the District of Columbia (*Adkins*) law, and the United States Supreme Court agreed.[165] However, in *Parrish* the state supreme court had upheld the law. *Practically*, however, the two cases were worlds apart. As has been noted, in *Morehead* the New York attorneys had not asked that *Adkins* be overruled, while in the present case the *Adkins* precedent was attacked.

The then assistant Attorney General Robert Jackson described the scene as the Chief Justice began reading his opinion:

> The room was crowded with spectators, and a long double line of those who could not get in extended through the majestic corridors to the outer portals of the building. The distinguished visitors' seats were filled with important personages. The wives of most of the Justices betrayed by their presence and gravity that something unusual was to happen. . . .
> To one who sat at the government counsel table the spectacle of the Court that day frankly and completely reversing itself and striking down its opinion but a few months old was a moment never to be forgotten. The Chief Justice read the opinion confessing error. But his voice was of triumph. He was reversing his Court, but not himself. He was declaring in March the law as he would have declared it the previous June, had his dissent been heeded. What made the June 1936 minority a June 1937 majority was the changed vote of Mr. Justice Roberts.[166]

Also, Carl Brent Swisher believed:

> The Chief Justice handled the opinion in such a way as to give a moderately plausible excuse for the different positions of Justice Roberts in the two cases, but the feeling of the public, and probably of the bar as well, was that Justice Roberts had deemed it expedient to change his position because of the movement to reorganize the Court.[167]

Swisher's view can be supported from the Chief Justice's comment that the appellees claim that *Adkins* is distinguishable is "obviously futile."[168] He continued:

> We think that the question which was not deemed to be open in the *Morehead* case is open and is necessarily presented here. The Supreme Court of Washington has upheld the minimum wage statute of that State. It has decided that the statutue is a reasonable exercise of the police power of the state. . . . We are of the opinion that this ruling of the state court demands on our part a reexamination of the *Adkins* case.[169]

The Chief Justice stated:

> The constitutional provision invoked is the due process clause of the Fourteenth Amendment governing the States, as the due process clause invoked in the *Adkins* case governed Congress. . . . What is this freedom [of contract]? The Constitution does not speak of freedom of contract. It speaks of liberty and prohibits the deprivation of liberty without due process of law. In prohibiting that deprivation the Constitution does not recognize an absolute and uncontrollable

liberty. . . . Liberty under the Constitution is thus necessarily subject to the restraints of due process, and regulation which is reasonable in relation to its subject and is adopted in the interests of the community is due process. . .Freedom of contract is a qualified and not an absolute right. There is no absolute freedom to do as one wills or to contract as one chooses. .... Liberty implies the absence of arbitrary restraint, not immunity from reasonable regulations and prohibitions imposed in the interest of the community.[170]

"We think," Hughes declared, "that the decision in the Adkins case was a departure from the true application of the principles governing the regulation by the State of the relation of the employer and employed,"[171] and the opinion quoted at length from the Nebbia opinion of Mr. Roberts. The majority then noted that poor wages places a burden on the whole community by increasing those on poor relief. "The community is not bound to provide what is in effect a subsidy for unconscionable employers. The community may direct its law-making power to correct the abuse which springs from their selfish disregard of the public interest."[172] The Court, through the Chief Justice, announced "our conclusion is that the case of Adkins v. Children's Hospital, supra, should be, and it is, overruled."[173]

Two months later, one commentator noted that the decision was an anticlimax because from the announcing of the Adkins opinion "until March 29th of this year, the minimum-wage problem in constitutional law was: How long would the precedent of the Adkins case be preserved by the Court against the pressure of prevailing judicial and legistlative thought?"[174]

Sutherland, whose opinion in the Adkins case was being repudiated, spoke for the four dissenters. Professor Swisher described the dissent as

> . . . an eloquent defense by the most fluent and the most scholarly of the four conservatives. It contains much with which any justice would agreee; when viewed in terms of its application, however, it was the expression of a dying philosophy. The time had passed when Justice Sutherland and others holding his point of view were to dominate the interpretation of constitutional law.[175]

"Correctly reading the Parrish decision as the beginning of the Court's capitulation to the New Deal fight," noted Walter F. Murphy and C. Herman Pritchett, "Sutherland tried to answer Stone's Butler dissent,"[176] but, as Robert McCloskey pointed out, the two dissents "are not a dialogue between men who share a common ground but disagree about its implications. The opinions represent wholly different realms of discourse."[177]

The dissent began with a statement that "a sufficient answer to all that is now said will be found in the opinions of the court in [past] cases."[178] A paragraph was then given over to the question whether a judge could rest his opinion upon the fact that the preponderance of judges, federal and state, had upheld the principle of minimum-wage control. The *United States Law Review* comments that "this statement seems to have no point unless one of the members of the Court was persuaded or urged to vote to uphold the statute on the ground that other members of the Court deemed it constitutional."[179]

Sutherland then answered Stone's *Butler* contention that the only restraint upon the exercise of judicial power is judicial self-restraint, terming it "ill considered and mischievous." He noted: "Self-restraint belongs in the domain of will and not of judgment."[180] In answer to the majority's view that economic necessity should be considered, the Justice replied: "The meaning of the Constitution does not change with the ebb and flow of economic events; to say that it does is to rob that instrument of the essential element which continues it in force as the people have made it until they, and not their official agents, have made it otherwise."[181] Because the freedom of contract principle under the due process of law clause of the Fourteenth Amendment is "no longer open to question," the Washington statute had to fall.[182]

Stone's illness was critical to the timing of the decision, as Roberts noted in his memorandum to Frankfurter:

> Justice Stone was taken ill about October 14.[183] The case was argued December 16 and 17, in the absence of Justice Stone, who at that time was lying in a comatose condition at his home. It came for consideration at the conference on December 19. I voted for affirmance. There were three other such votes, those of the Chief Justice, Justice Brandeis, and Justice Cardozo. The other four voted for reversal.
>
> If a decision had then been announced, the case would have been affirmed by a divided Court. It was thought that this would be an unfortunate outcome, as everyone on the Court knew Justice Stone's views.[184] The case was, therefore, laid over for further consideration when Justice Stone should be able to participate. Justice Stone was convalescent during January and returned to the sessions of the Court on February 1, 1937. I believe that the *Parrish* case was taken up at the conference on February 6, 1937, and Justice Stone then voted for affirmance. This made it possible to assign the case for an opinion, which was done. The decision affirming the lower court was announced March 29, 1937.[185]

Since the eight Justices wished to avoid another *Stettler* vote, they had postponed their decision. Therefore, when Roosevelt announced his Court

Plan request on February 5th, any subsequent decision handed down by the Court seemed to be in response to that threat. In fact, Hughes decided to withhold "his opinion for a short time to avoid the impression of an immediate response to the court-packing plan."[186]

Four years later Roosevelt wrote:

> I have confidence that after this decision and the other decisions mentioned [before] the due process clause will not soon again be misused so as to create a barrier to progressive social legislation. I have confidence that the protection of fundamental human rights afforded by the due process clause will be strengthened by this rejection of its perverted use to restrain the legitimate exercise of legislative power for the general welfare.[187]

Attorney General Cummings declared:

> Thus after twenty years of unabated struggle, minimum wage legislation is for the first time sustained by the Supreme Court by a bare majority vote. . . . Only by the vacillating vote of a single justice was the constitutional right of the state legislatures reinstated after what seemed to be a hopeless struggle.[188]

On April 6th the President notified the Speaker of The House and the President of the Senate that the Attorney General had advised him that the *West Coast Hotel* decision "has rendered the [District of Columbia minimum-wage] statute once more effective."[189]

A commentator in the *United States Law Review* noted in April, 1937 that "it should be observed that in upholding the Washington statute in the *Parrish* case, the Court went farther than it would have had to go in order to uphold the New York [Morehead] statute . . . ."[190] Robert E. Rhodes, Jr., assistant professor of law at the Notre Dame Law School, commenting on the case, declared that the principle behind the decision is "that a person who devotes his productive activity to a business is entitled to be supported, together with his dependents, by that business. . . ."[191]

Newspaper comments on the decision, while critical of the circumstances surrounding it, were fulsome in their praise. "A good day's work," quipped the New York *Herald-Tribune*[192] while the pro-New Deal New York *World-Telegram* asked: ". . . Did you notice that big judicial wash the nine elderly gentlemen hung out yesterday, a sizable day's work wasn't it?"[193] The editorial also noted that Senator Henry Ashurst had welcomed Justice Roberts into the school of inconsistency upon hearing of the decision.[194] Franklyn Waltman in *The Washington Post* declared that "the judicial 'No Man's Land' between state and federal governments has been wiped out."[195] And the Baltimore *Sun* noted that the Court was "true to itself."[196] The Philadelphia *Evening Bulletin* called it "a tremendous reversal,"[197] but the *Cleveland Plain Dealer* wrote that the law is now "as Justice Roberts holds."[198] "Owen J. Roberts, Rex," was the title of the *Philadelphia Record's* editorial which asked, "Is Owen J. Roberts, an ex-corporation lawyer, a king that he can safely govern our destinies?"[199] The attack on the Justice was accompanied by an editorial cartoon by Jerry Doyle entitled, "The Constitution is what one judge says it is."[200] Arthur Krock qualified that declaration to read thus: "The Constitution, in so far as the power of the states to fix minimum wages for women (and women only) is concerned, is today what Justice Roberts says it is."[201] And, finally, the *New York Times* instructed its readers that "not often in its long history has the Supreme Court handed down on a single day three major decisions of more immediate interest than those which were read on Monday, and part of this interest reflects the fact that each decision has helped in its own way to clarify some phase of the present controversy over the Court itself."[202]

Charles Curtis some time later reflected that "it was a bit ironical that in the battle between the Old Court and the New Deal, the Court's lines should break over what was not New Deal at all."[203]

In summary, in state power cases presented to the Court during the first five months of 1937, the Justices arrived at some very liberal decisions, though the overall record on state activity (78%) increased only six percentage points over the previous three and a half year period. Justice Roberts dissented in only one case,[204] again making his record almost a replica of the Court's line of decisions.

The total record of the Court, however, because of the support given to government in the federal cases, shows a more favorable posture. In forty-one of fifty cases discussed, the Justices rule favorably on the use of governmental power, which represents eighty-two percent as compared to sixty-two percent during the previous period and seventy percent in the 1930 to 1933 time bracket. Of the favorable opinions, twenty-four were unanimous, and in opinions against the government, five were unanimous; eleven favorable opinions were decided by the margin of one vote, while two anti-government opinions were five-to-four. These latter figures show that in a number of decisions, the vote of one justice could again have changed the position of the Court. This fear led the administration to continue its struggle for the court reorganization bill, despite the victories in 1937.

THE CONSTITUTION IS WHAT ONE JUDGE SAYS IT IS.

Notes

[1] J. Alsop & T. Catledge, *The 168 Days,* Chapter Title. Mr. Alsop confirmed that he was the originator of the quip "A Switch in Time Saves Nine" in a letter to the author dated July 7, 1964.

[2] *The Struggle for Judicial Supremacy,* p. xv.

[3] *University of Pennsylvania Law Review,* Vol. 104, p. 347.

[4] Corwin, pp. 64-65.

[5] B. Swartz, *The Supreme Court; Constitutional Revolution in Retrospect* (New York, 1957), p. 20.

[6] Dean Dunwoody, "Surprise Decision Widens the Commerce Clause," *New York Times,* April 18, 1937, sec. 4, p. 3.

[7] *Virginia Railway Co. v. System Fed. #40, A.F.L.,* 300 U.S. 515 (1937).

[8] 300 U.S. 379 (1937).

[9] E.S. Corwin, *Liberty v. Government* (Baton Rouge, 1948), p. 159.

[10] Swartz, p. 22.

[11] *The Judicial Process,* p. 113.

[12] 299 U.S. 334.

[13] *Ibid.,* at 346.

[14] *Ibid.,* at 345.

[15] *Hammer v. Dagenhart,* 247 U.S. 251 (1918).

[16] Jackson, p. 203.

[17] January 6, 1937, p. 18.

[18] 300 U.S. 515 (1937).

[19] Stern, p. 674, *Texas and New Orleans RR. v. Brotherhood of Railway Clerks,* 281 U.S. 584 (1930).

[20] V. Wood, *Due Process of Law* (Baton Rouge, 1951), p. 159.

[21] 11 F. Supp. 621 (E.D. Va. 1935).

[22] 84 Federal 2nd 641 (C.C.A. 4th 1936).

[23] *Roosevelt Library,* File 41-A, Cummings to Roosevelt, February 11, 1937.

[24] April 5, 1937, p. 12.

[25] Stone to Youngsters, April 1, 1937 quoted in A.T. Mason, "Harlan Fiske Stone and FDR's Court Plan." *Yale Law Journal* LXI (1952), 810-11.

[26] *American Constitutional Development, 948.*

[27] 300 U.S. 515 at 555-56.

[28] *Ibid.,* at 557, 559.

[29] p. 160.

[30] "Labor and the Liberals," *The Nation,* May 1, 1935 quoted in Schlesinger, 11, 401.

[31] Leutenberg, p. 150-51.

[32] Burns, p. 220.

[33] *F.D.R. Papers,* 1937 vol., pp. 272-73.

[34] Schlesinger, III, 490.

[35] Interview with the author, April 8, 1963.

[36] S. Cohen, *State Labor Legislation, 1937-1947* (Columbus, 1948), p. 108.

[37] *Op. cit.,* 214.

[38] *Boston Law Review* XIX (1939), 132.

[39] *Nine Honest Men* (New York, 1936), p. 38.

[40] 1 NLRB 1 (1935).

[41] Stern, p. 675n.

[42] *NLRB v. Jones and Laughlin Steel Corporation,* 301 U.S. 1; *NLRB v. Fruehauf Trailer Co.,*301 U.S. 49; *NLRB v. Friedman-Harry Marks Clothing Co.,* 301 U.S. 58 (1937).

[43] *Associated Press v. NLRB,* 301 U.S. 103; *Washington, Virginia and Maryland Coach Co.,* 301 U.S. 142 (1937).

[44] Stone, p. 460.

[45] 301 U.S. 1–25, 27.

[46] *Ibid.,* 30.

[47] *Ibid.,* 31.

[48] *Ibid.,* 32.

[49] *Ibid.,* 33-34.

[50] *Ibid.,* 36-37.

[51] *Ibid.,* 40-41.

[52] *Ibid.,* 43.

[53] 301 U.S. 58, 97.

[54] *Ibid.,* 99.

[55] April 13, 1937, p. 10.

[56] April 13, 1937, p. 12.

[57] April 13, 1937, p. 1.

[58] *F.D.R. Papers,* 1937 vol., p. 153.

[59] *Philadelphia Inquirer,* April 13, 1937, p. 14.

[60] 301 U.S. 103, 122.

[61] *Ibid.,* 127-130.

[62] *Ibid.,*132-33.

[63] *Ibid.,* 140.

[64] *Ibid.,* 141.

[65] Schlesinger, III, p. 457.

[66] April 14, 1937, editorial page.

[67] *F.D.R. Papers,* 1937 vol, p. 154.

[68] Roosevelt on occasion used the rhetorical strategem of "quoting others" in order to get a point across. See S. Rosenman, *Working with Roosevelt* (New York, 1952), p. 158.

[69] *F.D.R. Papers, loc. cit.*

[70] Stern, p. 885; M.G. Lee, "Notes on Wagner Decision," *Illinois Bar Quarterly* XXV (1937), 378.

[71] *The Court and the Constitution,* p. 49.

[72] Interview with Judge Charles Fahy; D. Yorkey, "Notes on Interstate Commerce Cases," *Cornell Law Quarterly* XXII (1937), 754.

[73] Interview with Merlo Pusey, March 14, 1963.

[74] A. Cox, "Federalism in the Law of Labor Relations," *Harvard Law Review* LXVII (1954), 1299.

[75] Yorkey, p. 569.

[76] April 13, 1937, p. 1.

[77] *Ibid.,* "In Washington," p. 24.

[78] 300 U.S. 352.

[79] *Ibid.,* 374.

[80] *Ibid.*, 378.

[81] *United States v. Hudson,* 299 U.S. 498 (1937)

[82] Rodell, p. 284.

[83] 300 U.S. 506 (1937).

[84] *Ibid.*, 513-14.

[85] "Social and Economic Control through Federal Taxation," *Minnesota Law Review* XVIII (1934), 764.

[86] 301 U.S. 308.

[87] *Ibid.*, 315.

[88] *Ibid.*, 324.

[89] 301 U.S. 337.

[90] Jackson, p. 233.

[91] page 12.

[92] *Roosevelt Library,* File 1710, Telegram from Winant to Roosevelt, September 28, 1936.

[93] Schlesinger, II, 298-312.

[94] 89 F (2d) 393.

[95] 89 Fed. (2d) 207 (1936).

[96] *Carmichael v. Southern Coal and Coke Co.,* 17 F Supp. 225 (1936).

[97] *Roosevelt Library,* File 1710.

[98] 300 U.S. 652.

[99] 301 U.S. 674.

[100] 301 U.S. 495 at 505.

[101] *Stewart Machine Co. v. Davis,* 301 U.S. 584; *Helvering v. Davis,* 301 U.S. 619.

[102] 301 U.S. 584, 587.

[103] *Ibid.*, 592-93.

[104] *Ibid.*, 593, 595.

[105] *Roosevelt Library,* 10 F "The Constitution," delivered on Station WMAL, Washington, D.C. for the NBC Network.

[106] 301 U.S. 619, 644-45.

[107] *Ibid.*, 639.

[108] 301 U.S. 495, 509, 514-15, 518-19.

[109] *Ibid.*, 552

[110] *Ibid.*, 526.

[111] Wood, p. 157.

[112] *The Court and The Constitution,* p. 61.

[113] Schlesinger, II, 315.

[114] May 25, 1937, p. 36.

[115] May 25, 1937, p. 6.

[116] May 25, 1937, A 10.

[117] May 25, 1937, p. 12.

[118] May 25, 1937, p. 10.

[119] 300 U.S. 324.

[120] 300 U.S. 440.

[121] April 5, 1937, p. 12.

[122] 299 U.S. 445.

[123] *Powell v. United States,* 300 U.S. 276.

[124] 306 U.S. 466 (1939).

[125] 300 U.S. 55.

[126] Wood, p. 183.

[127] *Henderson Co. v. Thompson*, 300 U.S. 258.

[128] *Midland Realty Co. v. Kansas City Power and Light Co.*, 300 U.S. 109.

[129] *Townsend v. Yeomans*, 301 U.S. 441.

[130] 301 U.S. 292.

[131] 301 U.S. 669.

[132] 13 *F. Sup.* 931 (1936).

[133] Krock wrote to the author on February 5, 1964 that he could not substantiate the speculation but "since my lifetime effort has been not to use such speculation without basing it on a source I considered authoritative and reliable, I assume that the one you cite was not an exception."

[134] "In Washington," The *New York Times*, June 8, 1937, p. 24.

[135] *Hartford Insurance Co. v. Harrison*, 301 U.S. 459.

[136] *Ibid.*, 463.

[137] *Ibid.*, 465.

[138] *New York ex rel. Rogers v. Graves*, 299 U.S. 401.

[139] *Great Northern Railway Co. v. Washington*, 300 U.S. 154.

[140] 300 U.S. 290.

[141] *New York ex rel. Cohn v. Graves*, 300 U.S. 308. The formal overruling came in *Madden v. Kentucky*, 309 U.S. 83 (1940).

[142] 300 U.S. 577.

[143] Swisher, *American Constitutional Development*, p. 979.

[144] *Great A. and P. Tea Co. v. Grosjean*, 301 U.S. 412 (1937).

[145] *Hague v. Chicago*, 299 U.S. 387; *Phelps v. Board of Education*, 300 U.S. 319; *National Fertilizer Association v. Bradley*, 301 U.S. 178; *Bourjois, Inc. v. Chapman*, 301 U.S. 183 (1937).

[146] 300 U.S. 608.

[147] 301 U.S. 468.

[148] *The Supreme Court Review, 1962,* "Economic Due Process and the Supreme Court," p. 37.

[149] 257 U.S. 312.

[150] R. Horn, *Groups and the Constitution* (Stanford, 1956), p. 71.

[151] *Carmichael v. Southern Coal and Coke Co.*, *supra*.

[152] 300 U.S. 379.

[153] "History of Labor and Realism in Constitutional Law." *Harvard Law Review* XXIX (1929), 363-64.

[154] *The Supreme Court and Labor* (published doctoral dissertation, The Catholic University of America, Washington, D.C., 1932.) p. 102.

[155] *Ibid.*, 117.

[156] 261 U.S. 525 (1923).

[157] 269 U.S. 385 (1926); O'Connor, pp. 15-55, O'Connor does not include the two cases based on *Adkins* cited by Curtis, *Lions under the Throne*, p. 163.

[158] The others dealt with specific industries.

[159] 243 U.S. 629 (1917).

[160] "Notes and Comment," *United States Law Review* LXXI (1937), 185.

[161] "Judiciality of Minimum Wage Legislation," *Harvard Law Review* XXXVII (1924), 555.

[162] *Roosevelt Library*, File 274, Resolution passed by Massachusetts House of Representatives on February 9, 1937, by the Senate on February 18, 1937.

[163] *Time*, April 5, 1937, p. 11.

[164] Frankfurter, "Mr. Justice Roberts," p. 315.

[165] Pusey, *The Supreme Court Crisis*, p. 49.

[166] Jackson, p. 207-08.

[167] *American Constitutional Development*, p. 946.

[168] 300 U.S. 388.

[169] *Ibid.*, 389-90.

[170] *Ibid.*, 391-92.

[171] *Ibid.*, 397.

[172] *Ibid.*, 399-400.

[173] *Ibid.*, 400.

[174] J.K. Cheadle, "The Parrish Case, Minimum Wages for Women and Perhaps for Men," *University of Cincinnati Law Review* XI (1937), 308.

[175] *American Constitutional Development*, p. 948.

[176] *Courts, Judges, and Politics* (New York, 1961), p. 632.

[177] McCloskey, p. 43.

[178] 300 U.S. 379, 401.

[179] "Notes and Comment," LXXI (1937), 186.

[180] 300 U.S. 379, 402.

[181] *Ibid.*, 403-04.

[182] *Ibid.*, 405-06.

[183] The exact date was October 12—See Mason, "Stone and FDR's Court Plan," p. 793.

[184] These had been expressed in discussion in conference on the *Morehead* case during the previous term.

[185] Frankfurter, "Mr. Justice Roberts," p. 315.

[186] Pusey, *Hughes*, p. 757.

[187] *F.D.R. Papers*, 1937 vol., p. 150.

[188] *Roosevelt Library*, File 41—Judicial Reorganization, filed May 27, 1937; Although there is no reference to an author, there are passages which are similar in wording to a statement made on March 31, 1937 by Cummings — See *Selected Papers of Homer S. Cummings*, ed. C.B. Swisher (New York, 1939), pp. 155-56.

[189] *F.D.R. Papers*, 1937 vol., pp. 146-48.

[190] "Notes and Comment," LXXI, 183.

[191] Rhodes, p. 25.

[192] March 30, 1937, p. 24.

[193] March 30, 1937, p. 18.

[194] Ashurst had been criticized for his switch from opposition to support of the President's Court Packing Plan. — See *Time*, April 5, 1937, p. 12n.

[195] March 30, 1937, p. 1.

[196] March 30, 1937, p. 12.

[197] March 29, 1937, p. 8.

[198] March 31, 1937, p. 6.

[199] March 30, 1937, p. 8.

[200] See Figure 2.
[201] "In Washington," The *New York Times,* March 30, 1937, p. 22.
[202] March 31, 1937, p. 22.
[203] *Lions under the Throne,* p. 140.
[204] *Hartford Insurance Co. v. Harrison, supra.*

Chapter IV

"...That Saved Nine."

1937

Professor Mario Einaudi tells us:

> The question fascinated observers of the American scene have tried to answer ever since 1937 has, of course, been this: Why did the Supreme Court reverse itself so drastically? Why did the Supreme Court apparently find it so simple, after 1936, to justify both the bold intervention and the expansion of federal and state governments in novel directions? Why, indeed, when during the worst period of the national emergency the Court had firmly refused to alter its constitutional thinking?[1]

The answer to these questions is one of the goals of the present analysis, at least as far as Mr. Justice Roberts can give us an answer.

Mr. Justice William J. Brennan, describing the process whereby a justice arrives at a decision, noted:

> In a very real sense, each decision is an individual decision of every justice. The process can be a lonely, troubling experience for fallible human beings conscious that their best may not be adequate to the challenge.... One does not forget how much may depend on his decision. He knows that usually more than the litigants may be affected, that the vital social, economic, and political currents may be directed. ...
>
> It is inevitable,...that Supreme Court decisions—and the Justices themselves—should be caught up in public debate and be the subjects of bitter controversy.[2]

And in a work cut short by his death, Justice Robert H. Jackson warned:

> When the Court goes too far in interfering with the processes of the majority, it will again encounter a drive against its power or personnel. ... Every Justice has been accused of legislation, and every one has joined in that accusation of others. When the Court has gone too far, it has provoked reactions which have set back the cause it is

designated to advance and sometimes called down upon itself severe rebuke.[3]

It was just such a situtation which faced the Court in early 1937, for while Chief Justice Hughes could declare on May 7, 1936, "I am happy to report that the Supreme Court is still functioning,"[4] the administration and many others throughout the nation were of the opinion that it was not functioning properly. When, therefore, in early 1937 the Court suddenly reversed itself, the nation could but wonder why, and the "swing man," Justice Roberts' failure to supply an answer, did not help to reduce the criticism which was heaped upon the Court and upon Roberts personally. Even close observers of the Court were unable to comprehend the change, as is seen, for example, in the following excerpt from a letter to Justice Stone from the then Professor Felix Frankfurter, following the announcement of the *Parrish* decision:

> Roberts' somersault is incapable of being attributed to a single factor relevant to the professional judicial process. Everything that he now subscribes to, he rejected not only on June first last, but as late as October 12th, when New York's petition for a rehearing was denied. ... I wish either Roberts or the Chief had the responsibility of conducting the class (on federal jurisdiction at Harvard) when we reach this case shortly. It is a very sad business.[5]

Professor Einaudi, himself, posits numerous reasons for the change: political pressure, the overwhelming victory of the administration at the polls in November, 1936, the labor strife, especially in the automotive industry, Roosevelt's Court Reorganization plan, and, "finally, Justice Roberts, even though reluctant to take the lead, remained open to persuasion and gradually became convinced of the need for change."[6] Which of these, all of these, or none of these, effected the change? These are questions which after thirty plus years have still not been answered.

Various Non-Political Factors

"There was ... evidence, " Einaudi comments, "which must have impressed with particular forcefulness judges who, like Hughes and Roberts, either were politically sensitive or occupied a middle-of-the-road position, of the damaging quality of some of the labor disturbances which were then sweeping the country."[7] Those in Detroit were especially violent, and the failure of local and state authorities to check the violence and to provide solutions to the problems demonstrated the need for a national approach. The General Motors "sit-down" strike in Flint, Michigan indirectly involved some 110,000 workers.[8] The turmoil resulted from the unionization of the automotive and steel industries by the Committee for Industrial Organization, which at this time was still within the American Federation of Labor, although it was becoming a dissident group within the parent organization.[9]

The failure of the Court to rule in favor of the power of the federal government to legislate in the area of labor-management relations in the *Carter Coal* case, as well as the decision in the *Schechter* case, caused organized labor to turn its guns on the supreme tribunal. William Green, President of the AFL, testifying before the Senate Judiciary Subcommittee on March 16, 1937 during the hearings on the Reorganization Bill, declared that "such majority opinions, adverse to such legislation, are certainly not the kind to be expected from judges trained and tested by the realities of current life and experienced in the facts and disorders with which such legislation has to deal."[10]

Indeed, in the *Carter* case Justice Cardozo had protested in his dissent that what was held in *Nebbia* regarding the milk business could be said "with equal, if not greater force, of the conditions and practices in the bituminous coal industry."[11] The Justice continued:

> There were strikes, at time nation-wide in extent, at other times spreading over broad areas and many mines, with the accompaniment of violence and bloodshed and misery and bitter feeling. The sordid tale is unfolded in many a document and treatise . . . in the weeks immediately preceding the passage of this Act the country was threatened once more with a strike of ominous proportions. The plight of the industry was not merely a menace to the owners and mine workers: it was and had long been a menace to the public, deeply concerned in a steady and uniform supply of fuel so vital to the national economy.[12]

Professor John Hannold of the University of Pennsylvania Law School, who served under Roberts when the latter returned to his alma mater as dean in 1948, as well as Vice-dean John J. Broderick of the Notre Dame Law School, believed that the influence of the 1936 strike epidemic can be seen in the *Jones and Laughlin* decision,[13] and the Chief Justice's words seem to support that view:

> The fact remains that the stoppage of those operations by industrial strife would have a most serious effect upon interstate commerce. . . . It is obvious that it would be immediate and might be catastrophic. We are asked to shut our eyes to the plainest facts of

our national life and *to deal with the question of direct and indirect effects* in an intellectual vacuum. ... [Italics supplied] Refusal to confer and negotiate has been one of the most prolific causes of strife. This is such an outstanding fact in the history of labor disturbances that it is a proper subject of judicial notice and requires no citation of instances. ... The fact that there appears to have been no major disturbance in that [the steel] industry in the more recent period did not dispose of the possibilities of future and like dangers to interstate commerce which Congress was entitled to foresee and to exercise its protective power to forestall.[14]

John H. Leek, in his study of *Government and Labor in the United States,* believes that such "reasoning may seem very commonplace and common sense to us today, but it comes very near marking a revolution in the interpretation of the Constitution."[15] And Justice Roberts, himself, while discussing the case some years later, noted the importance of the question of strikes in the thinking of Congress in the passage of the law and, by implication, in the thinking of the Court in upholding it:

Once the doctrine was established that, in order to protect the power of regulation in the national field, federal agencies might interfere with state regulation, a wide door was opened for economic and welfare legislation on a national scale, and much such legislation has followed. A few instances must suffice. One is the National Labor Relations Act. That act premises its provisions upon the proposition that industrial conflicts interfere with and limit interstate transportation and commerce. Albeit a strike is localized in a given community, the flow of goods to and from that community is interfered with. The interference may be so great as to be a matter of national concern. Therefore, such interferences should be dealt with at the source and however small at their inception. On this premise, Congress proceeded to legislate with respect to collective bargaining and to labor relations in general, even though the situations with which the statute deals are in their essence purely local.[16]

One area of influence on judicial thinking which is seldom investigated is that of the law journals. The opinions of the authorities in one's field is always important; and that this was true for the members of the Supreme Court during this period can be seen from the comments of Justice Stone. When Thomas Reed Powell wrote an imaginary judicial opinion lampooning Stone's opinion in *Educational Films Corporation v. Ward*[17] in 1931 in the *Harvard Law Review*, Stone told Powell that his article gave him "a good laugh," and "I should have preferred to have written your opinion than the one which will actually appear in the books."[18] And again, following the announcement of the *Schechter* decision, Stone wrote Powell that "I hope you will cut loose and tell us what you think,"[19] and later when Powell's

comments on that case did appear in the *Harvard Law Review,* Stone
wrote, "I am going to pray that I may avoid deserving the hiding you gave
one of my brethren in your law review article."[20] Stone, himself, insisted
that his own address given on the occasion of the tercentenary of Harvard
College be printed, because, according to his biographer, only then would it
be read by the "Supreme Court Justices—the most crucial target."[21]

In a number of opinions during this period Justices Brandeis and
Cardozo cited articles from various law journals.[22] Other extra-judicial
sources had their influence as well; Justice Roberts dissenting in *Hartford
Insurance Co. v. Harrison*[23] cited an article in the *Encyclopedia of The
Social Sciences.*

Paul Freund points out another influence, which, while not surprising,
is frequently forgotten:

> The company who share the lawmaking activity of the Supreme Court
> judges include at least the lower tribunals as well as counsel. The
> deference paid to the views of other judicial or administrative officers
> will necessarily be affected by the regard in which they are
> held. ... One may be permitted to wonder whether the decision in
> *Betts v. Brady* ... would have been the same had the opinion of the
> court below been written by someone less highly esteemed than Chief
> Judge Bond of Maryland, who is referred to by name in Mr. Justice
> Roberts' opinion no less than fifteen times.[24]

It has already been indicated that newspaper editorial comment varied
on the decisions of the Court during the 1930 to 1937 period. Although
highly favorable in the earlier period, the strict construction of the
constitutional powers of government during the economic crisis caused
more and more criticism after 1933. This change was obvious when it was
noted that only ten editorials in the country favored the *Morehead*
decision. Certainly, the Justices were affected by the criticism of the
newspapers. The whole issue of popular opinion at this time is clouded
because the newspapers of the period were on the whole controlled by
anti-New Deal elements of society.[25] Hughes' biographer tells us that the
Chief was disturbed by the outbursts following three adverse decisions: "in
three important cases within two weeks the Court repudiated his
leadership. That in itself was a minor matter, but the Chief Justice was
convinced, as his ringing dissent in the *Morehead* case showed, that the
Court was inflicting fresh wounds upon itself. ...Everywhere the prestige
of the judiciary was sinking."[26] Robert G. McCloskey analyzes the
question of judicial response to public opinion and finds:

> We now suspect that it was *lese majeste* to suggest in earlier days —

that judges were not entirely aware of public opinion. But we have not attempted to understand in what sense public opinion may affect the judicial process, unless indeed we make the completely unwarrantable assumption that our constitutional judges simply check the latest Gallup polls or election returns and then hasten to their courtrooms to vote accordingly. It may be in fact that what seems responsiveness to public opinion is something subtly different; *concurrence* with public opinion, arising from the fact that judges are themselves members of the public. The distinction, if valid, is surely significant; . . . and we should ask, incidentally, not only whether public opinion does play a part in determining the path of judicial doctrine, but whether it *should*.[27]

Professor McCloskey arrives at the conclusion that in certain fundamental areas it should not. On the other hand, Carl Brent Swisher writes that "the Court, for all its aloofness, cannot be regarded as completely separated from the populace,"[28] and he also notes that even individual justices are not certain about the part that should be played by popular opinion in their decisions. As an illustration, Swisher offers two quotes from the writings of Felix Frankfurter. In 1949 the Justices held that "a court which yields to the popular will thereby licenses itself to practice despotism, for there can be no assurance that it will not on another occasion indulge its own will,"[29] while one year earlier he had declared: "Our constitutional system makes it the court's duty to interpret those feelings of society to which the due process gives legal protection"[30] Professor Swisher concludes his observations with the incisive statement:

The Supreme Court is able to lead in constitutional development, then, only by virtue of that fact that its leadership is of such a character that the people and their representatives are willing to follow. To put the matter more simply, the Supreme Court succeeds in leading largely to the extent of its skill not merely as a leader but as a follower. Since the medium of its leadership is the law, or the decision of cases in terms of law, we can go further and say that the effectiveness of the Court's leadership is measured by its ability to articulate deep convictions of need and deep patterns of desire on the part of the people in such a way that the people, who might not be able themselves to be similarly articulate, will recognize the judicial statement as essentially their own. The Court must sense the synthesis of desire for both continuity and change and make the desired synthesis the expressed pattern of each decision.[31]

The Election of 1936

The election of 1936 seemed to indicate an articulation of the national will toward the New Deal. The convention began on June 23rd in Philadelphia's Franklin Field, where Alben Barkley, who was to become the majority leader of the Senate within a year, delivered the keynote address which Roosevelt had reviewed prior to its delivery.[32] Arthur Schlesinger described Barkley's attack on the Court thus:

> In more sober vein Barkley discussed the Supreme Court. "Over against the hosannas of Hoover for the tortured interpretation of the Constitution of this nation," he said to uproarious applause, "I place the tortured souls and bodies" of its working men, women, and children. The trouble lay, not with the Constitution, but with the men who interpreted it. The Democratic party wanted the Court to treat the Constitution "as a life-giving charter, rather than an object of curiosity on the shelf of a museum. Is the Court beyond criticism?" he asked. "May it be regarded as too sacred to be disagreed with?" The Convention roared back: "No! No!"[33]

The platform plank on the Constitution reflected the indecision of the President as to a solution of the Supreme Court "problem."[34] Although the first draft of the document was composed by Samuel Rosenman and Stanley High,[35] the plank on the Court decisions was assigned to Donald Richberg, the head of the court-slain N.R.A.[36] While Attorney General Cummings wanted to make the Court one of the main issues in the campaign,[37] Roosevelt decided on the more general attack and Richberg's draft was accepted with minor amendments.[38] The final phraseology was this:

> We have sought and will continue to seek to meet these problems through legislation within the Constitution.
> If these problems cannot be effectively solved by legislation within the Constitution, we shall seek such clarifying amendment as will assure to the legislatures of the several states and to the Congress of the United States, each within its proper jurisdiction, the power to enact those laws which the State and Federal legislatures, within their respective spheres, shall find necessary . . . .[39]

In his acceptance speech on the 27th, Roosevelt did make an oblique attack on "the nine old men" when he declared:

> These economic royalists complain that we seek to overthrow the institutions of America. What they really complain of is that we seek to take away their power. Our allegiance to American institutions requires the overthrow of this kind of power. In vain they seek to hide behind the Flag and the Constitution. In their blindness they forget what the Flag and the Constitution stand for. Now, as always, they stand for democracy, not tyranny; for freedom not subjection;

and against a dictatorship by mob rule and the overprivileged alike.[40]

However, during the campaign the President and his spokesmen carefully avoided a direct attack on the Court. Jackson tells us that Roosevelt said "almost nothing" about the Court.[41] In an address to labor's Non-Partisan League in August of 1936 the Chief Executive did note:

> During the past three years we have endeavored to correct through legislation certain of the evils in our economic system. We have sought to put a stop to certain economic practices which did not promote the general welfare. Some of the laws which were enacted were declared invalid by the Supreme Court. It is a notable fact that it was not the wage earners who cheered when those laws were declared invalid.[42]

The charge, made subsequent to the announcement of the Court Reorganization plan, that the President engaged in deception by keeping silent during the campaign, is denied by Justice Jackson. "The Republicans lost no opportunity," the then Attorney General declared,

> to identify themselves with the Court and the Court with themselves. Although the Court was helpless to prevent being thus publicly embraced, it had, as I have pointed out, at least encouraged the advances. The claim later made that the Supreme Court had not been an issue in the campaign is unfounded. It was merely an issue on which the President had no need to speak—one which his enemies could not win even by his default. The election had gone against the Court quite as emphatically as against the Republican Party, whose bedfellow it had been.[43]

Indeed in its platform, the GOP had committed itself to "resist all attempts to impair the authority of the Supreme Court of the United States, the final protector of the rights of our citizens against the arbitrary encroachments of the legislative and executive branches of Government."[44] And Arthur Krock reminded his readers on February 7, 1937 that "the Republicans in the campaign repeatedly notified the voters that the President was dissatisfied with the workings of the Judiciary and by new appointments to the Supreme Court and otherwise, would, if reelected, attempt sweeping reforms."[45]

The turnout at the polls was large for an American election; 37 percent of the total population participated, and Roosevelt won with an eleven million vote plurality, capturing all but eight of the 531 electoral votes. Alfred Landon won only the votes of Maine and Vermont.[46] While the labor vote was a dominant factor, Max Lerner maintains that the *Butler* decision "virtually handed over to Mr Roosevelt several million farm votes.[47] However, another commentator believes that because the Court had not been an issue in the campaign, "the President's great victory in November, 1936 did not, therefore, include a specific mandate to reform the Court,[48] and in this view he is supported by most other commentators.

Thomas G. Corcoran, a White House advisor at this time, holds that the popular support of the New Deal program manifested in the elections created "a popular weight which [the Court] could not indefinitely manage."[49] Fred Rodell, writing in 1955, the year of Roberts' death, speculated that "what effect this avalanche may have had in the marble temple, where the Court had convened for its new term a month before, must remain a matter of informed conjecture—at least until intimate memoirs are possibly published at a decent interval after the death of Roberts, the last survivor of the Nine Old Men."[50] It is highly unlikely that any such revelation will be forthcoming. However, the Justice in his Harvard Lectures in 1951 did intimate that the Court took cognizance of the popular will. In fact, one student of the reversal sees in Roberts' *The Court and The Constitution,* the title under which these lectures were printed, an admission that the elections of 1936 had an effect on the Court's activity in 1937.[51] Perhaps the following quotes from the printed edition of the 1951 Holmes Lectures substantiate MacColl's view:

> Looking back, it is difficult to see how the Court could have resisted the popular urge for uniform standards throughout the country — for what in effect was a unified economy.[52]

*****

> In summary, I think it fair to say that, progressively, the Supreme Court has limited and surrendered the role the Constitution was intended to confer on it. *Vox populi, vox Dei* was not the theory on which the charter was drawn. The sharp division of powers intended has become blurred. Perhaps this was inevitable. Perhaps it is a beneficial development.[53]

It is certain that the President viewed the election as a mandate to action, even though the Court, as an institution, had not been an issue in the campaign. In the first cabinet meeting after the election, we are told by Harold Ickes, Secretary of the Interior, that "there was a good deal of discussion" about the judiciary. "I think that the President is getting ready to move in on that issue."[54] When all the evidence is in, however, the condition of the public weal during 1936 and the public reaction to the Court's decisions seems to have been just as influential in the change in the Justices' views. Howard Brubaker's cynical comment in the *New Yorker* makes its point: "We are told that the Supreme Court's about face was not due to outside clamor. It seems that the new building has a soundproof room to which the judges may retire to change their minds."[55]

The Court Plan

"No event of twentieth-century American constitutional history," writes Professor William E. Leuchtenburg, "is better remembered than Franklin D. Roosevelt's ill-fated 'Court-packing' scheme of 1937 . . . ."[56] Popular opinion, at the time and since, has ascribed to the President's Judicial Reorganization Bill of 1937 the power of dynamite which broke the logjam of opposition to the economic programs of the New Deal. A detailed study of the history of that legislative proposal and the comments of the judicial participants in the "switch" seriously weaken the importance of the Court Bill in the change in interpretation of the Constitution during 1937 and after.

A bit of personal animosity was injected into the New Deal executive-judicial conflict because of a misunderstanding surrounding the annual visit made by the Chief Justice to the President at the beginning of the October term. The purpose of this ceremonial meeting is to inform the chief executive that the Court is in session and to give the President the opportunity to invite the Justices to the White House. In 1936 there was no such exchange of greetings, and the President took the omission as a personal affront, though Justice Roberts later protested that "no snub was intended."[57] According to Robert E. Sherwood, the President inquired through Marvin MacIntyre about the visit and was told by Justice Stone's secretary that there would be none that year,[58] but the conversation was subsequently denied by both the secretary and the clerk of the Justice. Merlo Pusey suggests that "in the three days the President spent in Washington between campaign trips, there was no mutually convenient time for the court to make its call."[59]

Further heat was added by the State of the Union message delivered on January 6th. Rosenman tells us that "even as we were working on this annual message, the Department of Justice was preparing the legislation and message and compiling the statistics that were to form the basis of the Supreme Court plan of the next month, but we knew nothing of this at the time."[60] And Harold Ickes made the following entry in his diary:

> The Pres' message was delivered before a joint session of the Senate and the House in the House of Repres. Wed. afternoon at two o'clock. . . .

The Pres told me afterward that it had been understood that the S.Ct. was to attend the joint session, but none of the justices showed up. The suspicion was they had gotten a tip as to the contents of the message. . . . I believe that we are on the eve of an era where the powers of the Court will be much more strictly limited than they have been in the past.[61]

The President told the attentive joint session of Congress:

The statute of the N.R.A. has been outlawed. The problems have not; they are still with us. . . . During the past year there has been a growing belief that there is little fault to be found with the Constitution of the United States as it stand today. The vital need is not an alteration of our fundamental law, but an increasing enlightened view with reference to it. Difficulties have grown out of its interpretation; but rightly considered, it can be used as an instrument of progress, and not as a device for the prevention of action;. . . it was the definite intent and expectation [of the founding fathers] that a liberal interpretation in the years to come would give to Congress the same relative powers over new national problems as they themselves gave to the Congress over the national problems of their day. . . . With a better understanding of our purposes and a more intelligent recognition of our needs as a Nation, it is not to be assumed that there will be prolonged failure to bring legislative and judicial action with closer harmony. Means must be found to adopt our legal forms and judicial interpretation to the actual present needs of the largest progressive democracy in the modern world.[62]

There have been incidents in the history of the Republic in which the executive was accused of "packing" the Court, attempting to do so, or thinking of doing so. Charles Warren, the authority on the history of the Supreme Court, tells us of rumors following the *Ex Parte Milligan* decision that the powers in government harbored such intentions,[63] but the most notable example prior to 1937 was the incident of appointments to the Court by President U.S. Grant in 1870. . . .There was an opportunity to appoint two justices, one to replace Justice Robert C. Grier, who resigned on February 1, 1870, and one to restore the number of Justices to nine as provided by congressional action. The result of the new appointments was a reversal of the precedent of one year standing in the greenback matter. In 1937 this incident was trotted out to justify President Roosevelt's Court bill, and emphasis was placed on the fact that Grant was a member of the party which happened to be in opposition in that year.[64]

One other incident of "court packing" is cited by A.C. Dicey in his authoritative work, *Introduction to the Study of the Constitution.* He notes:

Judges, further, must be appointed by some authority which is not judicial, and where decisions of a court control the action of government there exists an irresistible temptation to appoint magistrates who agree (honestly it may be) with the views of the executive. A stong argument pressed against Mr. [James G.] Blaine's election [1884] was that he would have the opportunity as President of nominating four judges, and that a politician allied with railway companies was likely to pack the Supreme Court with men certain to wrest the law in favour of mercantile corporations. The accusation may have been baseless; the fact that it should have been made, and that even "Republicans" should declare that the time had come when "Democrats" should no longer be excluded from the Bench of the United States, tells plainly enough of the special evils which must be weighed against the undoubted benefits of making the courts rather than the legislature the arbiters of the constitution.[65]

Finally, it might be pointed out that Sir James Bryce with amazing prophecy warned in his *American Commonwealth:*

The Fathers of the Constitution studied nothing more than to secure the complete independence of the judiciary. ... One thing only was forgotten or deemed undesirable, because highly inconvenient, to determine—the number of judges in the Supreme Court. Here was a weak point, a joint in the Court's armour through which a weapon might someday penetrate. ... This method is plainly susceptible of further and possibly dangerous application [increase in number of Justices during Grant's administration]. *The security provided for the protection of the Constitution is gone like the morning mist.* [Italics supplied.][66]

The theoretical basis for the attempt to add members to the Supreme Court was articulated by Dean Alfange when he wrote:

Precisely because the Supreme Court, by means of judicial review, has come to exercise political power, it must sedulously avoid even the appearance of playing politics. As a judicial body, it tends, by its very nature, to be more conservative on economic and social issues than state legislature or Congress, though it must not be forgotten that on questions involving civil liberty... and the other individual rights guaranteed by the Constitution, it has been far more liberal than legislative bodies, which are all too often subject to group pressures and mass passions. But the Court's inherent conservatism must not be allowed to crystallize into permanent identification with those groups, classes, or parties which are obdurately opposed to social change. Such identification could lower the Court's prestige and in the long run endanger its existence. Conservative institutions, especially in times of social crisis, must know how to bend in order not to break.[67]

As has been noted, the Court as an institution had been identified by many during the first years of the New Deal as a Republican stronghold. "Those dissatisfied with the trend of governmental policy," wrote Charles Black, "as such people always do and have a right to do, had taken their claims to the Court. And in the Supreme Court of the United States they had prospered far better than in the court of public opinion."[68] In so ruling, the Justices had decided economic matters "on a level too high for judicial governance, and imposed constitutional restraint so rigid that no popular government could tolerate them,"[69] or as Walter Murphy phrased it:

> In the New Deal period, some of the Justices, perhaps thinking that the triumph of judicial supremacy was permanent, tried to insist that public officials had no authority to tamper with the inexorable laws of the business cycle. These efforts to hold back the clock were doomed from the start, and the attack against the Court collapsed once again. In part this failure was due to the tactical blunders of an overconfident President; in part it was due to the Court's own strategic retreat. But there were also important institutional considerations involved. Congressional resentment against the Court was tempered by fear of executive dominance. Although it was inevitable that the Court's laissez-faire dogmas would be reversed either by legislative or judicial action, it was not inevitable—nor was it even probable—that jealous congressmen and senators would assist an ambitious Chief Executive to enhance substantially presidential influence over members of the Supreme Court.[70]

Ordinarily, the chief executive would have had an opportunity to appoint members to the Court during his term, but Roosevelt had not appointed any.[71] This seems to have been the *practical* reason for the attempt to "pack" the Supreme Court. Herbert Agar suggested to his readers in April, 1937 that "in judging the President's proposal, the following facts should be kept in mind: if, as was to be expected, three or four vacancies had come to Mr. Roosevelt's first term, the Court would now be safely and respectfully pro-New Deal and there would be no need for the present quarrel."[72] Joseph R. Saylor in his study of *The Constitutional Crisis of 1937* echoed the same view: "One might predict with a reasonable degree of accuracy that if Roosevelt had had the opportunity to appoint at least one or two justices prior to 1937, there would have been no proposal calling for an increase in the personnel of the Court."[73] And Attorney General Jackson charged:

> Life tenure was a device by which the conservatives could thwart a liberal administration if they could outlive it. The alternations of our national moods are such that a cycle of liberal government seldom exceeds eight years, and by living through them the Court could go on

without decisive liberal infusions. So well has this strategy worked that never in its entire history can the Supreme Court be said to have for a single hour been representative of anything except the relatively conservative forces of its day. It had worked to prevent Mr. Roosevelt from getting a single vacancy in four years, although six Justices had passed "the retiring age of 70." It seemed likely to work for four more and, as a matter of fact, but for retirement, Mr. Justice Van Devanter and Mr. Justice Sutherland would still be on the Court, and the only changes by death would be a replacement of the liberal Cardozo and the conservative Butler. The Court seemed to have declared the mortality table unconstitutional. And a nation was waiting for the President to move.[74]

It was, therefore, in an attempt to alleviate this condition that President Roosevelt unveiled his Judicial Reorganization Bill on February 5, 1937. It is difficult to recreate, a third of a century later, the emotions and tensions accompanying the event, but some of the thoughts which must have passed through the minds of the participants and public alike have been summarized by Professor McCloskey:

> It was, as it was called, a "court-packing plan," and its passage would set a precedent from which the institution of judicial review might never recover. It is not too much to say that the ambiguous and delicately balanced American tradition of limited government was mortally endangered by this bill. . . . Even the five or six judges who had provoked this threat must have slept rather uneasily for a few months.[75]

However, as Professor Mason points out, the plan was not completely a "bolt from the blue,"[76] and even though Secretary of Labor Frances Perkins protested that Roosevelt had no intention of "reforming, changing, or modifying the Supreme Court,"[77] Arthur Krock was able to trace Roosevelt's desire for a court receptive to the ideals of the Democratic Party to a speech delivered in Baltimore during the 1932 presidential campaign on October 5th of that year.[78] When the handwriting began to appear on the wall, as it did in the *Hot Oil* decision and to a certain degree in the *Gold Clause* cases, the President suggested to his associates that judges be added to the Court immediately.[79] Tom Corcoran was quoted "as saying that after [Roosevelt's] 'Horse and buggy' press conference (5-29-35) the President was thoroughly aroused 'and determined to prevent' the Court from blocking what he believed to be the very foundation of democracy."[80] In December Attorney General Cummings sent a memo to the assistant Attorney General outlining possible action should the Supreme Court decide "adversely to practically all New Deal legislation and sets up

constitutional standards which cannot be met. . . ."[81] A letter from the
Attorney General dated January 16, 1936 in reply to an inquiry from
Roosevelt about the *Ex Parte McCardle*[82] case reads thus:

> The case of *ex parte McCardle,* 7 Wallace 506, decided in December
> 1868, to which you refer in your memorandum, is one of the classic
> cases to which we refer when considering the possibility of limiting
> the jurisdiction of Federal Courts. This whole matter has been the
> subject of considerable study in this Department, and, in view of
> recent developments, is apt to be increasingly important.[83]

As noted above, the Democratic campaign avoided a direct position on the
Court, and Senator Henry Ashurst, who subsequently presided over the
Senate Judiciary Committee hearings on the Court Bill, answered
Republican campaign charges that if Roosevelt were reelected he would
pack the Court, by declaring "a more ridiculous, absurd, and unjust
criticism of the President was never made."[84]

The first inkling of what was afoot came in the state of the union
message in January, 1937 in which the President declared:

> With a better understanding of our purposes, and a more intelligent
> recognition of our needs as a nation, it is not to be assumed that
> there will be prolonged failure to bring legislative and judicial action
> into closer harmony. Means must be found to adapt our legal forms
> and our judicial interpretation to the actual present national needs of
> the largest progressive democracy in the modern world. . . .
> The judicial branch also is asked by the people to do its part in
> making democracy successful. We do not ask the courts to call
> non-existent powers into being, but we have a right to expect that
> conceded powers or those legitimately implied shall be made effective
> instruments for the common good.
> The process of our democracy must not be imperiled by the denial of
> essential powers of free government.[85]

There was an atmosphere of tension as Congress moved into its early
sessions. The votes were present, it seemed, for the working of the
President's will regardless of the expected defections. But Mr. Roosevelt
was tight-lipped at the press conference on January 22nd when the
following exchange took place:

> Q. Can you tell us whether you will join or support any legislation
> seeking a change of practice of the Supreme Court with respect to
> legislation?
> President. That is a sort of "iffy" question.
> Q. Have you selected any date or personnel yet for that conference
> about the courts that Senator Minton talked about?

President. There isn't any conference. Senator Minton is coming down to confer with me. The Attorney General will come down, but I suppose he will come down with a lot of other Senators.[86]

However, Washington was alive with rumors. Walter Lippmann noted that "since Congress came back to Washington, it has become evident that a storm is brewing over the judiciary. There is a large amount of accumulated resentment over the laws which have been outlawed and a strong feeling that all kinds of necessary or desirable reforms are prohibited. Those who voice this sentiment would say that the expressed will of the sovereign people is being frustrated."[87]

On February 2nd the annual dinner for the Judiciary was held, and the President presented an unusually jovial front, which with hindsight seems to have been a cover for his secret, since we now know that the decision to send the message and the bill to Congress had been made at the Presidential birthday luncheon a few days before. On the night of the 2nd, Cummings told Sam Rosenman: "I wish this message were over and delivered. It makes me uncomfortable; I feel too much like a conspirator."[88] A cabinet meeting was called for the morning of the 5th, and the leaders of Congress were invited to attend. At the meeting the President simply read the message to the group—there was no discussion. The press were informed in the same manner, and before the end of the conference the bill was on its way to Congress.[89]

The message began with a disarming statement:

I have recently called the attention of the Congress to the clear need for a comprehensive program to reorganize the administrative machinery of the executive branch of our Government. I now make a similar recommendation to the Congress in regard to the judicial branch of the Government, in order that it also may function in accord with modern necessities.[90]

However, a few paragraphs later the President came to the real issue when he stated:

The judiciary has often found itself handicapped by insufficient personnel with which to meet a growing and more complex business. It is true that the physical facilities of conducting the business of the courts have been greatly improved, in recent years, through the erection of suitable quarters, the provision of adequate libraries, and the addition of subordinate court officers. But in many ways these are merely the trappings of judicial office. They play a minor part in the processes of justice.[91]

And then further on, Roosevelt gave the opponents of the bill an opening
when he stated:

> A letter from the Attorney General, which I submit herewith, justifies
> by reasoning and statistics the common impression created by our
> overcrowded Federal dockets—and it proves the need for additional
> judges. Delay in any court results in injustice.
> Even at the present time the Supreme Court is laboring under a heavy
> burden. Its difficulties in this respect were superficially lightened some
> years ago by authorizing the Court, in its discretion, to refuse to hear
> appeals in many classes of cases. This discretion was so freely
> exercised that in the last fiscal year, although 867 petitions for review
> were presented to the Supreme Court, it declined to hear 717 cases. If
> petitions in behalf of the Government are excluded, it appears that
> the Court permitted private litigants to prosecute appeals in only 108
> cases out of 803 applications. Many of the refusals were doubtless
> warranted. But can it be said that full justice is achieved when a court
> is forced by the sheer necessity of keeping up with its business to
> decline, without even an explanation, to hear 87 percent of the cases
> presented to it by private litigants?[92]

Mr. Roosevelt took special delight in the fact that Justice McReynolds, as
Woodrow Wilson's Attorney General, had recommended a bill for an
increase in the membership of the lower courts. In 1913 James C.
McReynolds suggested an assistant judge for those on the federal bench
who refused to retire at the legal age limit. Roosevelt's Attorney General
simply had extended the idea to the Supreme Court.[93]

Looking back there were three lines of action open to the President in
his attempt to solve "the problem of the Court": to give new substantive
powers to the Congress; to limit the power of the Court; or to add justices
to the Court who would vote favorably on New Deal legislation.[94] Exactly
when the decision to attempt the last named was made is not known; but
an outline of a speech preserved at the Roosevelt Library, Hyde Park, New
York and marked "early 1937" indicates that all of the alternatives were
carefully examined and the decision "I have chosen the mildest as the first
thing to be done," was made by Roosevelt himself.[95] It seemed obvious to
the President from the first that the amending process used to increase the
powers of Congress would be futile, despite the fact that there was much
public clamor for such a solution and even though Senator George Norris
had spearheaded such an attempt in Congress. Professor Burns tells us that
Roosevelt had once declared, "Give me 10 million dollars and I can prevent
any amendment to the Constitution from being ratified."[96] And as
pointed out above, the President had inquired into the *Ex parte McCardle*

precedent as a possible base for congressional limitation on the appellate jurisdiction of the Supreme Court. It seems now that that solution was rejected some time during 1936.

Charles Black maintains that once the President had rejected the amendment route, the Court alone could legitimize the New Deal.[97] If this was so, then a change in the personnel through resignations or additional members or a change in the voting patterns of some of its present members were the only possibilities. On the first alternative Justice Roberts "later concluded that some of the bitterness of the Supreme Court fight might have been avoided had Roosevelt been able to appoint some new justices in his first term."[98] It was the view of some in Washington that a few of the older men on the Court felt that they were the bulwark against the wave of unconstitutional legislation proposed and enacted by the New Deal Congresses.[99]

Similarly, most of the observers of the Washington scene believe that the presentation and promotion of the Court Reorganization plan were poorly handled. Walter Murphy holds that F.D.R.'s decision "to keep his plan secret until the last moment... spelled disaster...."[100] Even Secretary of Labor Frances Perkins conceded that though Roosevelt "rarely got himself sewed tight to a program from which there was no turning back, Supreme Court reform...was one program to which he did get himself sewed tight. I have every reason to think that he later regretted it, although he made the best of his defeat and consoled himself with the belief that some good came out of the disturbance."[101]

The effect of the plan on the members of the Court is the most argued in the whole gamut of influences. The reluctance of the members of the Court to speak of the incident makes the facts more ethereal. We do have Brandeis' reaction. Tom Corcoran was sent by the President to forewarn the leading liberal on the high tribunal on the morning that the bill was to be sent to the Hill. Corcoran described the Justice's reaction: "Brandeis asked me to thank the President for letting him know but said that he was unalterably opposed to the President's action and that he was making a great mistake."[102]

Merlo Pusey describes the Court's first reaction to the news of the submission of the Court Reorganization Bill to Congress thus:

> News of the bill reached Chief Justice Hughes while he was presiding in the courtroom. Always alert for information of interest to the Court, the marshal, Thomas E. Waggaman, had secured copies of the President's message and the bill and immediately distributed them to the justices on the bench. Whatever inner excitement they may have

felt, the judges maintained a stoic silence. Even in the seclusion of their offices and conference room, there was very little discussion of the bill.[103]

In general, the Justices kept their own counsel on the whole issue. It is known from private conversations of some of the Court that, as a whole, the Justices took a dim view of the executive's attempt to tamper with the institutional form of the high tribunal. Similar to Brandeis' views expressed above, Justice Stone admitted to an acquaintance that "between ourselves the recent proposals about the Supreme Court are about the limit. To see it become the football of politics fills me with apprehension."[104] Again, writing to Professor Douglas W. Johnson, the Justice declared, "I have no hesitation in saying, for your personal information, that I think the present proposal is too high a price to pay for the correction of some of the decisions of the Court, which I, in common with a great many others, think unfortunate."[105] Justice Roberts, though not subject to the law had it been passed, was resolved to resign from the Court if judicial reorganization as the President envisioned it became law.[106]

The quasi-official position of the Court was expressed in the now famous letter from Chief Justice Hughes to Senator Burton K. Wheeler, which was read by the latter at the Senate Judiciary Subcommittee's hearings on S. 1392. It had been approved by Justices Van Devanter and Brandeis. Mr. Justice Hughes wrote, in part:

> An increase in the number of the justices of the Supreme Court, apart from any question of policy, which I do not discuss, would not promote the efficiency of the Court... It is believed that it would impair that efficiency so long as the Court acts as a unit. ... The present number of justices is thought to be large enough so far as the prompt, adequate, and the efficient conduct of the work of the Court is concerned.[107]

Because Brandeis and Van Devanter were the nominal leaders of the two "opposing" wings of the Court, it was supposed that their approval reflected that of the entire body. We know, however, that at least Justice Stone objected to any participation in the public debate by the members of the Court as much as he objected to the bill itself.[108]

The effect of the Court Reorganization Bill on the subsequent voting of the Court is impossible to assess. It was to be expected that the President would attribute the change in the Justices' viewpoint on social and economic legislation to his move to add members to the high bench. In June, 1941 he wrote thus: "I feel convinced, however, that the change would never have come, unless this frontal attack had been made on the philosophy of the majority of the Court. That is why I regard it as a turning point in our modern history."[109]

In addition, some of the most respected commentators on the Court during this period have agreed on the importance of the "plan" in the switch in the majority votes. Professor Carl Brent Swisher in his notable work, *American Constitutional Development,* wrote that "it is probable, however, that the change in interpretation was due largely to coercion in the form of the movement to reorganize the Supreme Court, backed by popular sentiment which strongly favored the substantive program of the New Deal, even if it did not include enthusiasm for direct interference with the Supreme Court,"[110] and Edward S. Corwin in his *Constitutional Revolution, Ltd.* stated that "the dramatic reversal by the Court of its attitude toward the principal constitutional tenets of the New Deal has provoked a good deal of speculation, and in this the coercive potentialities of the President's Court proposal of February 5, 1937, which preceded the decision in the *Jones-Laughlin* Case by about ten weeks, have loomed large."[111] Others felt that the plan had little or no effect on the Court's reversal. Mr. John Lord O'Brian, a member of the Supreme Court Bar for over fifty years and former government attorney, who was a close social as well as professional associate of the members of the Court during this period, told the author that in his opinion the personalities of the Justices precluded any sort of knuckling under to pressure from Congress or the White House. "I don't think the Court Plan had an influence on the Court. These men were strong-willed personalities. The introduction of the bill made them more stubborn than before."[112] One editorial cartoonist cited before in this work tended to disagree with Mr. O'Brian. (See illustration following.)

The man in the spotlight during this time was Owen J. Roberts; and his views, expressed some seventeen years after, are significant. Appearing before the Senate Judiciary Sub-committee, he declared, "Now I do not need to refer to the Court-packing plan which was resorted to when I was a member of the Court. Apart from the tremendous strain and the threat to the existing Court, of which I was fully conscious, it is obviously if ever resorted to, a political device to influence the Court and to pack it so as to be in conformity with the views of the Executive or the Congress, or both."[113] On the other hand, in his Oliver Wendell Holmes Lectures delivered at Harvard in 1951, the former Justice declared that "looking back it is difficult to see how the Court could have resisted the popular urge for uniform standards throughout the country—for what was in effect a unified economy."[114] In the memorandum which Roberts gave to Felix Frankfurter when he left the Court in 1945, the retiring Justice concluded his relating of the facts in the *West Coast Hotel* case with the

AS BUSY AS A ONE-ARMED BILLPOSTER WITH THE ITCH.

following comment: "These facts make it evident that no action taken by the President in the interim had any causal relation to my action in the *Parrish* case."[115] Nothing further can be offered in refutation of the accusation that Roberts bent to the wind of executive-legislative threat. The comment of the authors of *The 168 Days* is as valid today as when it was written a third of a century ago:

> Knowledge of the facts now merely serves to confuse the picture of what happened within the Court after the disclosure of the President's bill. How far had Roberts meant to go when he reversed himself on the New York statute? Had he intended simply to let the Court retreat from the untenable position of disapproving all social legislation, from whatever source, to the more defensible one of holding only federal government powerless to deal with social problems on the ground of states' rights? Or had he intended to throw wide the door for the federal as well as state governments? These are questions which cannot be answered. One can but guess at what really occurred. . . .[116]

NOTES

[1] *The Roosevelt Revolution* (New York, 1959), p. 219.

[2] *New York Times Magazine,* October 10, 1963, pp. 102-103.

[3] *The Supreme Court in the American System of Government* (Cambridge, 1955), pp. 79-80.

[4] *Vital Speeches* II (1936), p. 543, "Address to Meeting of the American Law Institute."

[5] *Stone Papers,* Felix Frankfurter to Harlan F. Stone, March 30, 1937.

[6] *Einaudi,* pp. 219-21.

[7] *Ibid.,* p. 220.

[8] W.E. Leutenberg, *Franklin D. Roosevelt & The New Deal* (New York, 1963), pp. 239-40.

[9] J.M. Burns, *Roosevelt: The Lion and the Fox* (New York, 1956), pp. 217-18.

[10] U.S. Senate, Committee on the Judiciary, 75th Congress, 1st. Session "Hearings on S. 1392, A Bill to Reorganize the Judicial Branch of the Government," (Washington, 1937) Part I, p. 99.

[11] 298 U.S. 328, 330.

[12] *Ibid.,* pp. 331-32.

[13] Interview with Author, April 17, 1963; many conversations with Dean Broderick in his office in the University of Notre Dame Law School.

[14] 301 U.S. 1, 41-43.

[15] (New York, 1952), p. 59.

[16] *Boston University Law Review,* "American Constitutional Government; The Blueprint & the Structure," XXIX January, 1949, p. 25.

[17] 282 U.S. 379 (1931).

[18] A.T. Mason, *Harlan F. Stone, Pillar of the Law* (New York, 1956), p. 308.
[19] *Ibid.,* p. 397.
[20] *Ibid.,* p. 399.
[21] *Ibid.,* p. 436.
[22] See 299 U.S. 101; 300 U.S. 74, 81; 301 U.S. 482, 592.
[23] 301 U.S. 459, 466-67.
[24] *On Understanding the Supreme Court* (Boston, 1949), pp. 78-79.
[25] C.L. Black, *The People and the Court* (New York, 1960), p. 60.
[26] Pusey, *Hughes,* p. 747.
[27] *Essays in Constitutional Law, "Introduction" (New York, 1957), p. 16.*
[28] *Supreme Court in a Modern Role* (New York, 1958), p. 166.
[29] *A.F.L. v. American Sash & Door Co., 335 U.S. 538, 557.*
[30] *Haley v. Ohio, 332 U.S. 596, 605 (1948).*
[31] *Supreme Court in Modern Role,* pp. 179-80.
[32] S.I. Rosenman, *Working With Roosevelt* (New York, 1952), p. 101.
[33] *The Politics of Upheaval* (Cambridge, Massachusetts, 1960), p. 580.
[34] Bruns, pp. 271-72.
[35] Rosenman, p. 101.
[36] *Ibid.,* p. 103.
[37] Schlesinger, p. 581.
[38] Rosenman, *loc. cit.*
[39] H.S. Commager, ed. *Documents of American History* (New York, 1941), p. 176.
[40] *F.D.R. Papers,* V. 5. 1936, p. 234.
[41] R.H. Jackson, *The Struggle for Judicial Supremacy* (New York, 1941), p. 176.
[42] *F.D.R. Papers,* V. 5. 1936.
[43] Jackson, p. 177.
[44] Commager, p. 543.
[45] *New York Times,* February 7, 1937, sec. 4, p. 3.
[46] *Nomination & Election of the Pres. & Vice Pres. of the U.S.* (Washington, D.C., 1964), Chart D.
[47] *Virginia Quarterly Review,* "The Great Constitutional War," XVIII, 538.
[48] Hirshfield, *The Constitution & the Court* (New York, 1962), p. 44.
[49] Interview with the author, April 2, 1963.
[50] *Nine Old Men* (New York, 1955), p. 243.
[51] E. Kimbark MacColl, "Supreme Court and Public Opinion: A Study of the Court Fight of 1937," unpublished doctoral dissertation, U.C.L.A. 1953, p. 133.
[52] (Cambridge, Massachusetts, 1951), p. 61.
[53] *Ibid.,* p. 95.
[54] H. Ickes, *The Secret Diary of Harold L. Ickes* (New York, 1953), p. 602.
[55] "Of All Things," Vol. 13, p. 34, April 10, 1937.
[56] "The Origins of Franklin D. Roosevelt's 'Court-packing' Plan," *The Supreme Court Review, 1966* (Chicago, 1966) p. 347.
[57] *Ibid.,* p. 750.
[58] *Roosevelt & Hopkins* (New York, 1948), p. 94.
[59] *Ibid.*
[60] Rosenman, p. 141.

[61] *The Secret Diary of Harold L. Ickes: The Inside Struggle 1936-1939* (New York), Simon & Schuster, 1954.

[62] *F.D.R. Papers*, Vol. 5, 1936, pp. 641-2.

[63] *Supreme Court in United States History* (Boston, 1926), II, 447.

[64] L.H. Leek, *American Federationist*, "'Packing' the Court," XLIV *(April, 1937), 278-87.*

[65] Dicey, p. 179.

[66] (London, 1888), pp. 268-69.

[67] The Supreme Court and the National Will (New York, 1937), pp. 232-33.

[68] Black, p. 58.

[69] R.G. McCloskey, *The American Supreme Court* (Chicago, 1960), p. 168.

[70] *Congress and the Court* (Chicago, 1962), p. 65.

[71] The personnel of the Court had remained the same for 63 months—March, 1932 to June, 1937—the second longest period of stability in the Court's history. See E.L. Barrett et al., *Constitutional Law* (Brooklyn, 1959), chart, pp. 1205-11.

[72] *The New Statesman & The Nation* "Mr. Roosevelt's Constitutional Crisis "XIII, 321.

[73] Unpublished doctoral dissertation, University of Texas, 1945, p. 97.

[74] Jackson, p. 187.

[75] McCloskey, *The American Supreme Court* p. 169.

[76] *Stone, p. 437.*

[77] *The Roosevelt I Knew* (New York, 1946), p. 331.

[78] *New York Times,* "In Washington," February 11, 1937, p. 22.

[79] Mason, *loc. cit.*

[80] Sherwood, p. 89.

[81] *Cummings Papers*, December 28, 1935, p. 147.

[82] 7 Wall. 506 (1869).

[83] *Roosevelt Library*, President's Secretarial File, 1936-42 folio.

[84] Pusey, p. 750.

[85] E.S. Corwin, *The President: Office and Powers* (New York, 1957) p. 290.

[86] *F.D.R. Papers*, 1937 Vol. p. 9.

[87] New York *Herald-Tribune* "Today and Tomorrow. The Court's in a Jam," p. 21, February 4, 1937.

[88] Rosenman, p. 154.

[89] *Ibid.*, pp. 155-56.

[90] *F.D.R. Papers*, 1937 Vol. p. 51.

[91] *Ibid.*

[92] *Ibid.*, pp. 52-53.

[93] Alsop and Catledge, *168 Days*, pp. 33-34.

94 Schlesinger, *The Politics of Upheaval*, p. 490; R.S. Hershfield, *The Constitution and The Court* (New York, 1962), p. 45.

[95] *Roosevelt Library*, President's Personal File 1820, Judicial Reform Material.

[96] *The Lion and the Fox*, p. 295.

[97] *The People and the Court*, p. 65.

[98] S. Krislov, *The Supreme Court in the Political Process* (New York 1965), p. 11.

[99] Confidential Source No. 1.

[100] *Congress and the Court,* pp. 57-58.

[101] *The Roosevelt I Knew* (New York, 1946), p. 137.

[102] Sherwood, p. 90.

[103] Pusey, p. 753.

[104] Mason, *Stone,* p. 445.

[105] Mason, *Yale Law Journal,* Harlan F. Stone etc., Vol. 61, p. 803.

[106] Pusey, p. 753. Mr. Pusey confirmed this statement in an interview with the author, assigning it to a statement of Roberts, himself, to Pusey when the latter was researching his book on Hughes.

[107] U.S. Senate, 75th Congress, 1st Session, part 3, p. 491.

[108] Mason, *Yale Law Journal,* "Harlan Fiske Stone . . ." p. 806.

[109] *F.D.R. Papers,* "The Constitution Prevails-Introduction" Vol. 1937, p. LXVI.

[110] P. 954.

[111] P. 72.

[112] Interview, in the offices of Covington and Burling, March 26, 1963.

[113] U.S. Senate, 83rd Congress, 2nd session, Committee on the Judiciary, Hearings on S.J. Res. 44 Proposing an amendment relating to the composition and jurisdiction of the Supreme Court, January 29, 1954, p. 9.

[114] *The Court and the Constitution,* p. 61.

[115] Frankfurter, *University of Pennsylvania Law Review,* p. 315.

[116] Alsop & Catledge, pp. 140-41.

Chapter V

The New View Continues, 1937-1941

Professor John R. Schmidhauser has noted:

> In many respects, the answers given to constitutional questions by the Hughes Court before 1937 were basically different from those given after that year. With few exceptions, the decisions of the pre-1937 Hughes Court were simply a continuation of the judicial policies of the Fuller, White, and Taft Courts. After 1937, however, came a tremendously important period of re-evaluation and sometimes of reversal of earlier doctrinal trends.[1]

Between the end of the 1936 term and the conclusion of the 1940 term, at which time Chief Justice Hughes resigned, there were several important cases which represented an extension or revision of positions taken during the vigorous second half of the 1936 term. Accompanying these legal changes was a gradual transition in the personnel of the Court, so that by the time that Harlan Fiske Stone was elevated to the chief justiceship on June 27, 1941, Owen Roberts was the only other remaining member of the pre-1937 Court,[2] and the only one who had voted against the extension of governmental controls and supervision in the economic sphere.

As the philosophical complexion of the High Bench changed, Roberts found himself more and more frequently to the right of the majority. As Judge Charles Fahy wrote:

> The change [in constitutional law] may be described in general terms as a greater receptivity by the Court to the validity of the exercise of legislative bodies of a discretion in adopting measures to cope with economic and social problems. . . . The change may be described generally as a movement of the Court as a whole from "conservatism" to "liberalism". . . .[3]

To some observers it seemed that Justice Roberts had again changed his judicial mind. A careful examination of the rulings of the high tribunal, however, demonstrates that it was the majority which had moved to a more liberal position while Roberts remained fairly constant. As Professor

Herman Pritchett points out:

> Justice Roberts stood out in his last years of service at the far outer
> reaches of the Court, as a reminder of how far it had moved from the
> days when, as middle man, he kept the Court suspended in uncertain
> balance. ... His conservatism was primarily of an economic sort. On
> all economic issues except the I.C.C., he took by far the most negative
> position on the Court.[4]

In reply to the allegation that Roberts' dissents were based on the
grumpiness of an old man, the same author declared that "clearly there
were larger and more powerful forces at work on the Supreme Court than
in judicial spleen and disgruntlement."[5]

Federal Legislation

The Court's view of the jurisdiction and power of the National Labor
Relations Board continued to widen. In *Santa Cruz Fruit Packing Co. v.
N.L.R.B.*[6] the Chief Justice declared for a five-to-two majority, which
included Justice Roberts, that "there is no question that the petitioner was
directly and largely engaged in interstate and foreign commerce. ... With
respect to the federal power to protect interstate commerce in the
commodities produced, there is obviously no difference between coal
mined, or stone quarried, and fruit and vegetables grown."[7] To the
challenge by the petitioner that the *Carter Coal Co.* precedent was
controlling in the case and should be used to uphold the view that the
labor dispute was of local character, the Chief Justice replied that *Jones
and Laughlin* was the present rule, concluding that "the direct relation of
the labor practices and the resulting labor dispute in the instant case to
interstate commerce and the injurious effect upon that commerce were
fully established."[8] Justice Butler dissented, however, because he felt that
the *Carter* precedent was still binding on the Court, and "at least until this
Court definitely overrules that decision, it should be followed."[9]

Robert L. Stern believes that this case "made it clear that industries at
the beginning of the flow, producing raw materials within the state for
shipment outside, were subject to the Act, since labor disputes in such
concerns would undoubtedly obstruct the interstate movement."[10]

Eight months later, the Chief Justice announced a further definition
of the jurisdiction of the labor board. The Consolidated Edison Company
of New York was held to be subject to the National Labor Relations Act
because "there is undisputed and impressive evidence of the dependence of
interstate and foreign commerce upon the continuity of the service of the

petitioning companies. . . . It cannot be doubted that these activities, while conducted within the state, are of federal concern."[11]

The *Fainblatt* decision[12] represented a total inclusion of all workers whose products entered the stream of interstate commerce. Justice Stone for seven of the Justices admitted that "the volume of commerce affected is smaller than in the other cases in which the jurisdiction of the Board has been upheld," but he contended that the fact "is in itself without significance."[13] One commentator viewed this decision as a marked judicial enlargement of the power of Congress over strikes in remote interstate commerce.[14]

The Court, without Roberts' participation, also ruled that refusal to hire a person solely because of union membership is an unfair labor practice.[15] The opinion, written by Felix Frankfurter, noted that "it is no longer disputed that workers cannot be dismissed from employment because of union affiliation. . .[16] Discrimination against union labor in the hiring of men is a dam to self-organization at the source of supply. The effect of such discrimination is not confined to the actual denial of employment; it inevitably operates against the whole idea of the legitimacy of organization." Therefore, the Court sustained the Board's order that two men be hired whose union membership had barred their employment. Justice Douglas considers this decision to have overruled *Adair v. United States*[17] and *Coppage v. Kansas*[18],[19]

However, on what Albert L. Warner called the worst day in court that the N.L.R.B. had experienced,[20] the Court affirmed a lower court's order setting aside the Board's decision in a "sit-down" strike.[21] The Chief Justice, with Justices Reed and Black dissenting in part and Frankfurter not participating, declared "that the employees had a right to strike, but they had no license to commit acts of violence or to seize their employer's plant. . . the seizure and holding of the buildings of itself was a wrong apart from any acts of sabotage."[22] With added emphasis Hughes warned that "to justify such conduct because of the existence of a labor dispute or of an unfair labor practice would be to put a premium on resort to force instead of legal remedies and to subvert the principles of law and order which lie at the foundation of society."[23] The Court then noted that the firing of the employees where there was no strike would have been justifiable, and it held that the N.L.R.B. had acted outside the meaning of the Act in ordering the reinstatement of the strikers.[24] The Baltimore *Sun* believed that in this decision the Court had placed "the first marker at the vast expanse of powers claimed by the N.L.R.B and [said] beyond this point the Board cannot go."[25]

In a similar case, but one involving a different legal point, the Court in *Apex Hosiery Co. v. Leader,*[26] over the objections of the Chief Justice, Mr. Justice McReynolds, and Mr. Justice Roberts, refused to apply the triple damage provision of the Sherman Anti-Trust Act against a union, which through a sit-down strike and violence had prevented the employer's goods from entering interstate commerce. In answer to Justice Stone's ruling the Chief Justice for the dissenters declared:

> This Court had never heretofore decided that a direct and intentional obstruction or prevention of the shipment of goods in interstate commerce was not a violation of the Sherman Act. In my opinion it should not so decide now. It finds no warrant for such a decision in the terms of the statute. I am unable to find any compulsion of judicial decision requiring the Court so to limit those terms. Restraints may be of various sorts. . . . When they are found to be unreasonable and directly imposed upon interstate commerce, both employers and employees are subject to the sanctions of the Act.[27]

In a parallel case, *United States v. Hutcheson,*[28] the Court by a vote of six to two refused to apply the Sherman Act to a carpenters' union which was engaged in a jurisdictional dispute with a machinists' union. Anheuser-Busch was the object of the strike. Justice Frankfurter declared for the majority: "It was precisely in order to minimize the difficulties to which the general language of the Sherman Law in its application to workers had given rise, that Congress [through the Clayton Act] cut through all the tangled verbalisms and enumerated concretely the types of activities which had become familiar incidents of union procedure."[29] Justice Roberts, joined by the Chief Justice, dissented. He clearly stated the reasons for his disapproval:

> The indictment adequately charges a conspiracy to restrain trade and commerce with the specific purpose of preventing Anheuser-Busch from receiving in interstate commerce commodities and materials intended for use in its plant; of preventing the Borsari Corporation from obtaining materials in interstate commerce for use in performing a contract for Anheuser-Busch, and of preventing the Stocker Company from receiving materials in like manner for the construction of a building for the Gaylord Corporation. . . . Without detailing the allegations of the indictment, it is sufficient to say that they undeniably charge a secondary boycott, affecting interstate commerce. This court, and many state tribunals, over a long period of years, have held such a secondary boycott illegal.[30]

In a bitter attack on his brethren of the majority, Roberts further declared:

By a process of construction never, as I think, heretofore indulged in
by this Court, it is now found that because Congress forbade the
issuing of injunction to restrain certain conduct, it intended to repeal
the provisions of the Sherman Act authorizing actions at law and
criminal prosecutions for the commission of torts and crimes defined
by the anti-trust laws. The doctrine now announced seems to be that
an indication of a change of policy in an Act as respects one specific
item in a general field of law, covered in an earlier Act, justifies this
Court in spelling out an implied repeal of the whole of the earlier
statute as applied to conduct of the sort here involved. *I venture to
say that no court has ever undertaken so radically to legislate where
Congress has refused to do so.* [Italics supplied] In the light of this
history, to attribute to Congress an intent to repeal legislation which
has had a definite and well understood scope and effect for decades
past, by resurrecting a rejected construction of the Clayton Act and
extending a policy strictly limited by the Congress itself in the
Norris-La Guardia Act, seems to me a usurpation by the courts of the
function of the Congress not only novel but fraught, as well, with the
most serious dangers to our constitutional system of division of
powers.[31]

Labor gained another victory in *United States v. Darby,*[32] in which
the constitutionality of the Fair Labor Standards Act was upheld. Robert
L. Stern, who was on brief with the Solicitor General Francis Biddle and
Assistant Attorney General Thurmond Arnold, commented in an article in
1946 that "the decisions in *West Coast Hotel* and *Jones and Laughlin*
cases... culminated in the passage of the Fair Labor Standards
Act...."[33]

The machinery for the wage and hour law was energized by the then
Senator Hugo L. Black, who later sat on the Court when it reviewed the
final form of the statute. Black's bill would have provided for a thirty-hour
week, and it received impetus from the destruction of the National
Industrial Recovery Act by the Supreme Court, as he noted in a letter
dated May 27, 1935 to President Roosevelt: "Believing further that
Congressional action constitutionally regulating hours and wages is vital to
the nation, I hope you will aid to accomplish that purpose by supporting
the pending Thirty Hour Week Bill. This bill is not at variance with the
opinion of the Supreme Court as rendered today."[34] However, even as late
as April 15, 1938, there was still doubt within White House circles, where
Marvin MacIntyre asked James Roosevelt to have his father get an opinion
from the Attorney General prior to the fight on the bill in Congress.[35]
These fears proved groundless, for when the statute came before the Court,
it was sustained. Justice Roberts later noted that "the effect of sustaining

the act was to place the whole matter of wages and hours of persons employed throughout the United States, with slight exceptions, under a single federal regulatory scheme and in this way completely to supersede state exercise of the police power in this field."[36] This interpretation is, of course, rather broad, but in view of the fact that he voted with the majority to uphold the law, his further comment makes the above sentence more meaningful. "As has usually been true, once the power of Congress in the premises was conceded, it became difficult for the Court to limit the legislative exercise of that power, however sweeping."[37]

Justice Stone for the unanimous Court declared:

> While manufacture is not of itself interstate commerce, the shipment of manufactured goods in such commerce and the prohibition of such shipment by Congress is indubitably a regulation of the commerce. . . . Such regulation is not a forbidden invasion of state power merely because either its motive or its consequence is to restrict the use of articles of commerce within the states of destination and is not prohibited unless by other Constitutional provisions.[38]

There followed a discussion of the precedents, and *Hammer v. Dagenhart*[39] was reviewed. Stone continued thus: "The conclusion is inescapable that *Hammer v. Dagenhart* was a departure from the principles which have prevailed in the interpretation of the Commerce Clause both before and since the decision, and that such vitality, as a precedent, as it then had, has long since been exhausted. It should be and is overruled."[40] And as for the *Carter* precedent, Stone disposed of it with the statement that it "is inconsistent with [the *Fainblatt* decision], its doctrine is limited in principle by the decisions under the Sherman Act and the National Labor Relations Act. . . ."[41] To the challenge based on the Tenth Amendment, Stone restates Justice Roberts' conclusion in *United States v. Sprague.*[42] "The amendment states but a truism," says Stone, "that all is retained which has not been surrendered."[43] Finally, invoking the *Parrish* decision, the Court ruled that the legislative power to fix maximum hours is no longer open to question under the due process clause of either the Fifth or Fourteenth Amendments.[44]

In a companion case, *Opp Cotton Mills v. Administrator,*[45] delivered immediately after the *Darby* decision, the Justices ruled that the Wage and Hour Law applied equally to the manufacturer of textile goods destined to enter interstate commerce.

In another area which had been a cause of controversy in 1936, the Court ruled on the question of price regulation of coal carried in interstate commerce. In *Sunshine Anthracite Coal Co. v. Adkins,*[46] speaking for all except Justice McReynolds, Mr. Justice Douglas recalled that "the labor provisions of the Bituminous Coal Conservation Act of 1935 had been held unconstitutional," but the price control provisions had never been ruled on in *Carter v. Carter Coal Co.*[47] In upholding the price fixing provisions the Justice declared:

> If the strategic character of this industry in our economy and the chaotic conditions which have prevailed in it do not justify legislation, it is difficult to imagine what would. To invalidate this Act, we would have to deny the existence of power on the part of Congress under the commerce clause to deal directly and specifically with those forces which in its judgment should not be permitted to dislocate an important segment of our economy and to disrupt and burden interstate channels of trade.[48]

Applying what Justice Roberts had held to be within the police power of the State in the *Nebbia* decision to the power granted to Congress under the commerce power, Douglas continues: "Certainly what Congress had forbidden by the Sherman Act, it can modify. It may do so by placing the machinery of price-fixing in the hands of public agencies."[49]

Following the voiding of the Agricultural Adjustment Act of 1933, Congress had sought to control farm surpluses through the stop-gap measure of the Soil Conservation Act of 1936, which paid farmers cooperating with the government program out of general funds.[50] When this proved inadequate, Congress was called upon to write a new bill, and the Agricultural Adjustment Act of 1938 was the result. The commerce power was substituted for the taxing and spending powers which had been invoked as a constitutional base in the 1933 statute.[51] The new law came before the Court in *Mulford v. Smith,*[52] and again Justice Roberts was called upon to announce the opinion of the majority of seven. The confidence of the President that the bill would be held valid was reflected in the press release which accompanied the signing ceremony. "It will be put into operation as quickly as possible, and in the meantime I ask that all those who are doing or will do spring planting govern their operations in the light of this new law."[53] His faith was well founded.

The Justice noted the difference between the present and earlier statutes when he declared that "the statute does not purport to control production. ... [Rather it is] solely a regulation of interstate commerce, which it reaches and affects at the throat where tobacco enters the stream of commerce—the marketing warehouse."[54]   To the challenge of an unconstitutional delegation of legislative power, Roberts replied that

"definite standards are laid down for the government of the Secretary . . . .
The Congress . . . has afforded both administrative and judicial review to
correct errors. This is not to confer unrestrained arbitrary power on an
executive officer. In this aspect the Act is valid within the decisions of this
court respecting delegation to administrative officers."[55] As an answer to
the contention that the application of the law to the appellants' 1938 crop
denies them of property without due process of law, Mr. Justice Roberts
stated:

> On the basis of these facts it is argued that the statute operated
> retroactively and therefore amounted to a taking of appellants'
> property without due process. The argument overlooks the
> circumstance that the statute operates not on farm production, as the
> appellants insist, but upon the marketing of their tobacco in interstate
> commerce. The law, enacted in February, affected the marketing
> which was to take place about August 1st following, and so was
> prospective in its operation upon the activity it regulated. The Act did
> not prevent any producer from holding over the excess tobacco
> produced, or processing and storing it for sale in a later year; and the
> circumstance that the producers in Georgia and Florida had not
> provided facilities for these purposes is not of legal significance.[56]

One is moved to agree with the dissenters, Justices Butler and
McReynolds, that this decision represents a reversal of the *Butler* decision.
As Professor Abraham comments: "True, the statutes were not exactly
alike, and the personnel of the Court had changed, but the essential
features and purposes of the statutes were unchanged."[57] The future
Justice Robert Jackson took a different view:

> The decision was followed by a good deal of uninformed comment to
> the effect that Mr. Justice Roberts had reversed his position and that
> the Court had reversed itself on the subject of control of agriculture.
> This was certainly untrue. . . . The two opinions by Mr. Justice
> Roberts are not legally inconsistent, since they are not concerned with
> the same power of Congress. I would agree, however, that the latter
> opinion indicates a broader and more tolerant approach to the
> constitutional problem than in his first opinion.[58]

On similar legislation, the Tobacco Inspection Act of 1935, the Court
ruled favorably in *Curran v. Wallace*,[59] and in *United States v. Carolene
Products Co.*,[60] the Filled Milk Act of 1923 was found to be neither
discriminatory nor unconstitutional. Justice Stone for six of the seven
members of the Court who participated noted that "Congress is free to
exclude from interstate commerce articles whose use in the states for which
they are destined it may be reasonably conceived to be injurious to public

health, morals, or welfare."[61] Further, in *United States v. Rock Royal Cooperative*[62] five justices upheld the Agricultural Marketing Act of 1937. Justice Stanley Reed announced a rule which was to have far-reaching implications. "Activities," he said, "conducted within state lines do not by this fact alone escape the sweep of the commerce clause."[63] The Chief Justice and Justices McReynolds, Butler, and Roberts dissented. The latter stated:

> I am of opinion, nevertheless, that Order No. 27 is not, in the respects to be discussed, authorized by the Act, but if it is authorized, deprives the appellees of their property without due process of law in violation of the Fifth Amendment.[64]

In a companion case, *Hood and Sons v. United States*,[65] the Chief Justice switched back to the majority, but Roberts dissented and was joined by McReynolds and Butler. His dissent was based on this fact:

> I am of the opinion that the Act unconstitutionally delegates legislative power to the Secretary of Agriculture. Valid delegation is limited to the execution of the law. If power is delegated to make a law, or to refrain from making it, or to determine what the law shall command or prohibit, the delegation ignores and transgresses the Constitutional division of power between the legislative and the executive branches of the government. . . .
> The statute is an attempted delegation to an executive officer of authority to impose regulations within supposed limits and according to supposed standards so vague as in effect to invest him with uncontrolled power of legislation. Congress has not directed that regulation shall be imposed throughout the United States or in any specified portion thereof. It has left the choice of both locations and areas to the Secretary. Congress has permitted such a variety of forms of regulation as to invest the Secretary with a choice of discrete systems each having the characteristics of an independent and complete statute. . . .
> Enough has been said to show that a law is to come into being on the basis of the Secretary's sole judgment as to its probable effect upon the milk industry, its probable effect upon the consumer, its probable consonance with the public interest, and its feasibility. The resolution of all such problems is of the essence of law making. . . .
> What was said concerning unconstitutional delegation of legislative power in *Panama Refining Co. v. Ryan*, 293 U.S. 388, and *Schecter Poultry Corp. v. United States*, 295 U.S. 495, applies with equal force here. Comparison of the provisions of the Act respecting flue-cured tobacco, which are summarized in *Mulford v. Smith, ante*, p. 38, with those applicable to milk, will disclose the fundamental difference between the administrative character of the powers delegated in the case of tobacco and the legislative character of those delegated in the

case of milk.

No authority cited by the Government presents a situation comparable to that here disclosed. It would not be profitable to analyze each of these cases, because in each the question of the nature of the statutory standard and its application in the administration of the statute involved depended upon the field which the legislation covers. Where delegation has been sustained, the court has been careful to point out the circumstances which made it possible to prescribe a standard by which administrative action was confined and directed. Such a standard, as respects milk marketing, is lacking in the Agricultural Marketing Agreement Act of 1937.

I think that the decree should be reversed.[66]

The extension of the federal government into the area of electric power was the subject of review in two cases during this period, *Tennessee Electric Power Co. v. Tennessee Valley Authority*[67] and *United States v. Appalachian Electric Power Co.*[68] In the former decision the Court ruled through Justice Roberts that T.V.A.'s competitive position did not constitute an unconstitutional regulation of private company rates. At the outset Roberts destroyed one of the basic claims of the appellants when he wrote:

The appellants invoke the doctrine that one threatened with direct and special injury by the act of an agent of the government which, but for statutory authority for its performance, would be a violation of his legal rights, may challenge the validity of the statute in a suit against the agent. The principle is without application unless the right invaded is a legal right, — one of the property, one arising out of contract, one protected against tortious invasion, or one founded on a statute which confers a privilege. The appellants urge that the Tennessee Valley Authority, by competing with them in the sale of electric energy, is destroying their property and rights without warrant, since the claimed authorization of its transactions is an unconstitutional statute. The pith of the complaint is the Authority's competition. . . .

The vice of the position is that neither their charters nor their local franchises involve the grant of a monopoly or render competition illegal. The franchise to exist as a corporation, and to function as a public utility, in the absence of a specific charter contract on the subject, creates no right to be free of competition, and affords the corporation no legal cause of complaint by reason of the state's subsequently authorizing another to enter and operate in the same field. The local franchises, while having elements of property, confer no contractual or property right to be free of competition either from individuals, other public utility corporations, or the state or municipality granting the franchise. The grantor may preclude itself by contract from initiating or permitting such competition, but no such contractual obligation is here asserted.[69]

In the latter case, which found the future Chief Justice Earl Warren on brief as attorney general of California, the Court was asked to rule on the licensing of a hydroelectric dam by the Federal Power Commission. The challenge was based on the question of the navigability of the New River. Justice Reed announced a broad principle for the majority of six: "A waterway otherwise suitable for navigation is not barred from that classification merely because artificial aids must make the highway suitable for use before commercial navigation may be undertaken."[70]

This time Justice Roberts, joined by McReynolds, dissented vigorously. He tore at the fabric of the majority opinion when he wrote:

> The judgment of reversal rests on the conclusion that New River is navigable. . . . the evidence will not support contrary findings if the navigability of New River be tested by criteria long established.
> 1. A river is navigable in law if it is navigable in fact. Indeed the issue of navigability *vel non* is so peculiarly one of fact that a determination as to one stream can have little relevancy in determining the status of another. . . . The evidence supports, — indeed I think it requires—a finding that, applying accepted criteria, New River is not, and never has been, in fact navigable. . . . As shown by the cases cited in the margin, a stream to be navigable in fact must have "a capacity for general and common usefulness for purposes of trade and commerce." Exceptional use or capability of use at high water or under other abnormal conditions will not suffice. Moreover, the stream must be used, or available to use "for commerce of a substantial and permanent character." Where the stream "has never been impressed with the character of navigability by past use in commerce,. . . commerce actually *in esse* or at least *in posse* is essential to navigability," and "a theoretical or potential navigability or one that is temporary, precarious, and unprofitable is not sufficient." The most important criterion by which to ascertain the navigability of a stream is that navigability in fact must exist under "natural and ordinary condition." Application of these tests by the court below to the evidence in the case led to but one conclusion: — that New River has not been, and is not now, a navigable water of the United States. . . .
> But further the court holds, contrary to all that has heretofore been said on the subject, that the natural and ordinary condition of the stream, however impassable it may be without improvement, means that if, by "reasonable" improvement, the stream may be rendered navigable, then it is navigable without such improvement; that "there must be a balance between cost and need at a time when the improvement would be useful." No authority is cited, and I think

none can be cited 'which countenances any such test.[71]

In a related case, *Oklahoma v. Atkinson Co.,*[72] the Court went further to hold that "it is clear Congress may exercise its control over the non-navigable stretches of a river in order to preserve or promote commerce on the navigable portions."[73] Justice William O. Douglas further on spelled out what this declaration meant:

> We have recently recognized that "Flood protection, watershed development, recovery of the cost of improvements through utilization of power are . . . parts of commerce control." *United States v. Appalachian Power Co., supra,* p. 426. And we now add that the power of flood control extends to the tributaries of navigable streams. For, just as control over the non-navigable parts of a river may be essential or desirable in the interests of the navigable portions, so may the key to flood control on a navigable stream be found in whole or in part in flood control on its tributaries. As repeatedly recognized by this Court from *M'Culloch v. Maryland,* 4 Wheat. 316, to *United States v. Darby,* 312 U.S. 100, the exercise of the granted power of Congress to regulate interstate commerce may be aided by appropriate and needful control of activities and agencies which, though intrastate, affect that commerce.[74]

This time there were no dissents.

The Court upheld the federal control of public utility holding corporations and their supervision by the Securities and Exchange Commission as prescribed by the Public Utilities Act of 1935,[75] but rejected an attempt to extend the control of the practices of a business purely within a state by the Federal Trade Commission.[76]

In these cases, which are mere samplings and therefore cannot be considered a basis for a statistical statement, Roberts participated in fourteen of the fifteen; he dissented against the extension of power three times—in *Hutcheson, Rock Royal,* and *Appalachiachian Electric Power.* He wrote the opinion of the Court in *Tennessee Electric Power* and *Mulford v. Smith,* both cases representing a continuation of the liberal views of the Court first expressed in 1937.

Erik M. Eriksson in his 1941 commentary on *The Supreme Court and The New Deal* points out:

> Justice Stone, generally considered to be liberal, has a record of eighty-two votes for the New Deal and twenty-six against it. Justice Roberts, whom many regard as conservative, has actually been almost as pro-New Deal as Justice Stone. Justice Roberts' record is seventy-two votes for and thirty-seven against New Deal measures.[77]

State Legislation

There were four landmark decisions in the period 1937 to 1941 in the area of state legislation affecting the incidents of interstate commerce.

In 1938 the Court ruled unanimously that in the absence of national legislation a state may regulate the use of its highways by interstate carriers for purposes of conservation and safety.[78] Justice Roberts, speaking for all except McReynolds and Butler in *Milk Control Board v. Eisenberg Farm Products*,[79] wrote that a state may require the licensing of milk distributors who receive some of their product from outside the licensing state and in turn ship all their products to another state. He opened his opinion with the declaration:

> We are called upon to determine whether a local police regulation unconstitutionally regulates or burdens interstate commerce.[80]

Justice Roberts found that:

> The question for decision is whether, in the absence of federal regulation, the enforcement of the statute is prohibited by Article 1, Sec. 8 of the Constitution. We hold that it is not.
> When the people declared "The Congress shall have Power.... To regulate Commerce ... among the several States, ..." their purpose was clear. The United States could not exist as a nation if each of them were to have the power to forbid imports from another state, to sanction the rights of citizens to transport their goods interstate, or to discriminate as between neighboring states in admitting articles produced therein. The grant of the power of regulation to the Congress necessarily implies the subordination of the states to that power. This court has repeatedly declared that the grant established the immunity of interstate commerce from the control of the states respecting all those subjects embraced within the grant which are of such a nature as to demand that, if regulated at all, their regulation must be prescribed by a single authority. But in matters requiring diversity of treatment according to the special requirements of local conditions, the states remain free to act within their respective jurisdictions until Congress sees fit to act in the exercise of its overriding authority. One of the commonest forms of state action is the exercise of the police power directed to the control of local conditions and exerted in the interest of the welfare of the state's citizens. Every state police statute necessarily will affect interstate commerce in some degree, but such a statute does not run counter to the grant of Congressional power merely because it incidentally or indirectly involves or burdens interstate commerce. This is so even though, should Congress determine to exercise its paramount power, the state law might thereby be restricted in operation or rendered

unenforceable. These principles have guided judicial decision for more than a century. Clearly they not only are inevitable corollaries of the constitutional provision, but their unimpaired enforcement is of the highest importance to the continued existence of our dual form of government. The difficulty arises not in their statement or in a ready assent to their propriety, but in their application in connection with the myriad variations in the methods and incidents of commercial intercourse.[81]

He concludes:

Only a small fraction of the milk produced by farmers in Pennsylvania is shipped out of the Commonwealth; there is, therefore, a comparatively large field remotely affecting and wholly unrelated to interstate commerce within which the statute operates. These considerations we think justify the conclusion that the effect of the law on interstate commerce is incidental and not forbidden by the Constitution, in the absence of regulation by Congress.[82]

Similarly, in *Ziffren v. Reeves*[83] the Court through Justice McReynolds upheld with only one dissent the right of the state to limit the transportation of intoxicating liquors within the state to specially licensed common carriers, even though such limitation did place some burden on interstate commerce. Finally, in *California v. Thompson*[84] the licensing by the state of agents who sold transportation on the state's highways was validated.

In the area of labor regulation the power of the state to prohibit all picketing in a labor dispute was held to violate the First and Fourteenth Amendments.[85] In *Olsen v. Nebraska,*[86] however, the power of the state to limit the fees charged by private employment agencies was upheld, which overruled a precedent of thirteen years' standing.[87]

In these cases involving state power, again too few to show a statistical trend, Justice Roberts agreed in all instances with the majority of his brethren. The liberal trend of the Court in general, and Roberts in particular, continued at least until 1941.

The drift of Justice Roberts to the right, or of the Court to the left, after 1941 as expressed in the comment of Professor Pritchett earlier in this chapter is not within the scope of this study. Therefore, its causes and effects are not within the area of our attention.

It is sufficient to point out that during the 1937 to 1941 period there was again a high coincidence of Justice Roberts with the majority of his brethren.

NOTES

[1] *The Supreme Court as Final Arbiter in Federal-State Relations,* 1789-1957 (Chapel Hill, N.C., 1958), p. 162.

[2] Herman Pritchett, *The Roosevelt Court* (New York, 1948), p.9.

[3] "Notes on the Development of Constitutional Law, 1936-1949," *Georgetown Law Journal* XXXVIII (1949), 3.

[4] Pritchett, p. 261.

[5] *Ibid.,* p. 30.

[6] 303 U.S. 453 (1938).

[7] 303 U.S. 453, 463-465.

[8] *Ibid.,* p. 468.

[9] *Ibid.,* p. 470.

[10] "The Commerce Clause and the National Economy, 1933-1946," *Harvard Law Review* LIX (1946), 683.

[11] *Consolidated Edison Co. v. N.L.R.B.,* 305 U.S. 197 (1938).

[12] *N.L.R.B. v. Fainblatt,* 306 U.S. 601 (1939).

[13] *Ibid.,* 609.

[14] A.L. Humes, "Trend of Decisions Respecting the Powers of Congress over Strikes in Remote Interstate Commerce," *American Bar Association Journal,* XXVI (19), 850.

[15] *Phelps-Dodge Corp. v. N.L.R.B.,* 313 U.S. 177 (1941).

[16] *Ibid.,* 183, 185.

[17] 208 U.S. 161 (1908).

[18] 236 U.S. 1 (1915).

[19] A. Blaustein & A. Field, "Overruling Opinions in the Supreme Court," *Michigan Law Review* LVII (1958), 154-155.

[20] New York *Herald-Tribune,* Feb. 28, 1939, p. 1.

[21] *N.L.R.B. v. Fansteel Metal Corporation,* 306 U.S. 240 (1939).

[22] *Ibid.,* p. 253.

[23] *Ibid.*

[24] *Ibid.,* pp. 254-55.

[25] February 28, 1939, p. 8.

[26] 310 U.S. 469 (1940).

[27] *Ibid.,* pp. 528-29.

[28] 312 U.S. 219 (1941).

[29] *Ibid.,* pp. 236-37.

[30] *Ibid.,* p. 243.

[31] *Ibid.,* pp. 245-46.

[32] 312 U.S. 100 (1941).

[33] Stern, p. 885.

[34] *Roosevelt Library,* Official File 372.

[35] *Roosevelt Library,* Confidential Memorandum MHM to JR, Official File 2730.

[36] *The Court and The Constitution* (Cambridge, Mass. 1951), p. 56.

[37] *Loc. cit.*

[38] *United States v. Darby* 312 U.S. 100, 113-14.

39 247 U.S. 251 (1918).
40 *Darby*, pp. 116-17.
41 *Ibid.*, p. 123.
42 282 U.S. 716 (1931).
43 *Ibid.*, p. 125.
44 312 U.S. 126 (1941).
45 310 U.S. 381 (1940).
46 *Ibid.*, 387.
47 *Ibid.*, 395-96.
48 *Ibid.*, 395-96.
49 *Ibid.*, pp. 395-96.
50 W.E. Leuchtenburg, *Franklin D. Roosevelt and The New Deal* (New York, 1963), p. 172.
51 Roberts, p. 54.
52 307 U.S. 38 (1939).
53 *Roosevelt Library,* Press Release of February 16, 1938, 1-K folio.
54 307 U.S. 38, 47.
55 *Ibid.*, pp. 48-49.
56 *Ibid.*, p. 51.
57 *The Judicial Process* (New York, 1962), p. 293.
58 *The Struggle for Judicial Supremacy* (New York, 1941), p. 238.
59 306 U.S. 1 (1939).
60 304 U.S. 144 (1938).
61 *Ibid.*, p. 147.
62 307 U.S. 533 (1939).
63 *Ibid.*, p. 569.
64 *Ibid.*, p. 583.
65 307 U.S. 588 (1939).
66 *Ibid.*, pp. 603-608, *passim.*
67 306 U.S. 118 (1939).
68 311 U.S. 377 (1940).
69 306 U.S. 137-139 (1939).
70 311 U.S. 407 (1940).
71 311 U.S. 429-433 (1940).
72 313 U.S. 508 (1941).
73 *Ibid.*, p. 523.
74 *Ibid.*, pp. 525-26.
75 *Electric Bond and Share Co. v. S.E.C.*, 303 U.S. 419 (1938).
76 *F.T.C. v. Bunte Brothers, Inc.*, 312 U.S. 349 (1941).
77 (Los Angeles), p.211.
78 *South Carolina Highway Dept. v. Barnwell Bros., Inc.*, 303 U.S. 177.
79 306 U.S. 346 (1939).
80 *Ibid.*, p. 349.
81 *Ibid.*, pp. 351 -53.
82 *Ibid.*, p. 353.
83 308 U.S. 132 (1939).
84 312 U.S. 109 (1941).

[85] *Thornhill v. Alabama*, 310 U.S. 80 (1940).
[86] 313 U.S. 236 (1941).
[87] *Ribnick v. McBride*, 277 U.S. 350 (1928).

Chapter VI

A Judgment

Surveying the evidence based on Mr. Justice Roberts' opinions and votes during the period from 1930 to 1941, we find that the Justice ranged from a somewhat strict reading of the economic clauses of the Constitution in his earlier years on the bench to a realization that constitutional interpretation must be adapted to the times. After 1941 this included a healthy respect for the legislative rather than judicial interpretation of the basic law. To phrase this development in a different way, we may say that the Justice's views went from a ready acceptance of the right of the state to legislate for the general good to a willingness to look with favor on the general government's right to do the same.

Three opinions of the many Mr. Roberts wrote seem best to exemplify this change. They are *Nebbia v. New York*,[1] *United States v. Butler*[2] and *Associated Press v. United States*.[3] In the first of these opinions the jurist declared: "So far as the requirement of due process is concerned, and in the absence of other constitutional restriction, a state is free to adopt whatever economic policy may reasonably be deemed to promote public welfare, and to enforce that policy by legislation adapted to its purpose."[4] While in the *Butler* decision, Roberts noted:

> While therefore, the power to tax is not unlimited, its confines are set in the clause which confers it, and not in those of sec. 8 which bestow and define the legislative powers of Congress. It results that the power of Congress to authorize expenditure of public moneys for public purposes is not limited by the direct grants of legislative power found in the Constitution.[5]

Some observers believe that even though *Butler* followed *Nebbia* chronologically, it preceded it in legal philosophical development. The end result in the *Triple A* case certainly would support such a view, but, as noted in Chapter II, a close reading of that controversial opinion demonstrates that in fact it *was* an extension of the "public welfare" doctrine announced in *Nebbia*. Nine years after *Butler* in his dissent in the *Associated Press* case, Roberts' last official pronouncement and one in

178

which Chief Justice Stone joined, he declared:

> For myself, I prefer to entrust regulatory legislation of commerce to the elected representatives of the people instead of freezing it in the decrees of courts less responsive to public will. I still believe that "the courts are without authority either to declare such policy, or, when it is declared by the legislature, to override it." (*Nebbia v. N.Y.*, 291 U.S. 502, 537)[6]

This comment seems to be an echo of these frequent calls for judicial self-restraint made by Justice Oliver W. Holmes, a colleague of Roberts on the Supreme Court some fifteen years before.

The spirit of the times during Roberts' service on the high tribunal was one which demanded that public figures take sides, and Justices of the Supreme Court are public figures. It may be that the Justice's wavering and his grasping at constitutional truth was the reason that he seemed a traitor to the "establishment" of the early '30's. "What is the matter with Roberts?" one of the conservative members of the Court asked when he announced his vote in the *Parrish* case.[7] Similarly, he was damned by the New Dealers for his refusal to seize the banner and lead the parade. One is led to conclude that Roberts, the top notch lawyer and an unquestionably honest man, had taken Alexander Pope's advice as his judicial motto in a time of radical changes: "Be not the first by whom the new are tried, not the last to lay the old aside."[8]

His conduct in the *Morehead-Parrish* switch is a case in point. While he had valid legal reasons for his voiding vote in *Morehead,* his decision to uphold the state law in *Parrish* demonstrated his willingness to change his judgment if the evidence was convincing. He was soundly condemned for his vacillation, especially since it involved an obscure technical point of law —a request for reversal—but those who knew the Justice intimately found just such a reason to be consistent with his regard to the proper processes of the law. We must agree with Justice Frankfurter, however, that in this matter "more needs to be said for Roberts than he cared to say for himself. As a matter of history it is regrettable that Roberts' unconcern for his own record led him from stating his position."[9] As Frankfurter further notes:

> The occasions are not infrequent when the disfavor of separate opinions, on the part of the bar and to the extent that it prevails within the Court, should not be heeded. Such a situation was certainly presented when special circumstances made Roberts agree with a result but basically disagree with the opinion which announced it.[10] *(Morehead)*

This observation is all the more valid in view of the fact that as Frankfurter points out the Chief Justice relied heavily on the *Nebbia* rationale in composing his opinion in *Parrish*, "for the reasoning of *Nebbia* had undermined the foundations of *Adkins*," which had been the precedent invoked in *Morehead*[11]

Roberts' failure to leave to history a detailed apologia for his constitutional exodus is not unique. The deposit of papers of the Justices who served on the High Court during his term is far from complete. Justice Jackson's papers were, in the main, destroyed as were large parts of those of Benjamin Cardozo.[12] It is dubious that we will ever get a clear picture of the inner workings of the Court at this time.

A line of development from Justice Roberts' earlier decisions through those of the 1937 period has been drawn in this study. It seems safe to say that this development of the Justice's thinking results from an honest search for the true meaning of the law. There is no *factual* justification for the accusation that the Justice's mind was determined by extrajudicial pressures for his later "liberal" decisions, though the Justice himself recognized that these pressures were present:

> Now, I do not need to refer to the Court-packing plan which was resorted to when I was a member of the Court. Apart from the tremendous strain and threat to the existing Court, of which I was fully conscious, it is obviously, if ever resorted to, a political device to influence the Court and to pack it so as to be in conformity with the views of the Executive, or the Congress, or both.[13]

Nothing appears in the record, except through political inuendo, upon which to base the implication that Mr. Justice Roberts had any but the most up right of motives in his wanderings through the maze of New Deal legislation, some of the more important of which was so poorly drafted that even such liberals as Brandeis and Stone among Roberts' brethren found them unpalatable. As indicated in the last chapter, one survey finds that Roberts and Stone were in high agreement on much of the legislation associated with the Roosevelt relief, recovery, and reform programs.

There are those who view the New Deal Court as unusual in American judicial history. However, the Supreme Court of the United States since the time of John Marshall has been periodically the center of controversy. It has not been unusual for the adherents of the losing side in a legal battle to attack the judiciary as "undemocratic, irresponsible, unpatriotic, inhuman," and even, on occasion, "traitorous." It is no mere coincidence that the vitriolic language currently used against the high tribunal, accused by some as the cause of the evils besetting the nation at the present time in the area of civil rights, has much the same ring as that used against the Marshall Court after *Gibbons v. Ogden,* the Taney Court after *Dred Scot,* and the Hughes Court after *Schechter.*

The "liberals" of the thirties, who, as we have seen, attacked the Court as the pillar of privilege, now see that same institution as the champion of the common man, while the "conservatives" who rejoiced in the pre-1937 bench as the grand protector of property rights, now see the high tribunal as the chief cause of the erosion of the *American system.* A cynic would be tempted to assess the popularity of the Supreme Court as a matter of "whose ox is being gored." A case in point was the appeal[14] during the 1968 presidential campaign by the supporters of George C. Wallace, one of the bitterest critics of the Court, of the refusal of the State of Ohio to place his name on the ballot. Evidently, these adherents of the former governor of Alabama failed to see that this request for the Supreme Court to intervene in the internal political processes of Ohio was inconsistent with the attacks their candidate was making on the Court during his campaign for interfering in the political affairs of Alabama.

An objective student of the Supreme Court is forced to conclude that its members are neither more nor less enlightened than their fellow citizens as to the nature of absolute truth. The Justices are subject to the same pressures and are prone to make the same errors as the rest of men. The judicial robe is not a mantle of infallibility. However, unless one is willing to deny the ability of man to rule himself, one cannot question the honesty of the attempts of the Justices of the Supreme Court of the United States to construct a body of legal principles which will keep the American System under the Constitution viable. In these days of civil turmoil this is a herculean task. How each judge performs this function is a matter for his own self-scrutiny. Former Justice Abe Fortas, whose judicial actions were as violently attacked and whose motives were as much questioned as those of Owen J. Roberts, in a speech delivered prior to his appointment to the Supreme Court characterized this search, when he declared:

> A Congressman, a Senator—even a President—may serve his term of office and still avoid the awesome question—"What do I really believe?"
>
>   Even for a Justice of the Supreme Court, beliefs may remain shrouded and ill-defined. . . . But for a Justice of this ultimate tribunal, the opportunity for self-discovery and the occasion for

self-revelation are unusually great. Judging is a lonely job in which a man is, as nearly as may be, an island entire. The moment is likely to come when he realizes that he is, in essential fact, answerable only to himself.[15]

NOTES

[1] 291 U.S. 502 (1934).
[2] 297 U.S. 1 (1936).
[3] 326 U.S. 1 (1945).
[4] *Nebbia v. New York*, 537.
[5] *United States v. Butler*, 66.
[6] *Associated Press v. United States*, 47.
[7] F. Frankfurter, *University of Pennsylvania Law Review*, Vol. 104, p. 315.
[8] *An Essay on Criticism*, line 335.
[9] Frankfurter, p. 315.
[10] *Ibid.*, pp. 315-16.
[11] *Ibid.*, p. 317.
[12] The author is indebted to Mr. Lloyd A. Dunlap of the Manuscript Division of the Library of Congress, Director of the Holmes Devise for the record of the papers of Supreme Court Justices.
[13] *United States Senate*, 83rd Congress, 2nd session, "Hearing before a Subcommittee of the Committee on The Judiciary on Senate Joint Resolution 44," January 29, 1954. Washington 1954, p. 9.
[14] *Williams v. Rhodes*, 393 U.S. 23 (1968)
[15] *The New Republic*, "Fortas to the Court," Vol. 153, No. 8-9, August 21, 1965, pp. 7-8.

Bibliographical Essay

Previously Unpublished Work in Area

It would seem that all that could be possibly told of this period of the New Deal has already been written, for as Walter Murphy comments in his *Congress and the Court,* "The story of the 1937 Court fight is a twice-told tale."[2] However, till the present, little has been written about the specific part played by Mr. Justice Roberts in the liberalization of the Court's social and economic decisions. There exists no biography of the Justice, and only one doctoral dissertation has been written on his work on the Court.

This unpublished thesis, entitled *The Constitutional Doctrines of Owen J. Roberts,* was submitted in 1943 to Cornell University by William O. Trapp. Dr. Trapp in a conversation with the author stated that the work was based mainly on personal interviews with the Justice at his estate in suburban Philadelphia. This study was made while Roberts was still on the bench, and it covers the entire spectrum of his judicial thinking up to 1942.[3]

In addition, there have been a number of doctoral dissertations written on the Supreme Court fight. James J. Anderson submitted one entitled *The President's Supreme Court Proposal* at Cornell University in 1941, which surveyed the relationship between the executive and judicial departments, up to and including the defeat of the Court proposal. Another dissertation entitled *The Court Crisis of 1937* was presented to the faculty of the University of Texas. It studies public opinion of the Court Bill of 1937 as expressed by various occupational groups. Its author was Joseph R. Saylor. E. Kimbark McColl wrote *The Supreme Court and Public Opinion: A Study of the Supreme Court Fight of 1937* as a doctoral dissertation for the University of California at Los Angeles. It presents an analysis of contemporary commentary on the struggle of 1937. Finally, Sam Krislov presented *The Supreme Court Since 1937: Nine Judges in Search of a Role* to the Princeton University faculty in 1955. He attempted to demonstrate that the Court has abandoned some of its jurisdiction in practice, if not in theory, in the area of economic legislation.

There have been numerous doctoral theses written about various aspects of the New Deal. The author was able to find forty-two dissertations in Political Science, listed in *Doctoral Dissertations, Dissertation Abstracts,* and the *American Political Science Review,*[4] which dealt with the New Deal or the judicial function in the area of New Deal legislation.

The Roberts Papers

Because primary sources are essential for a work of this nature, it was the obvious first step in researching for this paper to locate the Roberts Papers.

Justice Roberts' widow informed the author, through a member of the law firm of which the late justice had been a founder, that no body of papers exists.[5]

In an interview, Alfred Schneider, Roberts' law clerk from 1931 to 1945, confirmed the above and revealed that the late justice left little or no record of his work. Mr. Schneider characterized Roberts as a man who seldom put his thoughts on paper.[6]

Members of the Supreme Court, who served on the bench with Roberts, were contacted and the following replies were received. From Mr. Justice Hugo Black:

> Although I cannot be sure, my recollection is that Mr. Justice Roberts stated several times that it was his view that a justice should destroy papers in his office which related to the confidential work of the Court. This may be the reason you cannot find the papers. I have an idea, although again I cannot be sure, that Mr. Justice Roberts preferred that his work on the Court be appraised by his opinions and public statements.[7]

From Justice William O. Douglas:

> Under the date of December 2, 1954 the Manuscript Division of the Library of Congress was advised by Mr. Justice Roberts as follows: "Unfortunately, I have not preserved my papers, and I am not in possession of anything that should be of interest." In addition I am advised by the Justice's former secretary that some files were destroyed when Justice Roberts left the Court, and the remainder were destroyed after his death.[8]

From Justice Stanley Reed:

> It is my understanding that upon his retirement, Justice Roberts had destroyed his dockets containing his private records of

proceedings in the conferences during his years on the Court.[9]

From Justice Felix Frankfurter:

> Justice [Frankfurter] asked me to say that if neither Mrs. Roberts nor Mr. Schneider has any information concerning the material belonging to Mr. Justice Roberts, he doubts that there is any in existence.[10]

In response to an inquiry Mr. W. Brooke Graves of the Legislative Reference Bureau of the Library of Congress wrote: "We were informed by Mr. [Lloyd A.] Dunlap of the Holmes Devise in the Manuscript Division of the Library of Congress that the Roberts papers were not preserved. . . .He seemed very positive about it and offered no comment or explanation."[11] This information was later confirmed in conversations with Mr. Dunlap. Subsequently, Professors Paul A. Freund, Walter Murphy, and Alpheus Mason added their confirmation to the foregoing details.[12]

It is, indeed, a loss to the students of this period in the Court's history that Mr. Justice Roberts' personal records were not preserved for future analysis and study. Felix F. Frankfurter's comment on Roberts' silence in the *Morehead Case*[13] could well be extended to his entire career. "More needs to be said for Roberts than he cared to say for himself. As a matter of history it is regrettable that Roberts' unconcern for his own record led him from stating his position."[14]

Sources and Tools

The largest collected body of manuscripts associated with the New Deal period is to be found at the Franklin D. Roosevelt Library at Hyde Park, New York. The author spent two weeks searching the folios dealing with Mr. Justice Roberts, the Supreme Court fight, and those areas allied to Court decisions. The excellent cross-reference system permitted referral to other folios which contain papers related to the above topics.

Two months were employed in the use of the Supreme Court Library and the Library of Congress. The former contains the briefs and papers relating to the cases of the period and the latter provided access to periodicals and newspapers of the period under study.

While in Washington, the author interviewed former Justice Stanley Reed, who had been Solicitor General from 1935 to 1938,[15] and Federal Circuit Judge Charles Fahy, general counsel for the National Labor Relations Board from 1935 to 1940 and Solicitor General from 1941 to 1945.[16] He also spoke at length to John Lord O'Brian, Esq., a member of the Supreme Court bar for some fifty years and special counsel for T.V.A. in 1935–36,[17] and to Thomas G. Corcoran, an intimate member of the White House advisors during the New Deal.[18] Merlo Pusey, member of the editorial board of *The Washington Post* and author of the two-volume biography, *Charles Evans Hughes,* spoke at some length with the author of his interviews with the late Justice Roberts.[19] Finally, former Senator Burton K. Wheeler shared his memories of the Court fight in an interview in his law offices.[20]

Comments were also obtained from Arthur Krock of *The New York Times*[21] and Walter Trohan of the *Chicago Tribune,*[22] both of whom were in Washington during the period under study. Columnist Max Freedman, who, while this research was being done, was writing a biography of, and in conjunction with, former Justice Felix Frankfurter, was contacted also.[23]

The author conversed with George Haskins and John Honnold, colleagues of the former Justice at the University of Pennsylvania Law School.[24]

NOTES

[1] Not used.

[2] Walter F. Murphy, *Congress and the Court* (Chicago, 1962), p. 57.

[3] Telephone conversation on Jan. 18, 1963.

[4] *Doctoral Dissertations Accepted by American Universities* (New York, 1937–1955), vols. 5–22; *Dissertation Abstracts* (Ann Arbor, 1956 to present); *American Political Science Review,* August or September number each year.

[5] Letter from William A. Lathrop to author, May 29, 1962.

[6] Interview with the author in his office in the firm of Montgomery, Walker, McCracken & Rhoads, Phila., Penna., August 1, 1962.

[7] Letter to author, June 26, 1962.

[8] Letter to author, June 18, 1962.

[9] Letter to author, June 12, 1962.

[10] Letter from Elsie Douglas, Secretary, to author, June 26, 1962.

[11] Letter to author, May 14, 1962.

[12] Letter from Paul A. Freund to author, March 28, 1963; Letter from Walter F. Murphy to author, January 10, 1963.

[13] 298 U.S. 587 (1936).

[14] Glendon A. Schubert, *Constitutional Politics: The Political Behaviour of Supreme Court Justices and the Constitutional Policies That They Make* (New York, 1960), p. 171.

[15] Interview with the author in his chambers in the Supreme Court Building on February 18, 1963.

[16] Interview with the author in his chambers in the Federal Court Building, Washington, D.C., on April 8, 1963.

[17] Interview with the author in his office in the firm of Covington & Burling on March 26, 1963.

[18] Interview with the author in his office in the firm of Corcoran & Foley on April 2, 1963.

[19] Interview with the author in his office in *The Washington Post* Building on March 14, 1963.

[20] Interview with the author in his office in the firm of Wheeler & Wheeler on April 2, 1963.

[21] Telephone conversation on March 20, 1963.

[22] Telephone conversation on March 27, 1963.

[23] Telephone conversation on April 1, 1963.

[24] Interviews with the author in their offices at the University of Pennsylvania Law School on April 17, 1963.

Bibliography

PRIMARY SOURCES

Works of Owen J. Roberts

Roberts, Owen J. *The Court and The Constitution,* Cambridge, Harvard University Press, 1951.

-------. "Now is the Time: Fortifying the Supreme Court's Independence" *American Bar Association Journal* XXXV (January, 1949), 1–2.

-------. "Speech at Annual Dinner, 1932" Report of the 55th Annual Meeting of the American Bar Association LVII (1932).

-------. "American Constitutional Government: The Blueprint and The Structure" *Boston University Law Review* XXIX (January, 1949), 1–36.

General Collections

Cummings, Homer. *Selected Papers of Homer Cummings.* Edited by C.B. Swisher, New York: C. Scribner's Sons, 1939.

Holmes-Laski Letters. Edited by Mark De Wolfe Howe, Cambridge: Harvard University Press, 1953. 2 vols.

Ickes, Harold L. *The Secret Diary of H.I. Ickes,* New York: Simon & Schuster, 1954. 3 vols.

Preliminary Prints of the Official Reports of the Supreme Court. Washington: U.S. Government Printing Office, 1930 to 1945. Vols. 280 to 326.

Roosevelt, Franklin D. *Public Papers and Addresses of F.D.R.* Compiled & Edited by Samuel I. Rosenman. New York: Random House, 1938. 5 vols.

-------. *F.D.R.: His Personal Letters.* Edited by Elliot Roosevelt, New York: Duell, Sloan & Pearce, 1950. 2 vols.

Government Documents

U.S. Congress. *Congressional Record* LXXII 71st Congress, 2nd Session, May 19, 1930. Washington: U.S. Government Printing Office, 1930.

-------. *Congressional Record* LXXXI 75th Congress, 1st Session, July 22, 1937. Washington: U.S. Government Printing Office, 1937.

U.S. Government. *Second Annual Report of the National Labor Relations Board* for the Fiscal year ending June 30, 1937. Washington: U.S. Government Printing Office, 1937, 172 pp.

U.S. Senate. "Hearing before a Subcommittee of the Committee of the Judiciary on Senate Joint Resolution 44 Proposing An Amendment to the Constitution of the United States relating to the Composition and Jurisdiction of The Supreme Court." 83rd Congress, 2nd Session, January 29, 1954. Washington: U.S. Government Printing Office, 1954.

-------. "Hearings before the Committee on the Judiciary, 75th Congress, First Session on S. 1392. *A Bill to Reorganize the Judicial Branch of the Government* April 16 to 23rd, 1937. Washington: U.S. Government Printing Office, 1937. 2040pp.

Newspapers

Chicago Daily American
Chicago Daily News
Chicago Daily Tribune
Chicago Times-Herald
The Detroit Free Press
The Evening Bulletin (Philadelphia)
The Evening Star (Washington)
New York Herald Tribune
The New York Times
New York World-Telegram
The Philadelphia Inquirer
Philadelphia Record
The Cleveland Plain Dealer
The Sun (Baltimore)
The Wall Street Journal (New York)
The Washington Post

SECONDARY SOURCES
PUBLISHED WORKS

Abraham, Henry J. *The Judicial Process.* New York: Oxford University Press, 1962.

Alfange, Dean. *The Supreme Court and the National Will.* New York: Doubleday & Co., 1937.

Alsop, Joseph & Turner Catledge. *The 168 Days.* Garden City: Doubleday, Doran & Co., Inc., 1938.

Angell, Ernest. *Supreme Court Primer.* New York: Reynal & Hitchcock, 1937.

Barnes, William R. & A.W. Littlefield. *The Supreme Court Issue and The Constitution.* New York: Barnes & Noble, 1937.

Bartholomew, Paul C. *Summaries of Leading Cases on The Constitution.* Totowa, New Jersey: Littlefield, Adams & Co., 1965.

Bates, Ernest Sutherland. *The Story of the Supreme Court.* Indianapolis: The Bobbs-Merrill Co., 1938.

Beard, Charles A. & Mary. *American in Mid-Passage.* New York: Macmillan Co., 1939.

Beck, James M. & Merle Thorpe. *Neither Purse Nor Sword.* New York: Macmillan Co., 1936.

Berman, Edward. *Labor and the Sherman Act.* New York: Harper & Bros., 1930.

Black, Charles L. *The People and the Court: Judicial Review in a Democracy.* New York: The Macmillan Co., 1960.

Bickel, Alexander. *Unpublished Opinions of Justice Louis D. Brandeis.* Cambridge: Harvard University Press, 1957.

Bowen, Catherine D. *Yankee from Olympus.* New York: Bantam Books, 1960.

Brant, Irving. *Storm Over the Supreme Court.* Indianapolis: Bobbs-Merrill Co., 1936.

Bryce, James. *The American Commonwealth.* London, Macmillan & Co., 1888.

Burns, James M. *Roosevelt, The Lion and the Fox.* New York: Harvest Books, 1956.

Butler, Charles H. *A Century at the Bar with the Supreme Court of the United States.* New York: G.P. Putnam's Sons, 1942.

Cahill, Fred V. *Judicial Legislation: A Study in American Legal Theory.* New York: The Ronald Press Co., 1952.

Cahn, Edmund. *Supreme Court and Supreme Law.* Bloomington: Indiana University Press, 1954.

Cardozo, Benjamin. *The Nature of the Judicial Process.* New Haven: Yale University Press, 1921.

Carr, Robert. *The Supreme Court and Judicial Review.* New York: Holt, Rinehart and Winston, 1942.

Cohen, Sanford. *State Labor Legislation 1937–47.* Columbus Bureau of Business Research: The Ohio State University, 1949.

Commager, Henry S. *The American Mind.* New Haven: Yale University, 1959.

Corwin, Edward S. *Court Over Constitution.* Princeton: Princeton University Press, 1938.

———. Constitution of the U.S.A.: Annotated. Washington: U.S. Government Printing Office, 1952.

———. *Commerce Power V. States Rights.* Princeton: Princeton University Press, 1936.

———. *Constitutional Revolution, Ltd.* Claremont, California: Claremont College, 1946.

———. *Liberty Against Government.* Baton Rouge: Louisiana State University, 1948.

———. *The President: Office and Powers.* New York: New York University Press, 1957.

———. *Twilight of the Supreme Court.* New Haven: Yale University Press, 1934.

Crosskey, William. *Politics and the Constitution in the History of the U.S.* Athens, Ohio: University of Ohio Press, 1953.

Curtis, Chas. P. Jr. *Lions Under the Throne.* Boston: Houghton, Mifflin Co., 1947.

Danielski, D. *A Supreme Court Justice is Appointed.* New York: Random House, 1964.

Douglas, William O. *We, the Judges.* New York: Doubleday, 1956.

Eby, Herbert O. *The Labor Relations Act in the Courts: A Five Year Survey and Analysis of Legal Decisions Affecting the Rights and Responsibilities of Employers and Employees.* New York: Harper & Bros., 1943

Eriksson, Erik M. *Supreme Court and the New Deal.* Los Angeles: Lymanhouse, 1941.

Ewing, Cortez. *Judges of the Supreme Court, 1789–1937.* Minneapolis: University of Minnesota Press, 1938.

Frank, John P. *Marble Palace—The Supreme Court in American Life*. New York: A.A. Knopf, Inc., 1958.

———. *Mr. Justice Black: The Man and His Opinion*. New York: A.A. Knopf, Inc., 1949.

Frankfurter, Felix. *Mr. Justice Holmes and the Supreme Court*. 2nd Ed. Cambridge, Massachusetts: Harvard University Press, 1961.

———. & Nathan Green. *The Labor Injunction*. New York: The Macmillan Co., 1930.

———. & James M. Landis. *The Business of the Supreme Court: A Study in the Federal Judicial System*. New York: The Macmillan Co., 1927.

Freund, Paul A. *On Understanding the Supreme Court*. Boston: Little, Brown, 1949.

———. *The Supreme Court of the U.S.: Business, Purpose, Performance*. Cleveland: World Publishing Co., 1961.

Fuller, Raymond Garfield. *Child Labor and the Constitution*. New York: Thomas Y. Crowell Co., 1929.

Gellhorn, Walter. *Individual Freedom and Governmental Restraints*. Baton Rouge: Louisiana State University Press, 1956. viii+215 pp.

Goldman, Eric F. *Rendezvous with Destiny* New York: A.A. Knopf, 1956.

Gordon, Rosalie M. *Nine Men Against America*. New York: The Devin-Adair Co., 1958.

Gregory, Charles O. *Labor and the Law*. New York: W.W. Norton, Inc., 1946.

Gunther, John. *Roosevelt in Retrospect*. New York: Pyramid Publications, Inc., 1962.

Haines, Charles. *American Doctrine of Judicial Supremacy*. New York: Russell & Russell, Inc., 1959.

Hamilton, Walton H. & Douglas Adair. *The Power to Govern: The Constitution, Then and Now*. New York: W.W. Norton Co., 1937.

Harris, Joseph Pratt. *The Advise and Consent of the Senate*. Berkeley: University of California Press, 1953.

Hart, Henry, Jr. & Herbert Wechsler. *The Federal Courts and the Federal System*. Brooklyn: The Foundation Press, Inc., 1953.

Hendel, Samuel. *Charles Evans Hughes and the Supreme Court*. New York: King's Crown Press, 1951.

Hirshfield, Robert S. *The Constitution and The Court*. New York: Random House, 1962.

Horn, Robert A. *Groups and the Constitution*. Stanford: Stanford University Press, 1956.

Hughes, Charles Evans. *The Supreme Court of the United States: Its Foundation, Methods and Achievements: An Interpretation.* New York: Columbia University Press, 1928.

Jackson, Percival E. Compiler, *The Wisdom of the Supreme Court.* Norman: University of Oklahoma Press, 1962.

Jackson, Robert H. *The Supreme Court in the American System of Government.* Cambridge: Harvard University Press, 1955.

-------. *The Struggle for Judicial Supremacy.* New York: Alfred Knopf, 1941.

Johnson, Julia E. *Reorganization of the Supreme Court.* New York: H.W. Wilson Co., 1937.

Kallenbach, Joseph E. *Federal Cooperation with the States Under the Commerce Clause.* Ann Arbor: V & N Press, 1942.

Kelly, Alfred & Winifred Harbison. *The American Constitution, Its Origins and Development.* New York: W.W. Norton Co., 1955.

Konefsky, Sam J. *Chief Justice Stone and the Supreme Court.* New York: The Macmillan Co., 1945.

-------. *Legacy of Holmes and Brandeis.* New York: The Macmillan Co., 1956.

Krislov, Sam. *The Supreme Court in the Political Process.* New York: MacMillan, 1965.

Lawrence, David. *Nine Honest Men.* New York: Appleton-Century Co., 1936.

Leuchtenburg, William E. *Franklin D. Roosevelt and the New Deal, 1932–1940.* New York: Harper Torchbooks, 1963.

-------. "The Origins of Franklin D. Roosevelt's 'Court Packing' Plan," in *The Supreme Court Review 1966.* Chicago: University of Chicago Press, 1966.

Lippmann, Walter. *Supreme Court: Independent or Controlled?* New York: Harper & Bros., 1937.

Mason, Alpheus T. *Brandeis: A Free Man's Life.* New York: Viking Press, 1946.

-------. *Brandeis: Lawyer and Judge in the Modern State.* Princeton: Princeton University Press, 1933.

-------. *Harlan F. Stone: Pillar of the Law.* New York: Viking Press, 1956.

-------. *The Supreme Court from Taft to Warren.* Baton Rouge: Louisiana State University Press, 1958.

-------. *The Supreme Court: Palladium of Freedom.* Ann Arbor: University of Michigan Press, 1962.

-------. *The Supreme Court: Vehicle of Revealed Truth or Power Group, 1930–1937.* Boston: Boston University Press, 1953.

McCloskey, Robert C. *The American Supreme Court.* Chicago: University of Chicago Press, 1960.

------. *Essays in Constitutional Law.* New York: Alfred A. Knopf, 1957.

------. "Economic Due Process and The Supreme Court, An Exhumation and Rebuttal," *The Supreme Court Review, 1962* Chicago: University of Chicago Press.

McCune, Wesley. *The Nine Young Men.* New York: Harper & Bros., 1947.

Mendelson, Wallace. *Capitalism, Democracy and The Supreme Court.* New York: Appleton-Century-Crofts, 1960.

------. *The Constitution and The Supreme Court.* New York: Dodd, Mead & Co., 1959.

Miller, Perry. *The Legal Mind in America: From Independence to the Civil War.* Garden City, New York: Anchor Books, 1962.

Morrison, Samuel E. & Henry S. Commager. *Growth of the American Republic.* 2 vols. New York: Oxford Book Co., 1960, 1962.

Murphy, Walter. *Congress and the Court.* Chicago: University of Chicago Press, 1962.

------. "In His Own Image: Mr. Chief Justice Taft and Supreme Court Appointments," *The Supreme Court Review, 1961.* Chicago: University of Chicago Press, 1961.

O'Connor, John J. *The Supreme Court and Labor.* Washington: Catholic University of America Press, 1932.

Pascal, Joel F. *Mr. Justice Sutherland: A Man Against the State.* Princeton: Princeton University Press, 1951.

Pearson, Drew & Robert Allen. *The Nine Old Men.* Garden City: Doubleday, Doran & Co., 1936.

Peltason, Jack W. *The Federal Courts in the Political Process.* New York: Doubleday & Co., 1955.

Pepper, George W. *Philadelphia Lawyer, An Autobiography.* Philadelphia: J.B. Lippencott Co., 1944.

Perkins, Frances. *The Roosevelt I Knew.* New York: The Viking Press, 1946.

Perkins, Dexter. *Charles Evans Hughes and American Democratic Statesmanship.* Boston: Little, Brown & Co., 1956.

------. *The New Age of Franklin Roosevelt.* Chicago: University of Chicago Press, 1956.

Powell, Thomas R. *Vagaries and Varieties in Constitutional Interpretation.* New York: Columbia University Press, 1956.

Pound, Roscoe. *The Development of Constitutional Guarantees of Liberty.* New Haven: Yale University Press, 1951.

-------. *The Spirit of the Common Law.* Francestown H.M.: Marshall Jones Co., 1921.

Pritchett, C. Herman. *The Roosevelt Court: A Study in Judicial Politics and Values, 1937–47.* New York: The Macmillan Co., 1948.

-------. *The American Constitution.* New York: McGraw-Hill Book Co., Inc., 1959.

------- and Walter F. Murphy. *Courts, Judges, and Politics.* New York: Random House, 1961.

Pusey, Merlo. *Charles Evans Hughes.* New York: The Macmillan Co., 1952. 2 vols.

-------. *The Supreme Court Crisis.* New York: The Macmillan Co., 1937.

Robertson, Reynolds. *Practice and Procedure in the Supreme Court of the U.S.* Revised edition. New York: Prentice Hall, 1929.

Rodell, Fred. *Nine Men: A Political History of the Supreme Court, 1790–1955.* New York: Random House, 1955.

Roettinger, Ruth. *The Supreme Court and State Police Power.* Washington, D.C.: Public Affairs Press, 1957.

Rosenman, Sam I. *Working with Roosevelt.* New York: Harper & Bro., 1952

Schlesinger, Arthur, Jr. *The Age of Roosevelt.* Boston: Houghton, Mifflin Co., 3 vols.

-------. Volume 1. *The Crisis of the Old Order.* 1957.

-------. Volume 2. *The Coming of the New Deal.* 1959.

-------. Volume 3. *The Politics of Upheaval.* 1960.

Schmidhauser, John R. *Supreme Court as Final Arbiter in Federal – State Relations, 1789-1957.* Chapel Hill: University of North Carolina Press, 1958.

-------. *The Supreme Court: Its Politics, Personalities, and Procedures.* New York: Holt, Rinehart and Winston, 1961.

Schubert, Glendon A. *Constitutional Politics: Political Behavior of Supreme Court. Justices and the Constitutional Policies That They Make.* New York: Holt, Rinehart, Winston, 1960.

-------. *The Presidency in the Courts.* Minneapolis: University of Minnesota Press, 1951.

Schwartz, Bernard. *American Constitutional Law.* New York: Cambridge University Press, 1955.

-------. *Supreme Court: Constitutional Revolution in Retrospect.* New York: The Ronald Press Co., 1957.

Stern, Robert L. & Eugene Gressman. *Supreme Court Practice: Jurisdiction, Procedure, Arguing and Briefing Techniques, Forms, Status, Rules for*

Practice in the Supreme Court of the United States. Washington: The Bureau of National Affairs, Inc., 1950.

Sherwood, Robert E. *Roosevelt & Hopkins: An Intimate History.* New York: Harper & Bros., 1948.

Swisher, Carl Brent. *American Constitutional Development.* Cambridge: Houghton, Mifflin Co., 1954.

------. *Growth of Constitutional Power in the United States.* Chicago: University of Chicago Press, 1946.

------. *The Supreme Court in a Modern Role.* New York: University Press, 1958.

Tully Grace. *F.D.R. My Boss.* New York: Charles Scribner's Sons, 1949.

Twiss, Benjamin. *Lawyers and the Constitution.* New York: Russell & Russell, 1962.

Wehle, Louis B. *Hidden Threads of History: Wilson Through Roosevelt.* New York: The Macmillan Co., 1953.

Westin, Alan F. (ed.). *An Autobiography of the Supreme Court.* New York: The Macmillan Co., 1963.

Williams, Charlotte. *Hugo L. Black: A Study in the Judicial Process.* Baltimore: Johns Hopkins University Press, 1950.

Witte, Edwin E. *The Government in Labor Disputes.* New York: McGraw-Hill Book Co., 1932.

Wood, Virginia. *Due Process of Law.* Baton Rouge: Louisiana University Press, 1951.

Wormser, R.A. *Story of the Law.* New York: Simon and Schuster, 1962.

Wright, Benjamin. *The Contract Clause of the Constitution.* Cambridge: Harvard University Press, 1938.

------. *The Growth of American Constitutional Law.* New York: Henry Holt & Co., 1942.

LEGAL PERIODICALS

Alfange, Dean. "The Supreme Court Battle in Retrospect," *United States Law Review,* LXXI (September, 1937), 497-502.

American Bar Association Journal, "Justice Roberts Leaves the Court," XXXI (August, 1945), 407-435.

Arnold, Thurmond. "A Reply," *American Bar Association Journal,* XXIII (May, 1927), 364-8; 393-4.

Avakian, Spurgeon. "Comment on National Labor Relations Board Decision in the Supreme Court," *California Law Review,* XXV (July, 1937), 593-615.

Barrett, Edward L., Jr. "Substance' v. 'Form' in the Application of the Commerce Clause to State Taxation," *University of Pennsylvania Law Review*, C1 (April, 1953), 740-791.

Barrett, Harrison J. "Is There a National Police Power?" *Boston University Law Review*, XIV (April, 1934), 243-292.

Blaustein, Albert P. & Andrew H. Field. "'Overruling' Opinions in the Supreme Court," *Michigan Law Review*, LVII (December, 1958), 151-194.

Boston Law Review, "Note on N.L.R.B. v. Fainblatt," XIX (January, 1939), 129-133,

Boudin, Bouis B. "Truth and Fiction about the 14th Amendment,"*New York University Law Quarterly Review*, XVI (November, 1938), 19-82.

Browder, Olin L., Jr. "Note on Washington Minimum Wage Case," *Illinois Bar Journal*, XXV (April, 1937), 284-286.

Brown Leroy A. "Note on West Coast Hotel," *Southern California Law Review*, XI (April, 1937), 256-264.

Brown, Ray A. "Due Process of Law, Police Power, and the Supreme Court," *Harvard Law Review*, XL (May, 1926-27), 943-968.

-------. "Police Power—Legislation for Health and Personal Safety," *Harvard Law Review*, XLII (May, 1928-29), 866-898.

Carpenter, Charles E. "The President and The Court," *United States Law Review*, LXXI (March, 1937), 139-149.

Cheadle, J. Kennard. "The Parrish Case: Minimum Wage for Women and Perhaps for Men," *University of Cincinnati Law Review*, XI (May, 1937), 307-326.

Collier, Charles S. "Judicial Bootstraps and The General Welfare Clause: The AAA Opinion," *George Washington Law Review*, IV (January, 1936), 211-242.

Columbia Law Review. "Recent Decisions," XXXVII (May, 1937), 852-80.

-------, "State Views on Economic Due Process, 1937-53," LIII (June, 1953), 827-845.

Cook, Franklin H. "History of Rate Determination under the Due Process Clauses," *University of Chicago Law Review*, XI (June, 1944), 297-337.

Corwin, Edward S. "The Schechter Case-Landmark or What?" *New York University Law Quarterly*, XIII (January, 1936), 151-190.

Cox, Archibald, "Federalism in the Law of Labor Relations," *Harvard Law Review*, LXVII (June, 1954), 1297-1348.

Crosskey, William W. "Charles Fairman's 'Legislative History' and the Constitutional Limitation on State Authority," *University of Chicago Law Review,* XXII *(Autumn, 1954), 1-143.*

Cushman, Robert E. "Social and Economic Control Through Federal Taxation," *Minnesota Law Review,* XVIII (June, 1934), 757-783.

Dodd, E. Merrick. "The Supreme Court and Fair Labor Standards, 1941-1945," *Harvard Law Review,* LIX (February, 1946), 321-373.

Fahy, Charles. "Notes on the Development of Constitutional Law, 1936-1949," *Georgetown Law Journal,* XXXVIII (November, 1949), 1-31.

Fairman, Charles. "Does the 14th Amendment Incorporate The Bill of Rights? The Original Understanding," *Stanford Law Review,* II (December, 1949), 5-139.

Fellman, David. "Recent Tendencies in Civil Liberties Decision of The Supreme Court," *Cornell Law Quarterly,* XXXIV (Spring, 1949), 331-351.

Forrester, Ray. "Mr. Justice Burton and The Supreme Court," *Tulane Law Review,* XX (October, 1945), 1-21.

Fraenkel, Osmond. "The Constitution and The Supreme Court," *Columbia Law Review,* XXXVII (February, 1937), 212-222.

-------. "Five-to-Four Decisions of The Supreme Court," United *States Law Week,* II (May 12, 1935), 1010-1020.

Frankfurter, Felix. "Chief Justices I Have Known," *Virginia Law Review,* XXXIX (November, 1953), 883-905.

-------. "History of Labor and Realism in Constitutional Law," *Harvard Law Review,* XXIX (February, 1929), 353-373.

-------. "Mr. Justice Roberts," *University of Pennsylvania Law Review,* CIV (December, 1955), 311-317.

------- & Adrian S. Fisher. "Business of The Supreme Court at the October Term 1935 and 1936," *Harvard Law Review,* LI (February, 1937-38), 577-637.

------- & Henry M. Hart. "Business of The Supreme Court at the October Term, 1933," *Harvard Law Review,* XLVIII (December, 1935), 238-281.

-------. "Business of The Supreme Court at the October Term, 1934,'" *Harvard Law Review,* XLIX (December, 1935), 68-107.

Fuchs, Ralph F. "Judicial Method and the Constitutionality of the N.I. R.A.," *St. Louis Law Review,* XX (April 1935), 199-219.

Goldsmith, Irving S. & Gordon W. Winks. "Pricefixing: Nebbia To Guffey," *Illinois Law Review,* XXXI (June, 1936), 179-201.

Grant, J.A.C. "Commerce, Production and the Fiscal Powers of Congress," *Yale Law Journal,* XLV (May and June, 1936), 751-778; 991-1021.

Griswold, Erwin N. "Owen J. Roberts as a Judge," *University of Pennsylvania Law Review,* CIV (December, 1955), 332-349.

Hart, Henry M. "Business of the Supreme Court at the October Terms 1937 and 1938," *Harvard Law Review,* LII (February, 1940), 579-626.

Hays, Paul R. "Federalism and Labor Relations in The United States," *University of Pennsylvania Law Review,* CIV (June, 1954), 959-979.

Holmes, John W. "The Federal Spending Power and States Rights," *Michigan Law Review,* XXXIV (February, 1935), 637-649.

Humes, Augustine L. "Trend of Decisions Respecting the Powers of Congress To Regulate Interstate Commerce," *American Bar Association Journal,* XXVI (November, 1940), 846-851.

Jourolonom, Leon, Jr. "The Life and Death of Smyth v. Ames," *Tennessee Law Review,* XVIII (February, April, 1945), 347-355; 663-675; 756-761.

Keedy, Edwin R. "Owen J. Roberts and The Law School," *University of Pennsylvania Law Review,* CIV (December, 1955), 318-321.

Keneban, Edward F. "Note on Wagner Decision," *Illinois Bar Journal,* XXV (January, 1937), 376-78.

Lee, M.G. "Note on the Wagner Decision" *Illinois Bar Quarterly,* XXV (January, 1937); 378-85.

Lerner, Max. "The Constitution and Court as Symbols," *Yale Law Journal,* XLVI (June, 1937), 1290-1319.

McAllister, Breck P. "Lord Hale and Business Affected with the Public Interest," *Harvard Law Review,* XLIII (March 1930-31), 759-791.

McCloy, John J. "Owen J. Roberts' Extra Curricular Activities," *University of Pennsylvania Law Review,* CIV (December, 1955), 350-353.

McCracken, Robert T. "Owen J. Roberts-Master Advocate," *University of Pennsylvania Law Review,* CIV (December, 1955), 322-331.

McElwain, Edwin. "The Business of The Supreme Court as Conducted by Chief Justice Hughes," *Harvard Law Review* LXIII (1949) (451-490).

McGovney, D.O. "Reorganization of The Supreme Court," *California Law Review,* XXV (May, 1937), 389-412.

Mason, Alpheus T. "Harlan Fiske Stone and F.D.R.'s Court Plan," *Yale Law Journal,* LXI (June-July, 1952), 791-817.

-------. "Charles E. Hughes: An Appeal to History," *Vanderbilt Law Review,* VI (December, 1952), 1-19.

Swisher, Carl B. "Th Supreme Court — A Need for Re-evaluation," *Virginia Law Quarterly*, XL (November, 1954), 837-851.

United States Law Review, "Notes and Comment: 'Nine Old Men" LXX (January, 1936), 1-4.

------, "Notes and Comment: The Decision in the N.I.R.A. Cases," LXIX (June, 1935), 281-292.

------, "Notes and Comment: The President and The Court," LXXI (February, 1937), 61-73.

------, "What Was the Origin of the President's Supreme Court Proposal," LXXI (September, 1937), 488-493.

------, "Notes and Comment: The Minimum Wage Decision," LXXI, (April, 1937), 181-210.

Willcox, Alanson W. "Invasions of First Amendment through Conditioned Public Spending," *Cornell Law Quarterly*, XLI (Fall, 1955), 12-56.

Willis, High E. "Growth in the Constitution and Constitutional Law Since The Decision of the Case of *West Coast Hotel v. Parrish*," *Tulane Law Review*, XX (October, 1945), 22-55.

------. "Constitution Making by the Supreme Court Since March 24, 1937." *Indiana Law Journal*, XV (February, 1940), 179-201.

Wilson, Emmet H. "Property Affected with a Public interest," *Southern California Law Review*, IX (November, 1935), 1-13.

Yale Law Journal, "Note—Legislative Regulations of the New York Dairy Industry," XLII (June, 1933), 1259-1270.

Yorkey, Daniel G. "Notes and Comment on Interstate Commerce Codes," *Cornell Law Quarterly*, XXII (June, 1937), 568-76.

GENERAL PERIODICALS

Agar, Herbert. "Mr. Roosevelt's Constitutional Crisis," *The New Statesman and The Nation*, XIII (April 17, 1937), 321.

Bates, Ernest S. "McReynolds, Roberts and Hughes," *The New Republic* LXXXVII (July 1, 1936), 232-35.

Brunt, Irving. "How Liberal is Justice Hughes?" *The New Republic*, XCI (July 21-28, 1937), 295-298; 329-332.

Brennan, William J., Jr. "Inside View of the High Court," *The New York Times Magazine* " (October 6, 1963), 35, 100-103.

Burnham, Walter D. "Schizophrenia in the G.O.P.," *Commonweal*, LXXIX (September 27, 1963), 5-10.

Christian, Century, "Confirming Mr. Roberts," XLVII (May 28, 1930), 667-8.

Corwin, Edward S. "Curbing the Court," *The American Labor Legislation Review*, XXVI (1936), 85-88.

-------. "Some Probable Repercussions of "N.I.R.A." on Our Constitutional System," *The Annals of the American Academy of Politics and Social Science*, CLXXII (March, 1934), 1939-144.

Cushman Robert E. "Constitutional Law in 1933-34," *American Political Science Review*, XXIX (February, 1935), 36-59.

-------. "Constitutional Law in 1934-35," *American Political Science Review*, XXX (February, 1936), 51-89.

-------. "Constitutional Law in. 1935-36," *American Political Science Review*, XXXI (February, 1937), 253-279.

-------. "Constitutional Law in 1936-37," *American Political Science Review*, XXXII (February, 1938), 278-310.

-------. "Constitutional Law in 1937-38," *American Political Science Review*, XXXIII (April, 1939), 234-266.

Epstein, Abraham. "Governments Responsibility for Economic Security," *Annals of the American Academy of Political and Social Science* CCVI (November, 1939).

Fluno, Robert Y. "How Deep is the Supreme Court in Politics?" *Western Political Quarterly*, IX (June, 1957), 459-461.

Hughes, Charles E. "The Supreme Court is Still Functioning," *Vital Speeches*, II (February 10, 1936), 6542-44.

Johnston, Alva. "White House Tommy," *Saturday Evening Post*, CCX (July 31, 1937), 5-7; 65-70.

Kales, Albert M. "New Methods in Due Process Cases," *American Political Science Review*, XII (May, 1918), 241-50.

Lawrence, David. "Mr. Roberts and Mr. Roosevelt," *The United States News*, IX (May 10, 1937), Editorial.

Leek, L.H. "Packing The Court," *American Federationist*, XLIV (April, 1937), 378-387.

Lerner, Max. "The Great Constitutional War," *Virginia Quarterly Review*, XVII (1942), 530-546.

Mason, Alpheus T. "Labor, The Courts and Section 7(a)," *American Political Science Review*, XXVIII (December, 1934), 999-1015.

Murphy, Walter F. "Lower Courts' Check on Supreme Court Power," *American Political Science Review*, LIII (December, 1959), 1017-31.

The New Republic, "Fortas to the Court," CLIII (August 21, 1963), 7-8.

Newsweek, "Obituary," n., LVII (May 30, 1955), 45.

-------, "The Warren Court: Fateful Decade " (May 11, 1964), 24-33.

------. "Politics and The Supreme Court: President Roosevelt's Proposal," *University of Pennsylvania Law Review,* LXXXV (May, 1937), 659-677.

Morrison, Stanley. "Does The 14th Amendment Incorporate The Bill of Rights? The Judicial Interpertations," *Stanford Law Review,* II (December, 1949), 140-173.

Nathanson, Nathaniel L. "The Wagner Act Decision in Retrospect," *Illinois Law Review,* XXXII (June, 1937), 196-206.

Nicholson, Vincent D. "The Federal Spending Power," *Temple Law Quarterly,* IX (November, 1934), 3-24.

------. "Recent Decision on The Power To Spend for The Federal Welfare," *Temple Law Quarterly,* XII (July, 1938), 435-461.

O'Meara, Joseph. "Forward: The Supreme Court in the American Court System," *Notre Dame Lawyer,* XXXIII (August, 1958), 521-22.

Pepper, George W. "Owen J. Roberts-The Man," *University of Pennsylvania Law Review,* CIV (December, 1955), 372-380.

Post, Russell L. "The Constitutionality of Spending for the General Welfare," *Virginia Law Review,* XXII (November, 1935), 1-38.

Pound, Roscoe. "Liberty of Contract," *Yale Law Journal,* XVIII (May, 1909), 454-487.

Powell, Thomas R. "Changing Constitutional Phases," *Boston Law Review,* XIX (November, 1939), 509-532.

------. "Child Labor, Congress and The Constitution," *North Carolina Law Review,* I (February, 1922), 61-81.

------. "The Child Labor Law, The 10th Amendment, and The Commerce Clause," *Southern Law Quarterly,* III (August, 1918), 175-213.

------. "Commerce, Pensions and Codes," *Harvard Law Review,* XLIX (November, December, 1935), 1-43; 193-238.

------. "Judiciability of Minimum Wage Legislation," *Harvard Law Review,* XXXVII (March, 1924), 545-73.

------. "The Supreme Court and State Police Power 1922-1930," *Virginia Law Review,* VIII (April, 1931), 529.

Rodes, Robert E., Jr. "Due Process and Social Legislation in The Supreme Court—A Post Mortem," *Notre Dame Lawyer,* XXXIII (December, 1957), 5-33.

Stern, Robert L. "The Commerce Clause and The National Economy, 1933-1946," *Harvard Law Review,* LIX (May, July, 1946), 645-693, 883-947.

Streit, Clarance K. "Owen J. Roberts and Atlantic Union," *University of Pennsylvania Law Review,* CIV (December, 1955), 354-367.

O'Shaughnessy, Michael. "AAA and The Constitution," *Commonweal,* XXII (August 9, 1935), 357-8.

Outlook, "Trend of Events," CLV (June 4, 1930), 175-6.

------, "Backstage in Washington," CLV (May 21, 1930), 100.

Pritchett, C. Herman. "Justice Holmes and A Liberal Court," *Virginia Quarterly Review,* XXIV (Winter, 1948), 43-58.

Powell, Thomas R. "From Philadelphia to Philadelphia," *American Political Science Review,* XXXI (September, 1936), 1-27.

Spaulding, Thomas M. "The Supreme Court — 1937,'" *The Michigan Quarterly Review* (1963), 1-10.

Swisher, Carl B. "Supreme Court in Transition," *Journal of Politics,* I (November, 1939), 349-370.

Time, "Requiescat in Committee," XXX (August 2, 1937), 11.

——, "Judiciary—The Big Debate," XXIX (March 29, 1937), 14-15.

——, "Judiciary—Chambermaid Day," XXIX (April 5, 1937), 11-13.

——, "Judiciary—DeSenecture," XXIX (February 15, 1937), 16-19.

——, "Judiciary—Four 5-4; One 9-0," XXIX (April 19, 1937), 14-15.

——, "Judiciary—Jackson's Term," XXXIII (June 12, 1939), 16-17.

——, "Judiciary—Roberts' Dissent," XLVI (July 16, 1945), 16-17.

——, "Judiciary—Securely Secure," XXIX (May 31, 1937), 16-17.

------, XXVII No. 3 (January 13, 1936), 12.

------, XXVII No. 8 (February 24, 1936), 16.

------, XXVII No. 21 (May 25, 1936), 13.

------, XXVII No. 23 (June 8, 1936), 11.

------, XXVIII No. 22 (November 30, 1936), 13-14.

Veig, J.A. "The Supreme Court and Its Social Obligations,' *American Federationist,* XLIV (August, 1937), 835-843.

Wallen, Theodore C. "The Supreme Court—Nine Mortal Men," *Literary Digest,* CXVII (March 10, 1934), 9, 45-47.

Appendix

Membership of the United States Supreme Court, 1930-45

May 20, 1930 – January 12, 1932
Hughes, Holmes, Van Devanter, McReynolds, Brandeis, Sutherland, Butler, Stone, Roberts (replaced Sanford)

March 2, 1932 – June 1, 1937
Hughes, Van Devanter, McReynolds, Brandeis, Sutherland, Butler, Stone, Roberts, Cardozo, (replaced Holmes)

August 18, 1937 – January 18, 1938
Hughes, McReynolds, Brandeis, Sutherland, Butler, Stone, Roberts, Cardozo, Black (replaced Van Devanter)

January 27, 1938 – July 9, 1938
Hughes, McReynolds, Brandeis, Butler, Stone, Roberts, Cardozo, Black, Reed (replaced Sutherland)

January 20, 1939 – February 13, 1939
Hughes, McReynolds, Brandeis, Butler, Stone, Roberts, Black, Reed, Frankfurter (replaced Cardozo)

April 15, 1939 – November 16, 1939
Hughes, McReynolds, Butler, Stone, Roberts, Black, Reed, Frankfurter, Douglas (replaced Brandeis)

January 16, 1940 – February 1, 1941
Hughes, McReynolds, Stone, Roberts, Black, Reed, Frankfurter, Douglas, Murphy (replaced Butler)

June 12, 1941 – July 1, 1941
Hughes, Stone, Roberts, Black, Reed, Frankfurter, Douglas, Murphy, Byrnes, Jackson (replaced McReynolds)

February 11, 1943 – July 31, 1945
Stone, Roberts, Black, Reed, Frankfurter, Douglas, Murphy, Jackson, Rutledge (replaced Byrnes)

September 22, 1945
Burton replaced Robert.

Index of Names & Cases

(R) = Roberts wrote decision of the Court
(r) = Roberts participated in decision of the Court

205